Theories and Analyses of Twentieth-Century Music

J. Kent Williams

School of Music
University of North Carolina, Greensboro

Harcourt Brace College Publishers

Fort Worth   Philadelphia   San Diego   New York   Orlando   Austin   San Antonio
Toronto   Montreal   London   Sydney   Tokyo

Publisher	Christopher P. Klein
Senior Acquisitions Editor	Barbara J. C. Rosenberg
Developmental Editor	Terri House
Project Editor	Dee W. Salisbury
Senior Production Manager	Annette Dudley Wiggins
Art Director	Bill Brammer
Picture and Rights Editor	Carrie Ward
Permissions Editor	Aimé Merizon
Cover Design	Nick Welch/Design Delux

ISBN: 0-15-500316-X

Library of Congress Catalog Card Number: 95-75542

Harcourt Brace & Company may provide complimentary instructional aids and supplement packages to those adopters qualified under our adoption policy. Please contact your sales representative for more information. If as an adopter or potential user you receive supplements you do not need, please return them to your sales representative or send them to: Attn: Returns Department, Troy Warehouse, 465 South Lincoln Drive, Troy, MO 63379.

Address for Editorial Correspondence: Harcourt Brace College Publishers, 301 Commerce Street, Suite 3700, Fort Worth, TX 76102.

Address for Orders: Harcourt Brace & Company, 6277 Sea Harbor Drive, Orlando, FL 32887-6777, 1-800-782-4479, or 1-800-433-0001 (in Florida).

(Copyright Acknowledgments follow the Bibliography and constitute a continuation of this copyright page.)

Printed in the United States of America

6 7 8 9 0 1 2 3 4 5   016   10 9 8 7 6 5 4 3 2 1

PREFACE

To the Instructor

This book is intended as a basic text for upper-level undergraduate and lower-level graduate courses in music theory and analysis. It is organized in a spiral fashion whereby earlier chapters provide introductions to topics that are revisited and expanded upon later. Accordingly, Chapters 1–9 should be considered essential for the remainder of the text.

Several features make this text unique in comparison with others currently available. Its coverage is broad and eclectic with balanced treatment afforded to tonality, atonality, and neotonality. These three idioms are introduced briefly in Chapter 1 and then examined fully in later chapters.

Chapters 2–6 provide an introduction to pitch-class set theory (also called atonal or post-tonal theory), MIDI pitch numbers, and Brinkman's method of binomial representation. Additional competency in set theory and analysis is developed through exercises and projects in later chapters.

Chapters 7–8 balance the preceding concern about pitch with an introduction to meter, rhythm, and texture. Chapter 9 rounds off the introductory material by examining basic aspects of form, process, and temporality.

In Chapters 10–15 various systems of pitch organization are explored from both theoretical and analytical perspectives. Concepts and techniques presented earlier are applied here to the study of longer and more complex musical examples. Finally, Chapters 16–18 provide concise introductions to more recent approaches to composition.

Many of the musical examples in this text are available in the various published anthologies. Other anthologized works are cited at the end of each chapter. The emphasis, for the most part, is upon shorter and less complex excerpts and pieces.

Involvement with music and musical concepts is stressed throughout. Students are provided numerous opportunities to develop and test their understanding. They also participate by completing several musical examples and tables.

Creative problem solving is stressed in various ways. In several chapters, students are led step-by-step through a process of logical reasoning to the solution of a musical problem. They are also shown how to adapt previously introduced models or methods to the tasks at hand.

In addition to learning specific facts, procedures, and concepts, readers are introduced to critical issues in music theory and analysis: the importance of acknowledging one's assumptions, the inevitable trade-off between specificity and generality, the necessity for methodological rigor, and the gulf between musical conception and perception.

To my knowledge this book is the first of its kind to draw extensively upon the burgeoning literature in music psychology. Recent studies in that field have profound implications for the pedagogy of music theory. The works cited herein should provide an introduction to research that is especially relevant to the teaching of twentieth-century music.

To the Student

This book introduces you to a diverse and challenging repertoire: Western art music of the twentieth century. You will study that music from the perspective of music theory and analysis, two disciplines that attempt to explain how music works.

Your previous studies have deepened your understanding of key aspects of music. This understanding will serve as a foundation for studying twentieth-century music.

To increase your knowledge, you must become more familiar with the raw materials of music and more adept at using the analytical tools that you possess. In addition, you must add new tools to your toolbox. The most powerful of these is a new method for representing and comparing pitches, intervals, and pitch combinations. The necessity for these additions should become apparent as you read Chapter 1. Then, in Chapters 2–6, you'll be introduced to basic concepts, symbols, and method and learn how to apply them in solving simple musical problems. Additional opportunities are provided in later chapters where a certain level of competence is assumed and the problems are more complex.

In embarking upon this journey remember that you have already invested a considerable amount of time, money, and effort in becoming a musician. You may also have purchased this book and registered for a course of study. To derive the maximum value from those investments be sure to do the following:

1. Read the text carefully. Make sure that you understand the meaning of every term and can follow each train of thought. Test your understanding by answering the Questions for Review at the end of most chapters. If you don't understand certain points, ask your instructor to clarify them.
2. Study and listen thoughtfully to the musical examples. Some can be played on the piano; others should be heard in their original instrumentation. Be sure to concentrate upon the point that is being made about the example.
3. Do the assigned exercises and projects carefully. Make sure that you understand what you're doing and why you're doing it. If some of the tasks seem trivial or tedious, remember that analytical techniques, like performance techniques, are developed through practice and repetition.
4. Pause occasionally to reflect upon what you're learning. You'll be prompted to do so by questions that are enclosed in parentheses. (Do you understand what I mean?)
5. Pursue interesting topics by doing some of the Recommended Listening and Analysis at the end of each chapter.
6. Apply what you've learned to twentieth-century music that you have performed or are currently studying.
7. Make a special effort to attend recitals and concerts of twentieth-century music.
8. Take some composition lessons, even if you have no aspirations of being a professional composer.
9. Keep an open mind. Don't reject an unfamiliar work upon first hearing. Try to understand it from various perspectives and keep listening. You'll be a better musician for doing so.
10. When you have finished your course, retain this book for future reference as part of your professional library.

Acknowledgments

In writing this book I have been influenced by the work of numerous theorists, musicologists, and composers. I trust that I have acknowledged all of my intellectual debts in the appropriate manner.

I have also received helpful comments and suggestions from several reviewers who read earlier drafts of this manuscript. These include: Gregory Fritze, Berklee College of Music; Laura Nash, Hofstra University; Don Gibson, Ohio State University; Michael R. Rogers, University of Oklahoma; Allen Winold, Indiana University; and Daniel N. Wyman, San Jose State University.

A number of people at the University of North Carolina at Greensboro have helped this project along its way. These include Arthur Tollefson, Dean of the School of Music, James Sherbon, Director of Graduate Studies in Music, as well as Eddie Bass and Eleanor McCrickard, Chairs of the Division of Composition, History, and Theory. Arthur Hunkins, my colleague in that division, read and critiqued chapters in his areas of expertise. Richard Wursten, former Director of the Music Listening Center, helped with music reference tasks. Susan Quindag and James Barket helped to prepare certain musical examples. And, finally, a word of special thanks must go to my students who endured earlier drafts of this manuscript and made constructive suggestions for improving it.

The editorial staff at Harcourt Brace has been most supportive despite some trying times in the book publishing industry. My three developmental editors, Julia Berrisford, Mary Kay Bridges, and Terri House, provided their share of patience and encouragement.

The analytical examples and exercises were created on a Macintosh computer with the help of the Notewriter II music engraving program. I would like to thank Keith Hamel, the developer of this application, for his support.

Finally, I would like to acknowledge the support of those closest to me. These include my parents, Ken and Robert Williams, my sister and brother-in-law, Elaine and Nelson Stover, and my wife, Loretta. I could never have completed this project without them.

Greensboro, NC
September 1996

This book is dedicated to the memory of my father
Kenneth Edwin Williams
1914–1994

Key to Anthologies Cited

Arlin—Mary I. Arlin, et al., ed. *Music Sources.* 2nd ed., Englewood Cliffs, NJ: Prentice-Hall, 1989.

BHN—Thomas Benjamin, Michael Horvit and Robert Nelson, eds. *Music for Analysis.* 3rd ed., Wadsworth Publishing Co., 1992.

Burkhart—Charles Burkhart, ed. *Anthology for Musical Analysis,* 5th ed., Fort Worth, TX: Harcourt Brace College Publishers, 1994.

DeLio-Smith—Thomas DeLio and Stuart Sanders Smith, eds. *Twentieth Century Music Scores.* Englewood Cliffs, NJ: Prentice-Hall, 1989.

Godwin—Joscelyn Godwin, ed. *Schirmer Scores.* New York: Schirmer Books, 1975.

Kamien—Roger Kamien, ed. *The Norton Scores.* 5th ed., New York: W. W. Norton, 1990.

Morgan—Robert P. Morgan, ed. *Anthology of Twentieth-Century Music.* New York: W. W. Norton, 1992.

Palisca—Claude V. Palisca, ed. *Norton Anthology of Western Music.* New York: W. W. Norton, 1980.

Simms—Bryan R. Simms, ed. *Music of the Twentieth Century: An Anthology.* New York: Schirmer Books, 1986.

Turek—Ralph Turek, ed. *Analytical Anthology of Music.* 2nd ed., New York: McGraw-Hill, 1992.

Wen20—Mary H. Wennerstrom, ed. *Anthology of Twentieth-Century Music.* 2nd ed., Englewood Cliffs, NJ: Prentice-Hall, 1988.

WenAMSS—Mary H. Wennerstrom, ed. *Anthology of Musical Structure and Style.* Englewood Cliffs, NJ: Prentice-Hall, 1983.

CONTENTS

Part I

PITCH ORGANIZATION:
AN INTRODUCTION

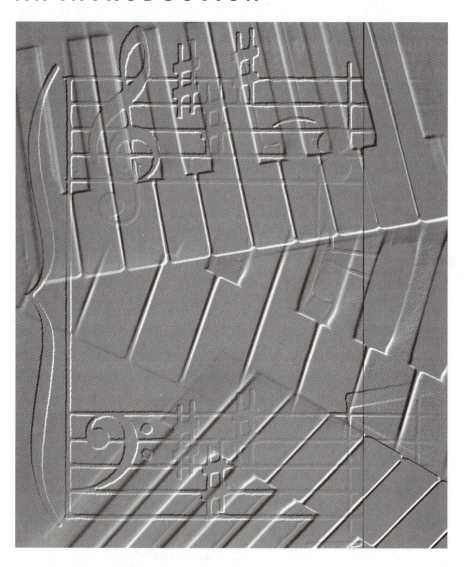

CHAPTER 1

Tonality, Atonality, and Neotonality

The term *tonality* concerns how pitches are organized and perceived. If certain pitches sound more stable and others less stable, then music can be described as *tonal*. In reading this text you'll encounter some musical examples that are unequivocally *tonal*, some that are definitely *atonal* (without tonality), and some that are *neotonal* (tonal, but in a new way). Figure 1–1 shows how these three categories can be represented on a continuum. To gain a deeper understanding we'll examine three representative works.

Functional Tonality

Berg, "Schliesse mir die Augen beide" (1907)

The score to Alban Berg's 1907 setting of "Schliesse mir die Augen beide" is given in Ex. 1–1. Example 1–2 is a diagram showing the song's phrase structure, melodic design, and tonal plan. From this we can see that:

- Mm. 1–2 form an *antecedent phrase* that ends with a *half cadence*. This phrase is divided into two *subphrases* by the rest on the first beat of m. 2.
- The second phrase, mm. 3–4, begins like the first but ends with an imperfect *authentic cadence* in A minor. Compare mm. 1 and 3 to locate the point of divergence.
- Mm. 5–6 comprise the *b* section where contrasting keys are implied but not firmly established.
- The return (in mm. 7–8) of the opening phrase, and of C major, the overall tonic key is veiled. (Can you explain how?)

Example 1–3 reveals that the vocal melody is built from three four-note motives. Phrases *a* and *a′* (mm. 1–4) are based on motives *x* and *y*; phrase *b* introduces motive *z* for contrast. Integers below the staff indicate the direction and size (in

---

Figure 1–1.

Tonal	Neotonal	Atonal

Example 1–1. Berg, "Schliesse mir die Augen beide" (1907 setting)

Example 1–2.   **Diagram of the 1907 setting**

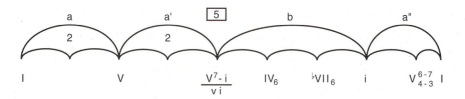

Example 1–3.   **Motivic analysis of the vocal melody**

semitones) of the melodic intervals in m. 1. Notice that motive *y* is almost an exact *inversion* of motive *x*. (Two motives are related by inversion if their corresponding intervals are identical in size but opposite in direction.)

The song's tonal structure can be represented with Schenkerian graphic notation. With only three basic elements (note heads, stems, and slurs), we can indicate three structural levels:

- Stemmed notes represent prominent chord tones.
- Unstemmed notes at the end points of slurs represent less prominent chord tones or nonchord tones.
- Unstemmed note heads enclosed by slurs indicate notes that embellish or connect other, more prominent notes.

Example 1–4. Diminution figures in traditional and Schenkerian notation

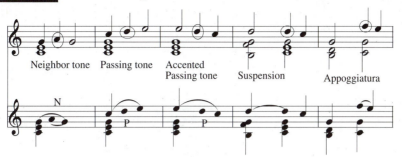

Neighbor tone   Passing tone   Accented
Passing tone   Suspension   Appoggiatura

Example 1–4 shows how conventional melodic figures are represented in Schenkerian notation. Example 1–5 is an analysis of the entire song.[1] Notice that:

- Phrases *a* (mm. 1–2) and *a″* (mm. 7–9) are based on the cyclic progression I–IV–V–I.
- Phrase *a* does not reach its harmonic goal, the tonic triad, but ends instead with a half cadence. The cadential V chord is "tonicized" by vii°7/V and Ger+6 chords.
- The keys of F major, B♭ major, and C minor are implied in the *b* section (mm. 5–6). These relate to C major as IV, ♭VII, and i, respectively.
- Phrase *a″* contains the only complete statement of the cyclic progression, I–IV–V–I, and ends with the only authentic cadence in the tonic key.

Example 1–5 also reveals that the song contains several accented dissonances. For the most part, these resolve directly to chord tones. Occasionally, however, one nonchord tone resolves while another appears, producing a *complex resolution.*

The same graph shows how Berg used dissonant and/or chromatic chords to *elaborate, expand,* or *prolong* the more consonant diatonic chords. Notice, for example, that in mm. 2 and 8 the cadential $^6_4$, vii°7/V, and +6 chords expand the cadential V chords. The crossed diagonal lines in m. 4 indicate that the outer voices form a 10–6 voice exchange pattern. Chords in mm. 1, 3, and 7 are expanded by a 6–6–10–10 voice exchange pattern.

A Schenkerian analysis is sometimes termed an *event hierarchy*, because it indicates the relative stability of pitch events in an actual piece of music.[2] Figure 1–2, a graph of the relative stability of chromatic scale degrees in the keys of C major and C minor based on data derived from psychological experiments is a *tonal hierarchy* . Notice that stemmed pitches in the event hierarchy (Ex. 1–5) correspond to higher ranking scale degrees in the tonal hierarchy (Fig. 1–2). For example, C,

[1]An alternative analysis can be found in Felix-Eberhard von Cube, *The Book of the Musical Artwork*, translated with an afterword by David Neumeyer, George R. Boyd, and Scott Harris (Lewiston, NY: The Edwin Mellen Press, 1988), 350–352.

[2]Jamshed Bharucha, "Anchoring Effects in Music: The Resolution of Dissonance," *Cognitive Psychology* 16 (1984): 485–518; and "Event Hierarchies, Tonal Hierarchies, and Assimilation: A Reply to Deutsch and Dowling," *Journal of Experimental Psychology: General* 113(3) (1984): 421–425.

Example 1–5. **Schenkerian analysis of the 1907 setting**

E, and G, the tones of the tonic triad, are prominent in the Schenkerian graph. F does not rank as high as C, E, or G, but it follows them closely. Notice, however, that F was stemmed only when it was the root of the IV chord in C major (mm. 1, 3, and 7), the tonic of F major (m. 5), or the dominant of B♭ major (m. 6).

Chromatic tones, the least stable members of the tonal hierarchy, occur as passing or neighboring tones in the Schenkerian graph. For the most part, their spelling reflects their voice-leading function, but there are a few discrepancies. The most interesting is the tenor register E♭$_4$/D♯$_4$, which first appears in m. 1 in the context of F–A–C–E♭.[3] Instead of resolving this apparent V⁷ chord to a B♭ major triad,

---

[3]Octaves are numbered as shown in Ex. 2–2, p. 31.

Example 1–5. *Continued*

b

5   6

4
2   7 -- 6   4
2   7 -- 6   6
5

IV   bVII   i

7   a"   8   9

6   6   10   10

7   6
4   4
2   6   6
4   b7   8 - - - - - - - - - - - - - 7
6 - - - - - - - - - - - - - 5
4 - - - - - - - - - - - - - 3

(I)   IV   V   I

Berg combined C and E♭ with F♯ and A♭ to form a *"diminished-third" chord* that he
resolved to a cadential $^6_4$, which, in turn, resolves to V (see Ex. 1–5). Berg might
have spelled the E♭s in m. 1 and m. 2 as D♯s, since they resolve to E naturals. The
E♭$_4$ in m. 2 (beat 4) is spelled correctly, since it leads to D. E♭$_4$ appears next in m.
3 where it is respelled as D♯, ♯4 of A minor. It also appears in m. 5 in the context of
an F7 chord (compare to m. 1). E♭$_4$ makes two more appearances in the tenor register
(m. 6, beat 4, and m. 7, beat 1) before it is transferred down an octave for two final
appearances (m. 7, beat 5, and m. 8, beat 3). In all but the first of these instances

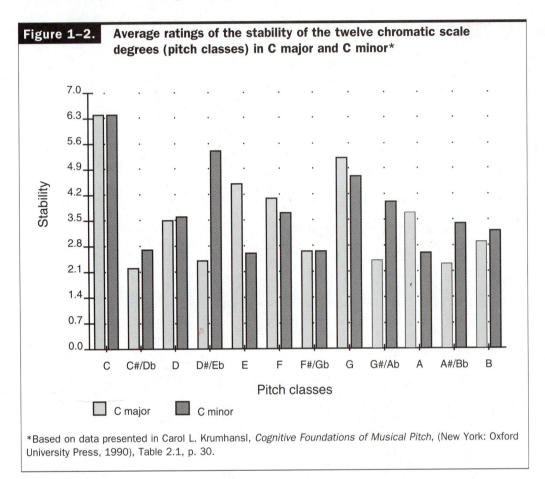

Figure 1–2. **Average ratings of the stability of the twelve chromatic scale degrees (pitch classes) in C major and C minor***

Pitch classes

☐ C major   ◼ C minor

*Based on data presented in Carol L. Krumhansl, *Cognitive Foundations of Musical Pitch*, (New York: Oxford University Press, 1990), Table 2.1, p. 30.

it functions as a lower chromatic neighbor to E and should, therefore, have been spelled as D♯. However, Berg wrote E♭ instead.[4]

Models of Functional Tonality

Music theorists and psychologists have developed various models of the tonal system; one was shown in Fig. 1–2. In Ex. 1–6, another such model, we see that a *fundamental* tone often has *harmonic partials,* pitches whose frequencies are integer multiples of the fundamental frequency.[5] The intensity of these partials usually decreases as one ascends in the series, but in certain cases higher partials can overpower the fundamental.

---

[4]For a more extensive discussion of chromatic notation in functional tonality see Edward Aldwell and Carl Schachter, *Harmony and Voice Leading*, 2nd ed. (San Diego: Harcourt Brace Jovanovich, 1989), Chapter 28, secs. 18–20.

[5]For a summary of the arguments for and against its relevance to tonal music see William Thomson, *Schoenberg's Error* (Philadelphia: University of Pennsylvania Press, 1991), Chapters 9 and 10.

4. What other keys are established? How stable are they? Describe the modulations to and from them.
5. What chord type does Wolf use extensively in mm. 19–37? With what poetic image(s) is this chord type associated?

"In der Frühe"

1. What keys are stated or implied? How are they related to each other? How are the modulations accomplished?
2. How does the vocal melody of mm. 1–10 compare with that of mm. 11–21?

Brahms, Capriccio in C, Op. 76, No. 8 (see Exx. 18–4b, 18–5b, and 18–7b, pp. 327–34)

1. Analyze each excerpt using Roman and figured-bass numerals. Show how each non-tonic key area relates to C major. How many V^7–I cadences can you find? How many accented dissonances?
2. Explain how Brahms avoided a strong cadence in mm. 56–57 of Ex. 18–7b.
3. Explain how the V^7 and I chords are prolonged in the last seven measures of Ex. 18–7b.

Atonality

Berg, "Schliesse mir die Augen beide" (1925) (see Ex. 1–7)

In this setting, the two quatrains (four-line stanzas) of Storm's poem are delineated by a slackening and resumption of tempo in mm. 10–11. Rhyming words from the original German and an English translation are shown in Table 1–1 (p. 14).

In Ex. 1–3 above we analyzed the vocal melody of the tonal setting in terms of four-note motives. The same approach can be applied to this setting, but we'll have to probe deeper to reveal similarities.

Example 1–8 shows three ways to represent the melodic intervals in mm. 1–2. Row *a* contains signed integers that indicate the direction of each interval and its size in semitones. Row *b* contains unsigned integers that denote size only. Row *c* contains plus and minus signs that indicate direction only. The angled brackets reveal that the directional pattern < – + – > occurs twice. Notice that both occurrences have identical durations and similar pitch contours.

Can the entire vocal melody be conceived in terms of this contour pattern, and perhaps one or two others? Example 1–9 shows that it can. As with the 1907 setting, there are three motives, each having a distinctive pitch contour. To represent these patterns, we'll use plus and minus signs to indicate ascending and descending melodic intervals.

Motive	Pitch contour
x	< – + – >
y	< – – >
z	< + + – >

Example 1–7.   **Berg, "Schliesse mir die Augen beide" (1925)**

Example 1–7. *Continued*

TABLE 1–1.   **Rhyme scheme and meter for the German and English texts of "Schliesse mir"**

Rhyme Scheme	German	English	Syllables
a	beide	parting	8
b	zu	much	7
a′	leide	suff'ring	8
b′	Ruh	touch	7
c	Schmerz	sea	7
d	leget	evening	8
d′	reget	beating	8
c′	Herz	thee	7
			60

Example 1–8.   **Types of melodic intervals in mm. 1–2**

a. ordered pitch intervals: -1   +8   -3   +10   -5   +6   -7

b. unordered pitch intervals: 1   8   3   10   5   6   7

c. interval directions: < -   +   - >   +   < -   +   - >

The melody of the tonal (1907) setting lies mainly within the octave C_4–C_5, but that span is raised to E_4–E_5 in mm. 3–4. In comparison, the melody of the atonal (1925) setting covers a much wider range, nearly two octaves from B^b_3 in m. 12 to A_5 in the very next measure. Even more significant are the ranges and contours of the individual phrases. Each phrase of the atonal setting spans considerably more than an octave, and the melodic motion is highly *disjunct*.

The accompaniment contains a variety of harmonic combinations. The F♯ major triads in mm. 12–13 are a familiar chord type, but they don't function in the traditional manner. Berg used dissonant intervals and chords more freely in this setting. Notice for example that in the final measure he piled up all twelve chromatic scale degrees to form the ultimate dissonance.

Example 1–9 shows that the eight vocal phrases are arranged in four groups of two. Example 1–10 shows that the melody can also be divided into five 12-note segments. Compare these five segments. Are any two exactly alike? If so, which ones? What feature do they all share?

Berg apparently composed this setting by arranging the twelve degrees of the chromatic scale to form an *ordered set* or *series*. He divided the sixty syllables of the

Example 1–9. Motive and phrase analysis of the vocal melody

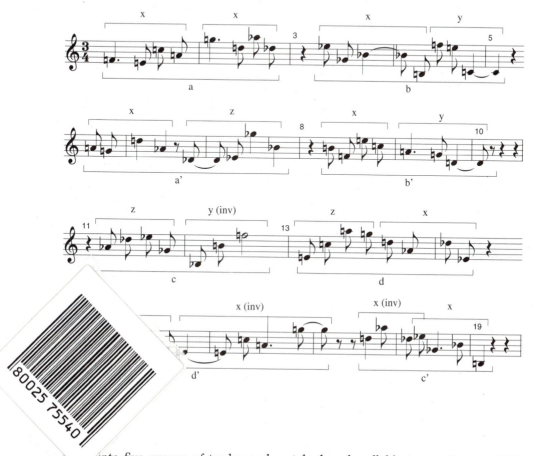

into five groups of twelve and matched each syllable to a scale tone. This enabled him to keep all twelve tones in constant circulation and to avoid undue emphasis on any one. Berg used *enharmonic notation* in a few places, most notably in mm. 12–13 where he replaced flatted pitches with their sharped equivalents.

The piano accompaniment is based on the same series used in the vocal melody. The accompaniment here is more *linear* and *imitative* than that of the earlier setting. Imitation begins in m. 7 where the piano echoes the vocal phrase "geht doch alles" with slightly altered rhythm, and it continues throughout the first half of the song. Notice that imitation occurs only at the unison or octave, never at another interval.

A similar procedure can be seen in mm. 4–7 where a melodic line is presented then restated with its pitches reversed. In Ex. 1–11, the original line is labeled *P* for *prime* and the reverse is labeled *RP* for *retrograde of prime*. The same labels appear in mm. 7–8, but note that the last two notes of the *RP* segment are two octaves higher than their counterparts in the *P* segment.

Example 1–10 also shows that each series of 12 tones can be divided into two hexachords that are labeled A and B. When the voice sings pitches from Hexachord

Example 1–10.   Statements of the basic set

Example 1–11.   Retrograde-related lines in mm. 4–8

A, the piano usually plays others from Hexachord B, and vice versa. As Fig. 1–3 illustrates, Hexachords A and B lie on opposite sides of the cycle of perfect fourths/fifths.

The 1925 setting ends with a delicate arpeggiation of its "mother chord." The arpeggio begins on F_4, the pitch that is connected by a dotted diagonal line to the final note of the voice part. In fact, Berg provided the direction "den Gesang fortsetzend" ("continuing the song") at that point. The arpeggio ends with F_1, the very last note in the piece. Notice that Berg did not tie the initial F_4 into the final measure, but he did tie each of the other notes. Perhaps he did not want F to be too prominent in the final sonority. How does this compare with his voicing of the final tonic triad of the 1907 setting?

SUMMARY

Atonality is a way of arranging pitches so as to preclude tonal focus. Atonal music is usually based on the entire chromatic scale. Composers have developed various procedures for keeping all twelve scale degrees in constant circulation and of avoiding emphasis upon any single degree. To emphasize pitch contour in the absence of a tonality, they have often used large melodic intervals. Atonal sonorities are often more varied than chords found in functional tonality. They often contain sharp dissonances and tritones. The texture of atonal music is often linear rather than chordal, and the various textural strands are often correlated through imitation by transposition, inversion, and/or retrograde.

EXERCISE 1-2

1. The 12-tone series listed above the staff has been divided into four trichords (sets of three pitches). A melodic interval pattern is shown in angled brackets beneath each measure. Realize each trichord by notating pitches that form the interval pattern. You may use either a sharped or flatted pitch for those degrees that require an accidental (for example, F♯/G♭). To avoid confusion, use natural signs for all of the other pitches. Use the completed measures as models.

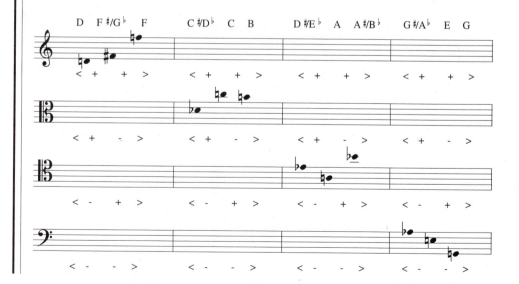

2. Now realize the same trichords as chords instead of melodic fragments. Notate four different realizations of each trichord, one on each staff. Because the pitches will sound simultaneously, you need not be concerned about preserving the original ordering. The only requirements are: 1) each chord must contain an instance of the three chromatic scale degrees; 2) the interval between adjacent pitches should not exceed an octave; and 3) the interval between adjacent pitches should not be an augmented unison (use a minor second instead). As above, use the completed measures as models.

3. Compare the vocal melody in mm. 1–4 of Ex. 1–7 with the violin phrase in Ex. 15–5b (p. 287). What do these two melodies have in common? How do they differ?
4. Continue Ex. 15–5b by writing three additional phrases of idiomatic melody for the violin. Create each phrase by using the pitches from rows 2, 3, and 4 of Ex. 1–10. Try to make your phrases sound like a logical continuation of Berg's.

Neotonality

The term *neotonal* describes compositions that belong somewhere between the extremes of tonality and atonality (see Fig. 1–1, p. 2).[7]

Copland, "The World Feels Dusty" (1951) (see Ex. 1–12)

Aaron Copland's song divides into three sections of nearly equal length as shown in Ex. 1–13. The first and last sections share the same tempo and melodic content,

---

[7]See Elliott Antokoletz, *Twentieth-Century Music* (Englewood Cliffs, NJ: Prentice-Hall, 1992), Chapter 11; also Robert P. Morgan, *Twentieth-Century Music* (New York: W. W. Norton, 1991), Chapter 4.

so the formal scheme is ternary or ABA′. The B section is marked by a faster tempo, a louder dynamic level (in mm. 11–13), and some harmonic-tonal contrast. The A′ section returns to the original tempo but with a first phrase that is rather different from its counterpart in section A. The song's final phrase is, however, virtually identical to *its* counterpart, except for the final note.

The vocal melody is less conjunct than Berg's 1907 setting, but more conjunct than his 1925 setting (compare Exx. 1–1, 1–7, and 1–12). Copland used consecutive thirds to subdivide a major seventh or ninth as shown in Ex. 1–14a. Perfect fifths can also be found between adjacent as well as nonadjacent notes. Within the various phrases, there are only a few intervals larger than a perfect fifth: sixths in mm. 4, 8, and 24–25, and octaves in mm. 14–16. Only one melodic seventh is present, but it is a "dead" interval that straddles the last two phrases (mm. 21–22). Diminished intervals occur only between nonadjacent notes (see Ex. 1–14b).

In contrast to Berg's atonal setting, Copland's entire melody includes only seven degrees of the chromatic scale: [D E F♯ ( ) A/A♯ B C♯].[8] Notice that A and A♯ never occur in direct succession within the vocal melody, but they do form a *cross relation* between voice and piano in mm. 19–20.[9]

Copland's accompaniment provides tonal and rhythmic support for the voice. It is chordal, but a melodic component is present as well in the form of two motives shared with the voice. Example 1–15 (p. 23) shows how the chords may be represented in three ways:

- in their original voicing with a box drawn around the root (see the grand staff)
- in root- and closed-position voicings with chord symbol labels (top staff)
- as simple or compound intervals above a bass note as represented by figured-bass numerals (below the bottom staff)

Each representation has its strong points. The original voicing preserves spacing and doubling and shows the placement of the root. The closed-position voicing (top staff) reveals that most chords can be built by stacking thirds to form *extended tertian* chords. The figured-bass numerals indicate the size of each harmonic interval in scale steps, but they do not show its "quality" (size in semitones) or position within the chord.

Ex. 1–15 also shows that some chords have strong roots, some have weak roots, and others lack a root. At times, chords on the first and second beats share the same root, but in other places (e.g., m. 15), the root changes within the measure. Several measures are ambiguous in this regard. For example, do you hear a change of root within mm. 1–6, 9–10, 17–23, 25–28? Furthermore, it is often difficult to identify root movement between measures.

In the absence of key-defining chord progressions, such as V⁷–I, the roots of the most stable and prevalent chords tend to sound like tonic scale degrees. For example, G is the tonic of mm. 11–15 because it is the root of all but two of the

---

[8]The empty parentheses indicate there is no pitch with letter name G in the vocal melody. The slashed combination A/A♯ indicates two pitches that have the same letter name.

[9]The term *cross relation* refers to the successive occurrence of pitches having the same letter name but differing accidentals in different voices of a texture.

Example 1–12.   Copland, "The World Feels Dusty" No. 4 of *Twelve Poems of Emily Dickinson* (1951)

chords. All of the G chords are in root position, and the G major triads in mm. 11 and 12 are the most consonant sonorities in the entire song. In contrast, the A and A′ sections consist mainly of chords whose root lies above their bass note (see Ex. 1–15). Notable exceptions are the unstable chords on the second beats of mm. 1–6, and the E-rooted chords of mm. 9–10 and 21–22.

G prevails as the harmonic root and apparent tonic of mm. 11–17, but it is entirely absent from the vocal melody. Instead of stressing G and D, tonic and dominant, in the voice part, Copland favored A, C♯, E, and F♯, the less stable degrees

Example 1–12.   *Continued*

Example 1–13.   **Sectional form and tonal plan**

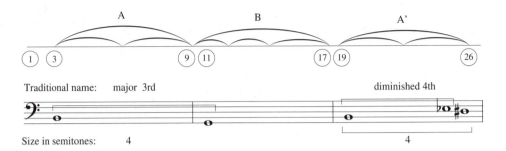

Example 1–14.   **Dissonant intervals formed between nonadjacent pitches in the vocal melody**

a. Major sevenths; major and minor ninths

b. Diminished fourths, elevenths, and twelfths

of the G Lydian scale [G A B C# D E F# G]. In fact, D does not appear until the end of m. 15 when the harmonic accompaniment takes a rest.

The tonal ambiguity of the A section is intensified in the A′ section where Copland introduced A# and D#, and pitted A sharp against A natural to create cross relations (see mm. 19 and 20). Notice that he wrote another sharp dissonance in m. 22 where the voice sings A_4 against the piano's $G\#_3$.

Example 1–15. Harmonic analysis of the piano accompaniment

The ending is most interesting. After leading us to expect a cadence on B in m. 25, Copland shifted abruptly to E♭ Lydian for the last three measures. But instead of using root-position chords, he used first-inversion triads similar to those in mm. 17–20. The combination of a non-tonic ending with these less stable sonorities lends the song a tentative but soothing quality that parallels the imagery of the text.

Copland's ending serves another purpose, as well. As Ex. 1–13 illustrates, E♭, the tonic of the ending, and G, the tonic of the middle section, lie the same distance

Example 1–15. *Continued*

above and below B, the apparent tonic of the A and A′ sections. The E♭ tonality of the ending acts, therefore, as a counterbalance to the G tonality of the middle section. Note, however, that these intervals are equal only when measured in semitones. They are unequal when measured by the traditional method: G–B is a major third, but B–E♭ is a diminished fourth.

Figures 1–4a and b show that the three tonics, B, G, and E♭, are equally spaced around the cycle of perfect fourths/fifths *and* around the cycle of minor seconds/major sevenths. Since each circle represents an octave, we can see that Copland divided the octave into three equal-sized parts.

Figure 1–4. Tonal plan of "The World Feels Dusty" (compare Ex. 1–13)

a. represented on the cycle of fourths/fifths

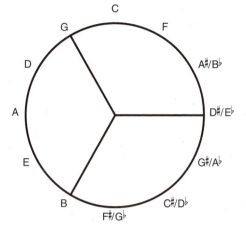

b. represented on the cycle of minor seconds/majors sevenths

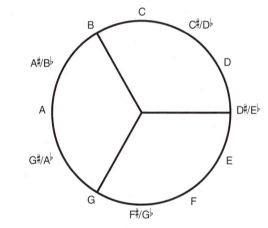

The ending (mm. 25–27) contains an apparent conflict between the voice ($A^\sharp_3$) and piano ($B^\flat_3$). This combination doesn't *sound* "wrong," it only *looks* "wrong." It appears that Copland used enharmonic notation to preserve legibility for both performers. If he had ended the vocal melody with $B^\flat_3$, the spelling would have agreed with the piano part (see Ex. 1–16a), but the final melodic interval would have been a descending augmented fifth, $F^\sharp_4 – B^\flat_3$, and the final $B^\flat$ would have formed a cross relation with B natural, the expected tonic of the phrase (compare mm. 9 and 25). The other alternative, adjusting the piano part to the voice, would have required the use of F double sharp to spell the first inversion $D^\sharp$ major triads (see Ex. 1–16b).

Example 1–16. Alternative notation for mm. 24–26

a.

b.

SUMMARY

Neotonality involves freer use of all twelve degrees of the chromatic scale, but in a way that usually projects a tonic pitch or sonority. Neotonal composers often avoid traditional major and minor scales, preferring the diatonic modes or other less familiar scale types. In addition, they often avoid the most common chord types of functional tonality: major and minor triads, and the dominant (major-minor) seventh chord. Instead they use extended tertian chords as well as chords built of other intervals. Perfect fourths and fifths occur frequently in neotonal music, both melodically and harmonically.

Neotonal harmony often avoids conventional chord progressions. Tonic chords can often be found, but they are established by means other than functional harmony. Several key areas may be established during the course of a neotonal work. These areas may be linked by common chords or common tones, but they are rarely connected by functional harmonic progressions. Enharmonic respelling can occur whenever successive key areas are distantly related. Neotonal pieces may begin and end on the same tonic or on different tonics.

EXERCISE 1–3

1. Realize the figured bass given below by providing soprano, alto, and tenor parts. Try to move the voices as smoothly as possible. When you have finished, compare your setting with Ex. 13–1a, mm. 1–5.

2. Provide a figured-bass and chord symbol analysis for mm. 1–14 of Britten's "Sonnet" from the Serenade for Tenor Solo, Horn and Strings, Op. 31 (Burkhart). How many different chord types can you find in this passage? Locate several examples of enharmonic respellings and cross relations.

QUESTIONS FOR REVIEW

1. Define the following terms: tonality, atonality, conjunct, disjunct, consonance, dissonance, harmonic function, harmonic expansion or prolongation, enharmonic, melodic inversion, modal mixture, tonicization, modulation, ordered set.
2. Compare and contrast the following:
   a. chord root vs. tonic scale degree
   b. cross relation vs. enharmonic respelling
   c. a scale vs. a collection of octave-related pitches
   d. figured-bass analysis vs. roman numeral analysis
   e. scale steps vs. semitones
   f. root motion vs. voice leading
3. Are the terms *consonant* and *tonal* synonymous? Is it possible for music to be consonant yet tonally unstable? Is it possible for music to be dissonant yet tonal?
4. What is the meaning of the term *chromatic* in functional tonality? Does it have the same meaning in atonality? In neotonality?
5. Explain the difference between a *tonal hierarchy* and an *event hierarchy*.
6. Explain how dissonant intervals and chords are treated differently in tonal and atonal music.

RECOMMENDED LISTENING AND ANALYSIS

Anthologies and musical examples are cited in parentheses. See the Key to Anthologies Cited (p. vi) for complete citations.

A. Functional Tonality

Brahms, Three Intermezzos (Burkhart)
———, "Wie Melodien zieht es mir" Op. 105, No. 1 (Burkhart)
Chopin, Seven Preludes (Burkhart)
Fauré, *Toujours* (Burkhart)
Mahler, *Adagietto* from Symphony No. 5 (Burkhart)
———, "Nun will die Sonn' so hell aufgeh'n" (Palisca; Turek)
———, "Um Mitternacht" (Godwin)
Wagner, *Tristan und Isolde* Prelude to Act I (Burkhart, Turek, WenAMSS), Excerpt from Act II (Turek), Prelude to and opening of Act III (WenAMSS), *Liebestod* (Burkhart)
Wolf, Two Songs (Burkhart)
———, "Gebet" from *Mörike Songs* (Turek)
———, "Wer sich der Einsamkeit ergiebt," No. 1 from *Goethe Songs* (Turek)

B. Atonality

Babbitt, Semi-Simple Variations (Burkhart; Morgan; Turek)
———, "Play on Notes" (Burkhart)
Bartók, Minor Seconds, Major Sevenths (Morgan)
Berg, Lyric Suite, first movement (Morgan)
Dallapiccola, *Quaderno musicale di Annalibera*, Nos. 4, 5, and 6 (WenAMSS), No. 11 (Burkhart)
Schoenberg, Three Piano Pieces, Op. 11, No. 1 (Burkhart)
———, Six Little Piano Pieces, Op. 19 (Nos. 2, 4, & 6 in Wen20; No. 6 in DeLio-Smith, Turek)
———, *Pierrot Lunaire*, Op. 21 (Nos. 1 and 8 in WenAMSS; No. 7 in DeLio-Smith; No. 8 in Turek)
Webern, Five Movements for String Quartet, Op. 5, No. 3 (Turek; WenAMSS) No. 4 (Burkhart)
———, Six Bagatelles for String Quartet, Op. 9, No. 1 (Godwin)
———, String Quartet, Op. 28, first movement (Morgan)

C. Neotonality

Bartók, Fourteen Bagatelles for Piano, Op. 6, Nos. 1, 4, 8, and 14 (Simms)
———, *Mikrokosmos*, IV/115 "Bulgarian Rhythm" and V/133 "Syncopation" (Burkhart); V/126 "Change of Time" and VI/148 Dance No. 1 in Bulgarian Rhythm (Wen20); II/59 "Major and Minor" and V/128 "Peasant Dance" (Turek)
Britten, Serenade for Tenor, Horn and Strings, "Sonnet" and Epilogue (Burkhart) "Dirge" (Simms; Turek; WenAMSS) "Nocturne" (Godwin)
Debussy. Preludes "Canope" (WenAMSS), "Des pas sur la neige" (Wen20), "La cathédrale engloutie" (Burkhart), "Danseuses de Delphes" (DeLio-Smith)
———, *Syrinx* (DeLio-Smith)
Dello Joio. Piano Sonata No. 3, first movement (WenAMSS)
Hindemith, *Six Chansons*, "A Swan" (Burkhart); "Spring" (Wen20)
———, *Ludus Tonalis*, Interlude in G (WenAMSS; Morgan) Interludium (Turek)
Prokofiev, Seventh Piano Sonata, III (Simms)
———, *Visions Fugitives*, No. 1 (DeLio-Smith)
Ravel, Sonatine, first movement (Burkhart)
Shostakovich, Twenty-Four Preludes, Op. 34, No. 1 (DeLio-Smith)
Stravinsky, Concerto for Piano and Winds, I (Morgan)
———, *Mass*, Kyrie (WenAMSS), Credo (Simms)
———, Sonata for Two Pianos, second movement (Theme with Variations) (Burkhart)

Part II

FUNDAMENTALS OF SET THEORY

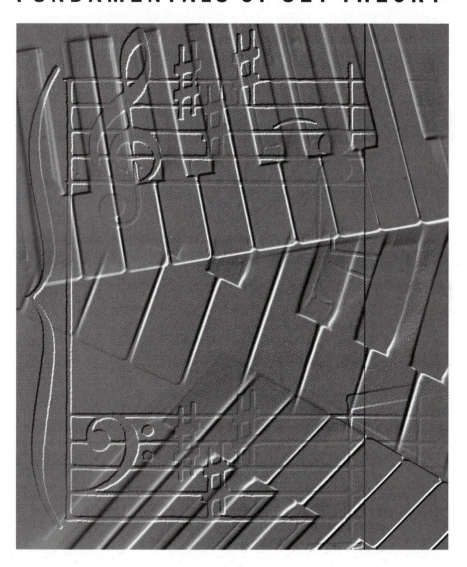

CHAPTER 2

Integer Representation

In order to study 20th-century music from a more objective point of view, one that is not biased toward functional tonality, music theorists have developed new ways to represent pitches and intervals. Their work comprises a branch of music theory that is often called *pitch class set theory, atonal theory,* or *post-tonal theory.*[1]

Pitch

For our purposes, *pitch* may be defined as the quality of musical tones that is perceived in terms of the spatial concepts of high and low. This definition implies that pitch can be measured. Indeed it can, and there are several ways of doing so. To limit the possibilities, let's assume that we intend to measure the discrete pitches of the equal-tempered system, the ones that form the so-called chromatic scale.

Example 2–1 shows two ways to represent pitches in *continuous pitch code.*[2] In the row labeled MIDI, the reference pitch (pitch zero) lies at the very bottom of the pitch gamut. This method is used for synthesizers and computer software that support the Musical Instrument Digital Interface. In the row labeled Rahn, zero is assigned to middle C, and the other pitches are numbered in both directions. Both schemes are useful, but one may be more convenient than another for certain tasks.

Octave Equivalence and Register

Continuous pitch code has a serious deficiency; it does not account for *octave equivalence*, the perceived similarity between octave-related pitches. To refer to specific pitches in an octave-based system we must indicate their octave and their position within the octave. Several systems of octave labeling are in current use. We'll use the one shown in Ex. 2–2.

---

[1]A number of theorists have made important contributions in this area. For an annotated bibliography compiled by Martha Hyde and Andrew Mead see *Music Theory Spectrum* 11/1 (1989). The concepts, terms, and symbols used in this text are primarily those found in John Rahn's *Basic Atonal Theory* (New York: Longman, 1980).

[2]See Alexander R. Brinkman, *Pascal Programming for Music Research* (Chicago: University of Chicago Press, 1990), Chapter 6.

Example 2–1. Two schemes for numbering pitches in continuous pitch code

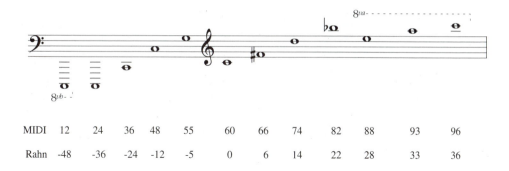

MIDI	12	24	36	48	55	60	66	74	82	88	93	96
Rahn	-48	-36	-24	-12	-5	0	6	14	22	28	33	36

Example 2–2. The ASA system of numbering octaves

Enharmonic Equivalence and Pitch Class

The term *enharmonic equivalence* refers to pitches that can be played by striking the same piano key. The term *pitch class* denotes a category of pitches that are related by both *octave equivalence* and *enharmonic equivalence*. Every pitch in the equal-tempered system can be assigned to one of twelve pitch classes (pcs) as shown by the rows of Table 2–1.

It is important at this stage to remind yourself that a pitch class is not a pitch. Rather, it is a group, class, or category of pitches. The pitches that you see notated in musical examples throughout this text, and the sounds they represent, are not pitch classes. They are *instances* of pitch classes.

If a pitch class can neither be seen nor heard, what purpose does it serve? Pitch class is a *concept* that enables us to overlook surface-level differences and focus on similarities that lie beneath the surface. Whenever we invoke this concept, we rely upon two mental operations. We *generalize* when we see or hear actual pitches and

TABLE 2–1. **Pitch class and name class numbers of common notes using C as reference***

Pitch Class	Name Class						
	0	**1**	**2**	**3**	**4**	**5**	**6**
0	C	D♭♭					B♯
1	C♯	D♭					B×
2	C×	D	E♭♭				
3		D♯	E♭	F♭♭			
4		D×	E	F♭			
5			E♯	F	G♭♭		
6			E×	F♯	G♭		
7				F×	G	A♭♭	
8					G♯	A♭	
9					G×	A	B♭♭
10	C♭♭					A♯	B♭
11	C♭					A×	B

*Alexander R. Brinkman, *Pascal Programming for Music Research* (Chicago: University of Chicago Press, 1990), Table 6.3, p. 128.

classify them as pitch classes. We *realize* or *instantiate* when we imagine or create actual pitches by assigning letter names and registers to pitch classes. As Figure 2–1 illustrates, these operations are reciprocal.

Name Class

Pitch class numbers allow us to ignore differences in letter-name spelling. For example, D♯ and E♭ can both be represented by 3; A♯ and B♭ by 10. There are times, however, when letter names are too important to disregard. On such occasions we'll use name-class numbers to represent pitch letter names, minus any qualifying accidental. As Table 2–1 shows, a name class includes any and all pitches that share the same letter name (for example, B♭, B, and B♯).

Figure 2–1.

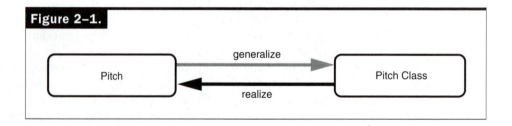

Binomial Representation

The position of a pitch within the chromatic octave *and* its position within the diatonic octave can be indicated by citing both its pitch class (pc) and name class (nc) numbers. Brinkman has coined the term *binomial representation* (br) to denote such a scheme.[3] Table 2–1 shows how any pitch can be represented as a binomial in the form <pc,nc>. To illustrate, C♯ has pc number 1 and nc number 0, so its br is <1,0>. B♭ would be represented as <10,6>. Example 2–3a lists brs for various pitches. Note that the binomial method allows us to distinguish between enharmonically equivalent pitches. For example, F♯ is <6,3> while G♭ is <6,4>. These two brs share the same pc number but have different nc numbers.

At other times, letter-name spelling may not be as important as specific registration. Then we can use pitch class-octave symbols (pc-octs), another type of binomial. Several pc-octs are shown in Ex. 2–3b.

Finally, when all three aspects (pitch class, name class, and octave) are essential, we can use a *complete binomial representation (cbr)*, a symbol whose prototype is <pc,nc,oct>. Ex. 2–3c shows cbrs for the same set of pitches.

EXERCISE 2–1

1. Provide a pitch number and a complete binomial (cbr) for each pitch. Refer to Ex. 2–1, Ex. 2–2, and Table 2–1.

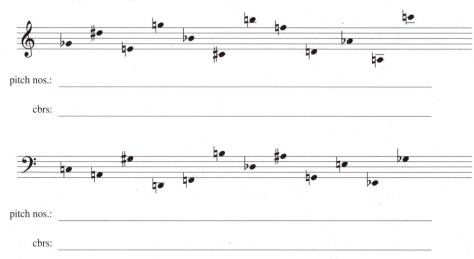

pitch nos.: _____

cbrs: _____

pitch nos.: _____

cbrs: _____

2. Notate pitches that correspond to the numbers given below each staff. Provide an accidental for every note, but do not use double sharps or double flats.

---

[3]*Pascal Programming for Music Research*, pp. 128–135.

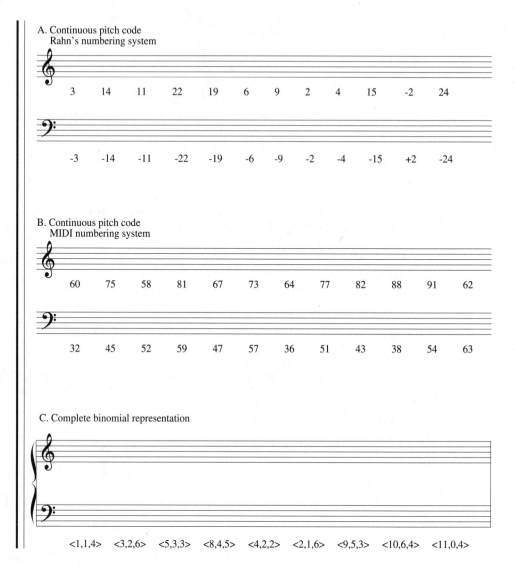

A. Continuous pitch code
Rahn's numbering system

| 3 | 14 | 11 | 22 | 19 | 6 | 9 | 2 | 4 | 15 | -2 | 24 |

| -3 | -14 | -11 | -22 | -19 | -6 | -9 | -2 | -4 | -15 | +2 | -24 |

B. Continuous pitch code
MIDI numbering system

| 60 | 75 | 58 | 81 | 67 | 73 | 64 | 77 | 82 | 88 | 91 | 62 |

| 32 | 45 | 52 | 59 | 47 | 57 | 36 | 51 | 43 | 38 | 54 | 63 |

C. Complete binomial representation

<1,1,4> <3,2,6> <5,3,3> <8,4,5> <4,2,2> <2,1,6> <9,5,3> <10,6,4> <11,0,4>

Absolute vs. Relative Representation

Pitch, pitch class, name class, and octave numbers may be assigned in an *absolute* or *relative* manner. With absolute representation, pitches are labeled as shown in Ex. 2–1, octaves as shown in Ex. 2–2, and pitch classes and name classes as shown in Table 2–1. This convention parallels the use of "fixed-do" solfège. Relative representation corresponds to "moveable-do" syllables, or scale-degree numbers, where the reference pc changes with the tonic key. While it may seem odd to use relative representation for atonal music, it is, nevertheless, done for various reasons. To illustrate, Ex. 1–10 (p. 16) shows a vocal line that consists of five statements of a series of twelve pcs. Each statement begins on F, so it makes sense to use F as the

Example 2–3. BRs, PC-octs, and CBRs for various pitches

a. brs   <0,0>   <7,4>   <2,1>   <9,5>   <1,1,>   <6,3>   <11,6>   <4,2>   <8,5>   <3,1>

b. pc-octs <0,2>   <7,2>   <2,3>   <9,3>   <1,4>   <6,4>   <11,4>   <4,5>   <8,5>   <3,6>

c. cbrs   <0,0,2> <7,4,2> <2,1.3> <9,5,3> <1,1,4>   <6,3,4>   <11,6,4>   <4,2,5>   <8,5,5>   <3,1,6>

reference pc (pc zero) and number the other pcs accordingly. If this method is adopted, then the name class and octave numbers should be adjusted, as well.

Intervals

We are often more concerned in musical analysis with distances between pitches than with pitches themselves. To measure these distances with varying degrees of precision, music theorists have devised various types of intervals. The rows of Table 2–2 show that intervals can be formed between *pitches, pitch classes, name classes,* and *octaves.* The columns show that intervals can be regarded as *ordered* or *unordered.* An *ordered interval* is formed by two pitches that occur successively; it has two properties: *size* and *direction.* The most familiar example is a melodic interval. *Unordered intervals* lack direction because their pitches occur simultaneously; they have only one property, *size.* The most familiar example is a harmonic interval.

TABLE 2–2. Types of intervals

	Ordered Intervals	Unordered Intervals
Pitches	Ordered Pitch Interval ip<a,b> = b − a	Unordered Pitch Interval ip(a,b) = | b − a |
Pitch Classes	Ordered PC Interval ipc<a,b>= mod12 (b − a)	Unordered PC Interval (Interval Class) ipc(a,b) = lesser of (ipc<a,b>, ipc<b,a>)
Name Classes	Ordered NC Interval inc<a,b> = mod7 (b − a)	Unordered NC Interval inc(a,b) = lesser of (inc<a,b>, inc<b,a>)
Octaves	Ordered Oct Interval ioct<a,b> = octb − octa	Unordered Oct Interval ioct(a,b) = | octb − octa |

In keeping with Rahn's conventions, we will use angle brackets to indicate ordered intervals. For example, if two pitches, *a* and *b*, occur in succession, they will be represented as <a,b>. If they occur simultaneously, or if the order of presentation is irrelevant, they will be enclosed in parentheses (a,b).

Intervals between Pitches

Let's begin by learning how to compute intervals between pitches that are represented with continuous pitch code (cpc).

Ordered Pitch Interval   To compute an ordered pitch interval, subtract the number of the first pitch from that of the second. This operation can be represented by the formula

$$\text{ip}<a,b> = b - a$$

where ip<a,b> stands for an ordered pitch interval, *a* is the number of the first pitch, and *b* is the number of the second pitch. It is important to subtract *a* from *b*, because this way the sign of the difference will indicate the direction of the interval. That is, positive numbers will denote ascending intervals and negative numbers, descending intervals.

To illustrate, let's compute intervals for the phrase given in Ex. 2–4. The cpc integers are shown beneath the notes in absolute representation. To compute the first interval, we simply replace *a* and *b* with the appropriate numbers and subtract.

MIDI	**Rahn**
ip<a,b> = b – a	ip<a,b> = b – a
ip<a,b> = 64 – 65	ip<a,b> = 4 – 5
ip<a,b> = –1	ip<a,b> = –1

The minus sign indicates that the interval's direction is descending.

Example 2–4.   **Pitch intervals in mm. 1–2 of "Schliesse mir"**

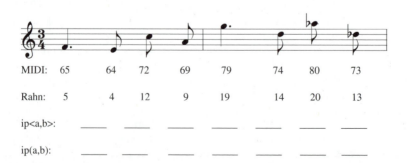

MIDI:	65	64	72	69	79	74	80	73
Rahn:	5	4	12	9	19	14	20	13
ip<a,b>:	___	___	___	___	___	___	___	
ip(a,b):	___	___	___	___	___	___	___	

The second interval would be computed as follows:

MIDI	Rahn
ip<a,b> = b − a	ip<a,b> = b − a
ip<a,b> = 72 − 64	ip<a,b> = 12 − 4
ip<a,b> = 8	ip<a,b> = 8

The result could be written as +8, but we'll assume that an integer other than zero is positive unless otherwise indicated.

EXERCISE 2–2

Using the integers given in Ex. 2–4, compute the remaining ordered pitch intervals for the Berg melody. Record them in the first row of blanks, the one labeled ip<a,b>.

Unordered Pitch Interval   The formula for this type of interval is:

$$ip(a,b) = |\, b - a \,|$$

where the vertical lines indicate the *absolute* value of b − a, that is, the number without any plus or minus sign. Thus, | 7 − 4 | = | +3 | = 3; and | 5 − 9 | = | −4 | = 4.

To compute the size of a harmonic interval, we'll regard the lower pitch as *a* and the higher pitch as *b*. If the computation is done this way, the difference will always be a positive integer, and its absolute value will be the unordered pitch interval.

EXERCISE 2–3

1. Compute unordered pitch intervals for the phrase shown in Example 2–4. Record your answers in the second row of blanks, the one labeled ip(a,b).

Ordered Pitch Class Interval   An ordered pc interval is computed by subtracting the first pc number from the second and applying the mod 12 function to the result. Expressed as a formula, the operation is

$$ipc<a,b> = mod12\ (b - a)$$

To find the *residue mod 12* of a positive number or zero, divide the number by 12 and take the remainder. Thus,

$$mod12\ (4) = 4\ div\ 12 = 0\ rem\ 4 = 4$$
$$mod12\ (19) = 19\ div\ 12 = 1\ rem\ 7 = 7$$

To find the residue mod 12 of a negative number, add twelve until the result falls within the range of 0–11. Thus,

$$\text{mod12} \ (-3) = (-3 + 12) = 9$$
$$\text{mod12} \ (-17) = (-17 + 12 + 12) = 7$$

Mod 12 arithmetic should be familiar from everyday activities. For example, if the time is 10:00 AM and you agree to meet a friend in four hours, the two of you will meet at 2:00 PM. Thus, mod12 (10 + 4) = mod12 (14) = 2. Similarly, if the time is 1:00 PM and you tell someone you've been up for six hours, then you arose at 7:00 AM. Thus, mod12 (1 − 6) = mod12 (−5) = (−5 + 12) = 7.

EXERCISE 2–4

Write pc numbers below the notes and compute the ordered pc intervals. The bottom two rows should be left blank for now. For this exercise assign zero to F and number the other pcs accordingly.

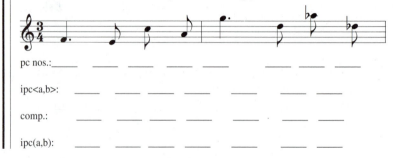

Unordered Pitch Class Interval   To find an unordered pc interval, compute the ordered interval between pcs *a* and *b*, then reverse the pcs and compute the ordered interval between pcs *b* and *a*. The unordered interval, ipc(a,b), will be the lesser of these two numbers. The formula is, therefore:

$$\text{ipc}(a,b) = \text{the lesser of ipc}\langle a,b\rangle \text{ or ipc}\langle b,a\rangle$$

To illustrate:

$$\text{ipc}\langle 5,10\rangle = \text{mod12} \ (10 - 5) \qquad \text{ipc}\langle 10,5\rangle = \text{mod12} \ (5 - 10)$$
$$\text{ipc}\langle 5,10\rangle = \text{mod12} \ (5) \qquad\qquad \text{ipc}\langle 10,5\rangle = \text{mod12} \ (-5)$$
$$\text{ipc}\langle 5,10\rangle = 5 \qquad\qquad\qquad \text{ipc}\langle 10,5\rangle = 7$$
$$\text{ipc}(5,10) \ = 5$$

Actually, we only need to compute one interval because every pair of ordered pc intervals is *complementary*, that is, they sum to 12, the *modulus* of the pc system. The six pairs of complementary intervals, often called interval classes, are shown in Table 2–3. Notice that an interval class (ic) is always named by the *smaller* of its two ordered pc intervals.

Unordered pc intervals can also be computed with the aid of the pc clock face (Fig. 2–2). We can define the unordered interval between pcs *a* and *b* as the number of "hours" from pc *a* to pc *b* as measured in *either* direction, whichever is shorter. Thus,

$$\text{ipc}(1,6) = 5 \text{ (measured clockwise)}$$
$$\text{ipc}(1,8) = 5 \text{ (measured counterclockwise)}$$

EXERCISE 2–5

Determine the complement of each ordered pc interval in Exercise 2–4. Compare these two numbers to determine which is the unordered pc interval. Record your answers in the bottom two rows of the worksheet.

Intervals between Name Classes

Intervals between name classes can be computed in the same way as those between pitch classes. However, the two systems have a different modulus: 12 for the pc system, 7 for the nc system. To compute an ordered interval between two name classes, subtract the first number from the second and apply mod 7 to the result. The formula, therefore, is:

$$\text{inc}\langle a,b\rangle = \text{mod7}\,(b - a)$$

The first phrase of Berg's 1925 setting is given in Exercise 2–6 below. Name class numbers have been assigned to the first two pitches using relative representation (F = 0). The ordered nc interval between these pitches would be computed as follows:

$$\text{inc}\langle a,b\rangle = \text{mod7}\,(b - a)$$
$$\text{inc}\langle F,E\rangle = \text{mod7}\,(6 - 0) = \text{mod7}\,(6) = 6$$

EXERCISE 2–6

Provide nc numbers for the remaining pitches and compute the remaining ordered name class intervals as shown above.

ncs: 0   6

inc⟨a,b⟩:   6

TABLE 2–3.   Interval classes and complementary ordered pc intervals

Interval class	1	2	3	4	5	6
Complementary pc intervals	1	2	3	4	5	6
	11	10	9	8	7	6

Figure 2–2. **Clock face of pitch class numbers**

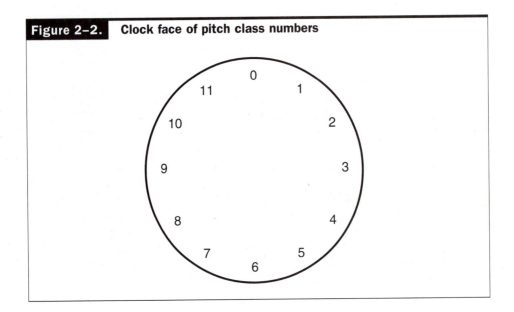

It is also possible to compute unordered name class intervals, but we will rarely have occasion to do so.

Figure 2–3 is a clock face that can be used to compute nc intervals. The methods are the same as those for pc intervals. Ordered intervals are measured in a *clockwise* direction; unordered intervals are measured in *either* direction, whichever is shorter.

Intervals between Octaves

The two motives shown in Ex. 2–5 have different melodic contours, but their ordered pc interval patterns are identical. To acknowledge these different contours, we must compute octave intervals, by subtracting the octave number of the first pitch from that of the second. The formula, therefore, is:

$$ioct<a,b> = oct<b> − oct<a>$$

Since octave numbers do not form a cycle, we need not apply any mod function to the result. If the sign of the octave interval is retained, we have an *ordered octave interval*. If the sign is discarded, we have an *unordered octave interval*. Example 2–5

Figure 2–3. **Clock face of name class numbers**

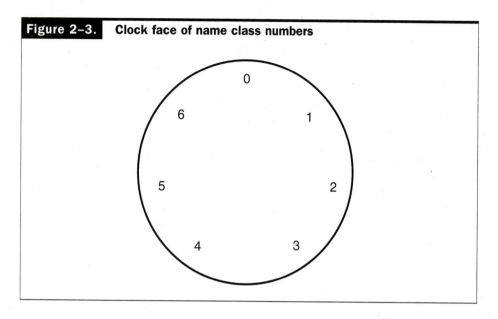

Example 2–5. **Pitch class, name class, and octave intervals for two Webern motives**

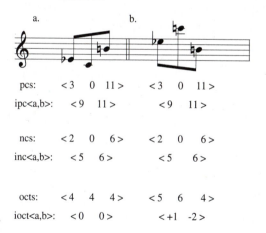

lists the octave number for each pitch and the ordered octave interval formed by each pair of adjacent pitches. As you can see, the two motives differ considerably in this respect.

Polynomial Intervals

It is often advisable to name an interval in more than one way. This can be done by combining pitch class, name class, and octave intervals to form various types of polynomial intervals.

PC-Oct Intervals   A pc-oct interval consists of an ordered pc interval and an ordered octave interval. To illustrate, the pc-oct intervals for Ex. 2–5b would be computed as follows:

First interval		**Second interval**	
pc-oct of pitch b:	<0, 6>	pc-oct of pitch b:	<11, 4>
pc-oct of pitch a:	<3, 5>	pc-oct of pitch a:	< 0, 6>
ipc-oct:	<9, +1>	ipc-oct:	<11, –2>

PC-NC Intervals   A pitch br (binomial representation) has the form <pc,nc>. An interval formed by two brs has two terms, as well: an ordered pc interval and an ordered nc interval. In computing an interval br (abbreviated as ibr), remember that the pc system has a modulus of 12, but the nc system has a modulus of 7. To illustrate, the br intervals for Ex. 2–5b would be computed as follows:

First interval		**Second interval**	
br of pitch b:	<0, 0>	br of pitch b:	<11, 6>
br of pitch a:	<3, 2>	br of pitch a:	< 0, 0>
ibr:	<9, 5>	ibr:	<11, 6>

CBR Intervals   Computing a complete binomial interval (icbr) involves finding the ordered interval between the corresponding terms of two pitch cbrs. Using the same example as above, the operations would be performed as follows:

First interval		**Second interval**	
cbr of pitch b:	<0, 0, 6>	cbr of pitch b:	<11, 6, 4>
cbr of pitch a:	<3, 2, 5>	cbr of pitch a:	< 0, 0, 6>
icbr:	<9, 5, +1>	icbr:	<11, 6, –2>

Interval Patterns

An *interval pattern* is an ordered listing of the intervals formed between adjacent pitches. It may consist of any type of interval, but all of its intervals must be of the same type.

   To compute an interval pattern, first represent each pitch with the appropriate integer (cpc, pc, nc, and/or oct). Then isolate successive pairs of integers and compute the appropriate type of interval for each pair.

EXERCISE 2–7

1. For each note provide a pitch, pitch class, name class, and octave number on the appropriate line. Then compute the ordered and unordered intervals for each type of number and write these on their respective lines.

cpc:
nos: _____

ip<a,b>: _____

ip(a,b):

_____

pcs: _____

ipc<a,b>: _____

ipc(a,b): _____

ncs: _____

inc<a,b>: _____

inc(a,b): _____

octs: _____

ioct<a,b>: _____

ioct(a,b): _____

2. Compute the following interval patterns for each staff in Ex. 1–10: ordered pitch interval, unordered pitch interval, ordered pc interval, unordered pc interval. Then compare patterns of the same type, for example, all of the ordered pc interval patterns. Are any of them identical? If so, can you explain why?

3. Build trichords (3-note chords) by notating pitches at the intervals specified below the given pitch. Notice that two types of intervals are used. The first chord of each staff has been notated for you. Provide an accidental for each pitch, but avoid double sharps and double flats.

Pitch intervals

a.

Pitch class intervals

c.

| 4 | 5 | 10 | 9 | 6 | 4 | 11 | 2 |
| 2 | 6 | 2 | 5 | 3 | 2 | 3 | 1 |

d.

| 3 | 11 | 8 | 10 | 9 | 7 | 4 | 6 |
| 1 | 4 | 6 | 5 | 2 | 3 | 1 | 4 |

SUMMARY

Pitches can be represented with varying degrees of precision. Pitch numbers are useful for indicating the location of a pitch with respect to a reference pitch, but they do not account for octave equivalence. To retain this important aspect, musicians use pitch class or name class numbers. Pitch class numbers indicate the position of pitches within the chromatic octave; name class numbers indicate their position within the diatonic octave. To locate pitches precisely in pitch space, we must also cite their octave numbers.

Intervals are distances between two elements of the same type: pitches, pitch classes, name classes, or octaves. When notes occur successively, the vertical distance between them may be regarded as an ordered interval having both size and direction. Notes that occur simultaneously form unordered intervals that have only one property: size. The size of intervals can be represented in more than one way by combining pitch class, name class, and octave intervals.

QUESTIONS FOR REVIEW

1. Define the following items: pitch, pitch class, octave equivalence, enharmonic equivalence, ordered interval, unordered interval, interval class, interval pattern.
2. List the properties of ordered and unordered intervals.
3. Write from memory the formula for: ordered pitch interval, unordered pitch interval, ordered pc interval, unordered pc interval, ordered nc interval, and unordered nc interval. Give the numerical range for each type of interval.

CHAPTER 3

Transposition

The Concept of Set

A set is a collection of objects of the same type. The objects that comprise a set are called its *elements*. To qualify as a set, a collection may not contain any duplicate elements. Thus, [C E G] is a set but [C E G C] is not. The term *cardinality* denotes the number of elements within a set. A set of three elements, such as [C E G], has a cardinality of three, a four-element set, such as [C E G B], has a cardinality of four, etc. Most sets used in musical analysis contain *integers* (whole numbers) that represent pitches, pitch classes, or name classes.

Sets, like intervals, can be classified as *ordered* or *unordered*. An *ordered set* is one whose elements are listed in a specific order. An *unordered set* is one whose elements may be listed in any order. Ordered sets have two properties: their *content* and the *ordering* of their elements; unordered sets have only one property: their *content*. We will enclose ordered sets in angle brackets: <G B D>, <B D G>, and <D G B>, and unordered sets in curly braces: {G B D}, {B D G}, and {D G B}.

Performing the Operation

Pitch Transposition

In tonal theory, a melodic line is transposed by raising or lowering each of its pitches by a constant interval. The operation is the same in atonal theory, but the pitches and the interval are represented by integers. Example 3–1 shows how a line can be transposed for alto saxophone. Here +9, the equivalent of an ascending major sixth, is added to each element of set A to produce set B.

Ex. 3–2 shows another transposition problem, this one for E-flat clarinet. That instrument sounds an octave higher than the alto saxophone, so its parts must be transposed *down* a minor third, which is represented here by –3.

The transposition of a single pitch can be represented as

$$T^p_n(p) = p + n$$

where p represents the pitch to be transposed, n represents the interval of transposition, and $T^p_n(p)$ represents the result.[1] A set of pitches can be transposed by adding the same interval to each pitch as shown in Exx. 3–1 and 3–2.

---

[1]The formulas and symbology in this chapter are modeled after those in John Rahn, *Basic Atonal Theory* (New York and London: Longman, 1980).

Example 3–1. **Pitch transposition for E♭ alto saxophone**

Rahn: 0   10   6   7   1   9   19   15   16   10

MIDI: 60 70 66 67 61   69   79   75   76   70

Rahn pitch numbers

A:	<0	10	6	7	1>
n:	+9	+9	+9	+9	+9
B:	<9	19	15	16	10>

MIDI pitch numbers

A:	<60	70	66	67	61>
n:	+9	+9	+9	+9	+9
B:	<69	79	75	76	70>

Example 3–2. **Pitch transposition for E♭ soprano clarinet**

Rahn: 21 17   13   10   16   18   14   10   7   13

MIDI: 81 77 73 70 76   78 74 70 67 73

Rahn pitch numbers

A:	<21	17	13	10	16>
n:	−3	−3	−3	−3	−3
B:	<18	14	10	7	13>

MIDI pitch numbers

A:	<81	77	73	70	76>
n:	−3	−3	−3	−3	−3
B:	<78	74	70	67	73>

EXERCISE 3–1

Represent each line or chord as a set using continuous pitch code. Transpose the set by the specified interval and notate the result. In some cases, you'll need to change the clef sign to avoid excessive leger lines. The first example has been done for you.

Pitch Class Transposition

Pitch classes are transposed in essentially the same manner as pitches, but there are a few differences:

- The element(s) to be transposed must be pc numbers, that is, they must fall within the range 0–11.
- The interval of transposition must be an ordered pc interval (these also must be within the range 0–11).

- The mod 12 operation must be applied to the result to ensure that it remains within the allowable range.

The formula for pc transposition is, therefore,

$$T_n(pc) = \text{mod}12\ (pc + n)$$

where pc represents the pitch class to be transposed, n represents an ordered pc interval, and $T_n(pc)$ represents the result. As Ex. 3–3 shows, a set of pcs can be transposed by adding the interval to each pc number and applying mod 12 to each sum. This means dividing each sum by twelve and taking the remainder. The results of division are shown on the line labeled mod 12; the first integer is the remainder and the second is the quotient. To preserve the contour of the original line, we could add the quotients to the octave numbers of the original pitches as shown. In this way we can *realize* the pitch classes by assigning them to a definite octave.

You may find it helpful to visualize pitch class transposition with the aid of the pc clock face (see Fig. 2–2, p. 40). To transpose a pc, locate its number on the clock face, then advance clockwise by the interval of transposition. Your stopping point will be the transposed pc. For example, to transpose pc 9 by interval 5, start at "9:00," advance 5 "hours," and you'll be at "2:00." The result, therefore, is pc 2.

EXERCISE 3–2

Represent each line as a set of pc numbers, transpose the set by the specified interval, and record the result in the spaces provided. Notate two realizations of the transposed pcs on the staff provided. One should preserve the melodic contour of the original line; the other should alter it. The first exercise has been done for you. Remember to use pc numbers instead of pitch numbers.

Example 3–3. Pitch class transposition (compare Ex. 3–1)

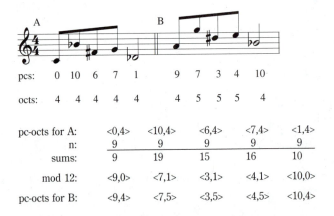

pcs:	0	10	6	7	1		9	7	3	4	10
octs:	4	4	4	4	4		4	5	5	5	4

pc-octs for A:	<0,4>	<10,4>	<6,4>	<7,4>	<1,4>
n:	9	9	9	9	9
sums:	9	19	15	16	10
mod 12:	<9,0>	<7,1>	<3,1>	<4,1>	<10,0>
pc-octs for B:	<9,4>	<7,5>	<3,5>	<4,5>	<10,4>

Name Class Transposition

It is also possible to transpose within a diatonic collection. To illustrate, suppose that we wish to transpose the line shown in Ex. 3–4 so that it remains within the G major scale. The interval of transposition will be an ascending sixth, or five scale steps. This can be done by assigning name class numbers to the pitches, adding 5

Example 3–4. Diatonic transposition using name class numbers

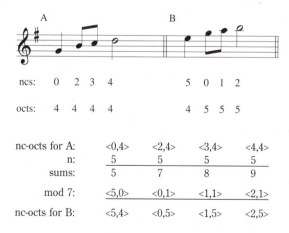

ncs:	0	2	3	4	5	0	1	2
octs:	4	4	4	4	4	5	5	5

nc-octs for A:	<0,4>	<2,4>	<3,4>	<4,4>
n:	5	5	5	5
sums:	5	7	8	9
mod 7:	<5,0>	<0,1>	<1,1>	<2,1>
nc-octs for B:	<5,4>	<0,5>	<1,5>	<2,5>

to each nc number, and applying mod 7 to each sum. This means dividing each sum by 7 and taking the remainder. Thus, the formula for nc transposition is:

$$T_n(nc) = mod7 \ (nc + n)$$

where nc represents the integer to be transposed, n the interval of transposition, and $T_n(nc)$ the result. If the quotient is added to the octave number, the transposed ncs can be realized in the proper octave.

EXERCISE 3–3

Each line is a fragment of a major or minor scale. Determine the most appropriate key and write its name under the meter signature. Using the tonic scale degree as the reference (nc zero), provide an nc number for each note. Transpose the set by the specified nc interval, and record the result in the two spaces provided. Remember to apply mod 7 to each sum so that the nc integers remain within the range 0–6. Notate two realizations of the transposed ncs on the staff provided. One should preserve the melodic contour of the original; the other should alter it. The first exercise has been done for you.

Recognizing T-Related Sets

Pitch Sets

In analyzing music we often need to determine whether lines or chords are related by transposition. T^p-related melodic lines have essentially the same pitch contour; T^p-related chords have essentially the same spacing between pitches. The qualifier "essentially" was used because staff notation and enharmonic spellings can obscure T relations.

To illustrate, let's assume that we have found two lines which may be T^p-related. We'll label the first set A and the second set B as shown in Ex. 3–5.

To determine whether two lines or **pitch sets** are $\mathbf{T^p_n}$**-related:**

1. Compare their ordered interval patterns (see Ex. 3–5a). If the interval patterns are identical, the lines are T^p-related.
2. Compute the differences between corresponding pitches (see Ex. 3–5b). If the differences are constant, then the lines are T^p-related, and the constant difference is the interval of transposition.

Example 3–5. Determining transpositional equivalence between pitch sets

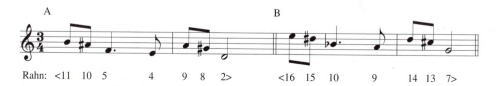

Rahn: <11 10 5   4   9 8 2>   <16 15 10   9   14 13 7>

a. compare ordered interval patterns

```
         -1    -5   -1   +5   -1   -6
A:   <11    10    5    4    9    8    2>
```

```
         -1    -5   -1   +5   -1   -6
B:   <16    15   10    9   14   13    7>
```

b. subtract pitch numbers

B:	16	15	10	9	14	13	7
A:	−11	−10	−5	−4	−9	−8	−2
n:	5	5	5	5	5	5	5

c. validate interval of transposition

A:	11	10	5	4	9	8	2
n:	+5	+5	+5	+5	+5	+5	+5
B:	16	15	10	9	14	13	7

If we already know that two sets are T^p_n-related, the interval of transposition can be computed by subtracting any pitch of set A from the corresponding pitch of set B. To validate we can transpose set A by interval n to show that it "maps onto" set B. In the present case, we could say that set A maps onto set B under T^p_5 (pitch transposition by ordered pitch interval +5), because for every pitch in set A the operation produces a corresponding pitch in set B. The validation process is shown in Ex. 3–5c.

EXERCISE 3–4

Determine whether each pair of lines or chords is related by pitch transposition. When you discover a T^p_n-related pair, compute the interval of transposition and validate it by demonstrating that set A, when transposed by interval n, maps onto set B.

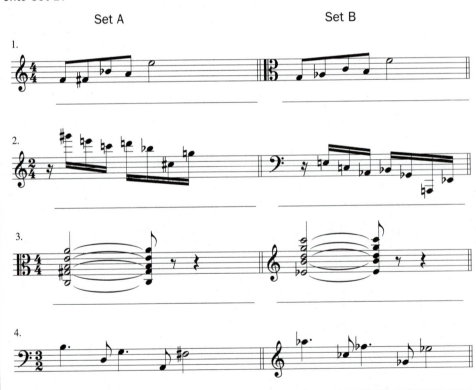

Pitch Class Sets

The same procedure can be used to determine whether two pc sets are T_n-related. Consider the lines shown in Ex. 3–6. It is obvious that they are *not* related by pitch transposition, since they have different melodic contours. They may, however, be related by pc transposition.

Example 3–6. Determining transpositional equivalence between pitch class sets

pcs: <0   1   4   5   8   9>   <6   7   10   11   2   3>

a. compare ordered pc interval patterns

```
        1    3    1    3    1
A:   <0    1    4    5    8    9>
```

```
        1    3    1    3    1
B:   <6    7    10    11    2    3>
```

b. subtract pc numbers (mod 12)

B:	<0	1	4	5	8	9>
A:	<6	7	10	11	2	3>
n:	6	6	6	6	6	6

c. validate interval of transposition

A:	<6	7	10	11	2	3>
n:	6	6	6	6	6	6
B:	<0	1	4	5	8	9

To determine whether two **pc sets** are **T$_n$-related:**

1. Compare their ordered pc interval patterns, or
2. Subtract the pc numbers of set A from those of set B.

Since the ordered interval patterns are identical (Ex. 3–6a), and the differences are constant (Ex. 3–6b), the sets are T$_n$-related and the interval of transposition is 6. This result may be validated by adding 6 to each element of set A to produce set B (Ex. 3–6c).

EXERCISE 3–5

Derive an ordered pc set from each line, then determine whether each pair of sets is T$_n$-related. If so, compute the interval of transposition. Remember that a pc set contains no duplicate elements. You should, therefore, list only one integer for repeated pitches. Be sure to enclose the pcs in angle brackets to indicate that the sets are ordered.

Analysis Projects

In the analysis of atonal music, smaller segments (motives, chords, etc.) are typically reduced to sets, which are then compared in various ways. An appropriate problem at this stage would be to discover T_n-related sets.

There are two degrees of T_n-relatedness: pitch and pitch class. Sets related by pitch transposition are also related by pc transposition. The converse, however, is not necessarily so. Sets related by pc transposition *may not* be related by pitch transposition. So if you think that two pitch sets are T^p_n-related, test first for that relation. If the test proves true, then their corresponding pc sets are also T_n-related. If, however, you find that two pitch sets are *not* T^p_n-related, their corresponding pc sets *may* still be T_n-related.

Composers often make slight adjustments when transposing musical segments. In tonal music, these are often made to conform to a prevailing scale or chord type. In atonal or neotonal music, they may be made for other reasons. Whatever the reason, it is important to acknowledge these "near misses" as well as the "perfect hits." In fact, the misses are often more interesting than the hits.

Transposition is especially valuable for writing imitative counterpoint because it enables a composer to present a melodic idea at various pitch levels. Several 20th-century composers have written pieces that use imitation extensively. Analysis projects for some of these works are provided below.

A. Bartók, "Chromatic Invention" (Mikrokosmos, III/91; WenAMSS)

1. The piece can be understood as a series of points of imitation in which a subject presented by the leading voice (the *dux*) is answered by the trailing voice (the *comes*). Locate these points by drawing a diagonal line from the first note of the *dux* to the first note of the *comes*. Notice how Bartók varied the time interval between the *dux* and *comes*. What happens to the subject during the passage beginning at the *mf* in m. 6 and ending at the *p* in m. 11?
2. Locate points of imitation where the *dux* and *comes* appear to be T-related. For each of these points:
   a. Determine whether the lines are related by pitch transposition (T^p_n) or pc transposition (T_n).
   b. Determine whether the transposition is exact or altered. If you discover any alterations, try to explain why Bartók made them. To do so, compare the effect of an exact transposition with that of Bartók's alteration.
   c. Compute the interval of transposition between *dux* and *comes* and write it beside the diagonal line that connects them.

   Note: it will be best to use relative pitch numbers for this assignment. You should assign zero to A_3 and number the other pitches accordingly (using Rahn's system). With this numbering scheme the first note, A_4, would be pitch number 12. Pitch class numbers and octave numbers should also be assigned in the same manner. That is, any A would be pc zero, any $A^\sharp$ or $B^\flat$ would be pc 1, etc. The octaves would begin with A rather than C.

B. Webern, Five Pieces for String Quartet, Op. 5; Piece No. 3
(see Ex. 14–11, pp. 264–65)

1. Locate any points of imitation by drawing diagonal lines from the first note of the *dux* to the beginnings of as many *comes* as you find.
2. If *dux* and *comes* appear to be T-related, determine the type of transposition (T^p_n or T_n) and compute the interval.

   N.B.: For this piece, it is recommended that you assign pitch number zero to $C^\sharp_4$ and pc number zero to $C^\sharp$. Can you explain why?
3. In addition to looking for T-related motives that are stated successively, find some that are stated simultaneously. One example would be the first two notes in the first violin, second violin, and viola parts.

C. Webern, Five Pieces for String Quartet, Op. 5, Piece No. 4 (Burkhart)

1. Into how many sections does this short movement divide? Explain your answer by citing musical events that are divisive.
2. How many different musical ideas are contained in this movement? Identify each by a letter or descriptive term and cite all of its occurrences by instrumental part and measure number (e.g., Violin I, mm. 1–2).
3. Locate several T-related melodic lines. For each pair describe the relationship with a formula.

D. Britten, "Dirge" from Serenade, Op. 31 (Simms, WenAMSS)

1. The cellos and string basses present a fugue subject in mm. 5–9, and the fugal exposition continues through m. 24. Locate subsequent entries of the subject in mm. 10–24, and compare each of these entries with the first. Determine whether a given entry is a chromatic or diatonic transposition of the original, and note whether the composer has made other adjustments.

2. The climax of this movement occurs at the entrance of the French horn in m. 31. Transpose the horn part to its sounding key using the procedure shown in Exx. 3–1 and 3–2. First, number the pitches of the written part. Then add the interval of transposition to each pitch number to compute the number of the sounding pitch. Finally, notate these pitches on a separate staff. (The horn part is in F, which means that it sounds a perfect fifth lower than written.)

3. How is the horn part of mm. 31–33 related to the cello part of mm. 6–8? Indicate the type of transposition (chromatic or diatonic) and the interval of transposition. Be sure to use the sounding pitches for both instruments in solving this problem.

QUESTIONS FOR REVIEW

1. Define the following terms: ordered set, unordered set.
2. Write from memory the formulas for pitch transposition, pc transposition, and nc transposition.
3. Explain how to determine whether two melodic lines or chords are related by:
   a. pitch transposition
   b. pc transposition
   c. nc transposition

CHAPTER 4

Inversion

The term *inversion* has several meanings in music theory. It can refer to changing the relative position of the pitches that form a harmonic interval or a chord (Ex. 4–1a). It can also mean reversing the intervals of a melodic line (Ex. 4–1b).

When inversion is applied to pitches and pitch classes it is best understood in relation to a fixed point of reference called an *axis.* The inversion of a pitch or pc is the pitch or pc that lies the same distance from the axis but on the *other side* of it. Figure 4–1 shows how "I-related" pairs of elements balance with respect to their axes.

Performing the Operation

Pitch Inversion

Let's begin by exploring inversion in the pitch domain. For the present, we'll assume that the axis is middle C (C_4), to which we'll assign pitch number zero. As Ex. 4–2a shows, the inversion of pitch 5 is –5, and the inversion of pitch –9 is +9 (Ex. 4–2b).

Example 4–1.

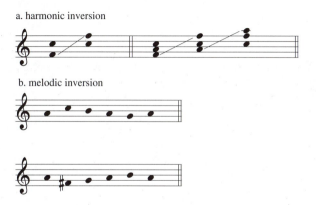

a. harmonic inversion

b. melodic inversion

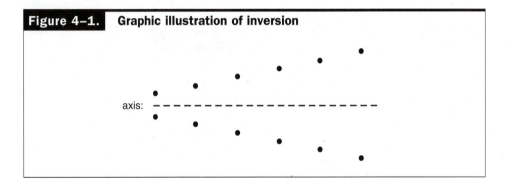

Figure 4–1. **Graphic illustration of inversion**

Example 4–2. **Inversionally-related pitches**

Thus, when zero is the axis, a pitch can be inverted by negating (changing the sign of) its number. This operation can be expressed as:

$$I(p) = -p$$

As you can see, Rahn's method of numbering pitches is more suitable for inversion problems than the MIDI method.

EXERCISE 4–1

Number each pitch to form an ordered pitch set, then invert the set by inverting each of its elements. Show your work in both integer and staff notation. Use Rahn's method of pitch numbering.

Pitch Inversion Followed by Transposition

Pitch inversion is often followed by transposition. When the two operations are combined, inversion must be performed first because inversion and transposition are not commutative. That is, transposing an inverted pitch will not produce the same result as inverting a transposed pitch. In keeping with Rahn's symbology, we'll represent pitch inversion followed by transposition as T^p_nI. The formula for inverting and transposing pitch p by interval n is:

$$T^p_nI(p) = -p + n$$

which tells us to negate p, then add n to the result. The formula can also be written as:

$$T^p_nI(p) = n - p$$

which subtracts p from n. A set of pitches can be inverted and transposed by performing this operation upon each of its elements.

EXERCISE 4–2

Invert and transpose each line or chord as indicated. Show each result in staff notation.

Tp3I

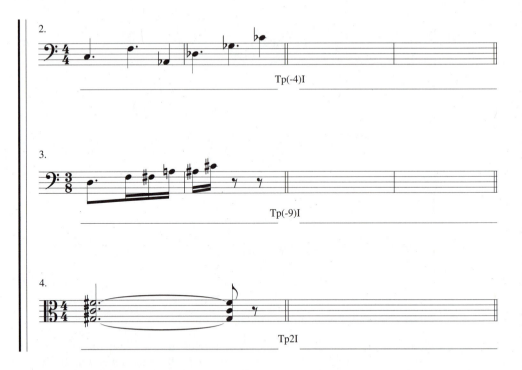

Pitch Inversion about a Non-Zero Axis

In some cases we will invert a pitch about an axis other than middle C. There are two ways to do so:

1. Renumber the pitches, assigning zero to the new axis, and then invert in the usual manner. Example 4–3a shows several I-related pairs of pitches with $E\flat_4$ as the axis.
2. Invert the pitch, transpose the result by the interval between the axis pitch and pitch zero, then transpose *that* result by the same interval. Since the interval between the axis pitch and pitch zero will be equal to the axis pitch, the formulas for pitch inversion about a non-zero axis resemble those for inversion followed by transposition. Example 4–3b shows the same I-related pairs with $E\flat_4$ as the axis but middle C as the reference pitch.

$$I(p) = (-p + axis) + axis$$

or

$$I(p) = (2 \times axis) - p$$

Pitch Inversion Using MIDI Pitch Numbers

Inversion Only Since the MIDI reference pitch lies five octaves below middle C, it could never be an axis. (Can you explain why?) Therefore, we will always be inverting about some other, non-zero axis.

Example 4–3. **Pitch inversion about a non-zero axis (using Rahn's numbering system)**

a. with E♭₄ as the axis and reference pitch

b. with E♭₄ as the axis and C₄ as the reference pitch

Let's begin with the familiar case: middle C as the axis. Example 4–4a shows several pairs of I-related pitches. Here, however, the pitches have MIDI numbers. Notice that the numbers of each I-related pair sum to 120, which equals two times 60, the number of C_4, the axis pitch. This proves that we can use the formulas listed above. To invert a pitch about a non-zero axis, simply subtract its pitch number from two times the axis pitch. To demonstrate, let's invert the pitches in the treble staff by subtracting their MIDI numbers from 120 (2 times 60). As shown below, the results are the MIDI numbers of the pitches in the bass staff.

2 × axis:	120	120	120	120	120	120
treble:	−63	−67	−70	−74	−77	−81
bass:	57	53	50	46	43	39

Since these pitches form I-related pairs, we could also invert the pitches in the bass staff to obtain those in the treble staff.

2 × axis:	120	120	120	120	120	120
bass:	−57	−53	−50	−46	−43	−39
treble:	63	67	70	74	77	81

Example 4–4. **Pitch inversion about a non-zero axis (using the MIDI numbering system)**

a. with C₄ as the axis

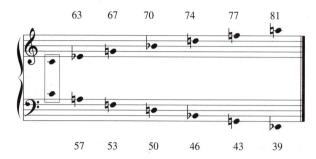

b. with E♭₄ as the axis

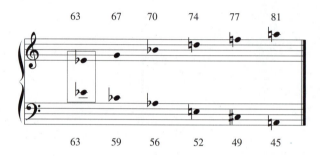

The operation remains the same for any other axis pitch, as well. Example 4–4b is comparable to Ex. 4–3b in that the axis for both is $E^{\flat}_4$. In both cases, the numbers of the I-related pitches sum to twice the number of the axis pitch.

Inversion Followed by Transposition As noted earlier, when inversion is combined with transposition, inversion should be performed first. The formula for inversion about a non-zero axis followed by transposition is, therefore:

$$T^{p}_{n}I(x) = ((2 \times axis) - x) + n$$

or

$$T^{p}_{n}I(x) = ((2 \times axis) + n) - x$$

Pitch Class Inversion

A pitch class can be inverted by negating its number and applying mod 12 to the result. This operation can be expressed by the formula

$$I(pc) = mod12 \ (-pc)$$

The same result can be obtained by subtracting the pc number from 12, the modulus of the pc system. Thus,

$$I(pc) = 12 - pc$$

The axis of pc inversion can be represented as a line connecting two pcs or pairs of pcs that lie diametrically opposite each other on the clock face. Example 4–5 shows three different axes: The arrows point to I-related pcs. Notice that, in each case, these pcs lie the same distance from their axis but on *opposite sides* of it.

EXERCISE 4–3

Write the pc number of the notated pitch in the space provided (assume that pc 0 = B♯/C). Compute the inversion of that pc, and notate at least three realizations of the inversion. Be sure to demonstrate both octave and enharmonic equivalence in your notations. For example, if the pc number is 10, do not write three B♭'s in the same octave; instead, notate B♭'s and A♯'s in various octaves.

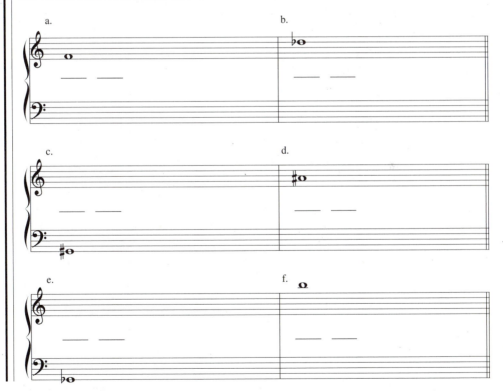

Pitch Class Inversion Followed by Transposition

As in the pitch domain, when pitch class inversion and transposition are combined, inversion must be performed first. The combined operation can be represented as:

$$T_nI(pc) = mod12 \ (-pc + n)$$

or

$$T_nI(pc) = mod12 \ (n - pc)$$

Example 4–5. **I-related pitch classes**

a. with 0/6 as axis

 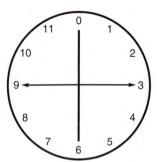

b. with 11/5 as axis

 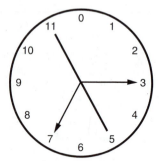

c. with 1.5/7.5 as axis

 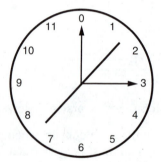

The second formula may be the easier to remember, so let's apply it to an example. Suppose that we wish to invert <0 1 4 5 8 9> and transpose the result by interval 3. This requires subtracting each pc number (pc) from the interval of transposition (n) and applying mod 12 to each result. In the present case, we must add 12 to any negative integers.

n:	3	3	3	3	3	3
pcs:	<0	1	4	5	8	9>
differences:	<3	2	−1	−2	−5	−6>
mod 12:	<3	2	11	10	7	6>

EXERCISE 4–4

Using 0/6 as the axis, invert then transpose each set of pcs. Notate two different realizations of the transposed inversion on the staff provided. Remember to provide a meter signature and the correct number of beats for each measure.

a.
Prime: <7 11 0 2 3>

T_4I: _____

b.
Prime: <3 6 9 0>

T_6I: _____

c.
Prime: <0 1 4 5 8>

T_5I: _____

d.
Prime: <10 0 1 5 6>

T_9I: _____

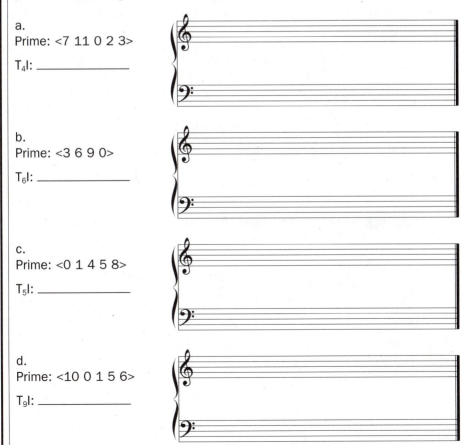

Diatonic Inversion

A set can be inverted within a *diatonic* scale by using *name class* numbers. The formula for nc inversion parallels that for pc inversion.

$$I(nc) = mod7 \; (-nc)$$

A name class integer can be inverted by subtracting it from 7, the modulus of the nc system. Expressed as a formula, this would be

$$I(nc) = 7 - nc$$

Example 4–6 shows how a line may be inverted by applying the second formula. The original line is labeled P for prime; the inverted line is labeled I for inversion. To mirror the contour of the original line, the octave numbers must be adjusted as shown.

Diatonic inversion and transposition can be combined by subtracting a name class integer from n, the interval of transposition, as shown in Ex. 4–7. The formula for this compound operation is, therefore:

$$T_nI(nc) = mod7 \; (n - nc)$$

Example 4–6. **Diatonic (name class) inversion**

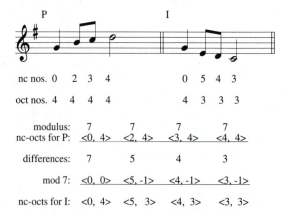

	P				I			
nc nos.	0	2	3	4	0	5	4	3
oct nos.	4	4	4	4	4	3	3	3

modulus:	7	7	7	7
nc-octs for P:	<0, 4>	<2, 4>	<3, 4>	<4, 4>
differences:	7	5	4	3
mod 7:	<0, 0>	<5, -1>	<4, -1>	<3, -1>
nc-octs for I:	<0, 4>	<5, 3>	<4, 3>	<3, 3>

Example 4–7. Diatonic (name class) inversion followed by transposition

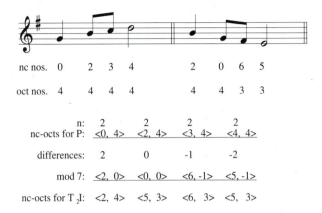

nc nos.	0	2	3	4		2	0	6	5
oct nos.	4	4	4	4		4	4	3	3

	n:	2		2		2		2	
nc-octs for P:		<0, 4>		<2, 4>		<3, 4>		<4, 4>	
differences:		2		0		-1		-2	
mod 7:		<2, 0>		<0, 0>		<6, -1>		<5, -1>	
nc-octs for T₂I:		<2, 4>		<5, 3>		<6, 3>		<5, 3>	

EXERCISE 4–5

Invert each set of name classes and transpose the result by the specified nc interval. Then notate two different realizations of the transposed inversion within the scale indicated. Remember to use mod 7 for this task.

a.
<2 5 0 1 6>

T_4I: _____
D major

b.
<3 6 1 0>

T_6I: _____
F harmonic minor

c.
<0 1 4 5 2>

T_1I: _____
G natural minor

d.
<4 0 1 5 6>

T_5I: _____

F♯ Major

Recognizing I-Related Sets

Pitch Inversion

The procedure for determining whether two sets are I-related is similar to that used for T-related sets. First, compare. I-related melodic lines will have mirror-related contours as shown in Exx. 4–1b and 4–8a. I-related chords will have mirror-related spacing as shown in Ex. 4–8b.

If inversion appears likely, it should be proven by computation. If the two sets represent melodic lines, their corresponding pitches should produce constant sums as shown below for the lines in Ex. 4–8a.

	Rahn numbers					**MIDI numbers**			
P:	< 5	14	12	10 >		< 65	74	72	70 >
T^p_nI:	<–3	–12	–10	–8 >		< 57	48	50	52 >
sums:	2	2	2	2		122	122	122	122

Example 4–8.   **I-related lines and chords**

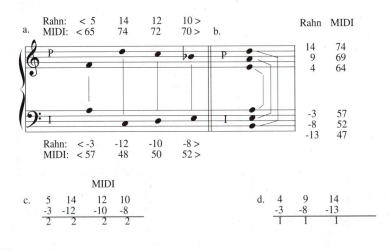

e. axis = 2 / 2 = 1   f. axis = 1 / 2 = 0.5

If the sets represent chords, their corresponding pitches will lie at *opposite* ends of each chord, and the pairs should produce constant sums as shown below for Ex. 4–8b.

	Rahn numbers			**MIDI numbers**		
P:	< 4	9	14 >	< 64	69	74 >
T^p_nI:	<−3	−8	−13 >	< 57	52	47 >
n:	1	1	1	121	121	121

The sum of any pair is the interval of transposition. Either set maps onto the other when inverted and then transposed by this interval. To demonstrate, we can subtract the inverted pitch numbers from the interval of transposition.

Melodic lines (see Ex. 4–8a)

	Rahn numbers				**MIDI numbers**			
P:	< 5	14	12	10 >	< 65	74	72	70 >
n:	< 2	2	2	2 >	<122	122	122	122 >
I of P:	<−5	−14	−12	−10 >	<−65	−74	−72	−70 >
T^p_nI:	<−3	−12	−10	−8>	< 57	48	50	52 >

Chords (see Ex. 4–8b)

	Rahn numbers			**MIDI numbers**		
P:	< 4	9	14 >	< 64	69	74 >
n:	1	1	1	121	121	121
I of P:	<−4	−9	−14 >	<−64	−69	−74 >
T^p_nI:	<−3	−8	−13>	< 57	52	47 >

The relation between the I-related lines (Ex. 4–8a) can be symbolized as:

$$T^p_2I \quad < 5 \quad 14 \quad 12 \quad 10 > = < -3 \quad -12 \quad -10 \quad -8 > \text{ (Rahn)}$$
$$T^p_{122}I \quad < 65 \quad 74 \quad 72 \quad 70 > = < 57 \quad 48 \quad 50 \quad 52 > \text{ (MIDI)}$$

The relation between the I-related chords (Ex. 4-8b) can be symbolized as:

$$T^p_1I \quad < 4 \quad 9 \quad 14 > = < -3 \quad -8 \quad -13 > \text{ (Rahn)}$$
$$T^p_{121}I \quad < 64 \quad 69 \quad 74 > = < 57 \quad 52 \quad 47 > \text{ (MIDI)}$$

To determine whether two **lines** or **pitch sets** are T^p_nI-**related:**

Add their corresponding pitches.
If the sums are constant, the lines or sets are T^p_nI-related, and the sum is the interval of transposition.

EXERCISE 4–6

Determine whether each pair of lines or chords is related by pitch inversion. For those that are, compute the interval of transposition, validate it, and express the relationship in a formula as shown above.

Pitch Class Inversion

Example 4–9 shows two lines that are obviously *not* related by pitch inversion, since they do not have mirror-related contours. They may, however, be related by pitch class inversion (T_nI). To test for that relation we would *add* the corresponding pc

---

Example 4–9.   **Melodic lines related by pc inversion**

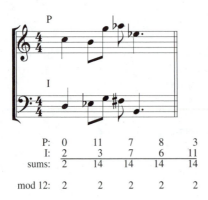

P:	0	11	7	8	3
I:	2	3	7	6	11
sums:	2	14	14	14	14
mod 12:	2	2	2	2	2

numbers (mod 12). If each pair sums to the same number, then the lines are T_nI-related, and the interval of transposition is the constant sum of the pairs.

To determine if two **ordered pc sets** are **T_nI-related:**

Add their corresponding pc numbers (mod 12).
If the sums are constant, the sets are T_nI-related.

EXERCISE 4–7

Determine whether each pair of lines is related by pc inversion. If so, compute the interval of transposition, and show that the first line will map onto the second under T_nI.

Locating the Axis

To compute the axis between two I-related pitches or pcs, add the two numbers and then halve the sum. The operation can be expressed as

$$\text{axis } (x,y) = (x + y) / 2$$

where x and y represent the two pitches or pcs.

To illustrate, let's compute the axes for the I-related lines and chords shown in Example 4–8. As above, we'll add the numbers of the corresponding pitches to obtain n, the interval of transposition. Then we'll halve n to compute the axis of inversion.

Melodic lines (see Ex. 4–8a)

	Rahn numbers				MIDI numbers			
P:	< 5	14	12	10 >	< 65	74	72	70 >
T^p_nI:	<–3	–12	–10	–8 >	< 57	48	50	52 >
sums:	2	2	2	2	122	122	122	122
axis:	1	1	1	1	61	61	61	61

Chords (see Ex. 4–8b)

	Rahn numbers			MIDI numbers		
P:	< 4	9	14 >	< 64	69	74 >
T^p_nI:	<–3	–8	–13 >	< 57	52	47 >
n:	1	1	1	121	121	121
axis:	.5	.5	.5	60.5	60.5	60.5

Since the interval of transposition for the melodic lines is an even number (2), the axis is an integer (1). This integer represents $C^\sharp_4/D^\flat_4$, the pitch that lies halfway between each pair of I-related pitches in Ex. 4–8a.

The interval of transposition for the chords is an odd number, so the result of dividing it by 2 is a fraction. The pitch number .5 represents a quarter tone that lies halfway between pitches 0 and 1. We will indicate such an axis by listing the pitches that lie on either side of it. In this case, we could write the axis as $C_4/C^\sharp_4$.

EXERCISE 4–8

List a pitch number for each pitch. Write these numbers above and below the staff. Then compute the axis of inversion. Write that number between the staves and notate the corresponding pitch, or in the case of a quarter tone, the adjacent pitches. The first example has been done for you.

As mentioned earlier, the axis for a pair of I-related pcs can be represented by a line that connects two diametrically opposite points on the pc clock face. This line bisects the angles formed by the arrows that point to the I-related pcs. Six such diagrams were shown in Ex. 4–5. In 4–5a and b the axis lines connect diametrically opposite pcs, one of which is half the sum of the I-related pcs. In 4–5c the I-related pcs sum to an odd number so the axis lines connect points that lie halfway between adjacent pc numbers.

The procedure for computing the axes for each of the clock diagrams of Ex. 4–5 is shown below.

I-related pcs	Sum	Sum / 2	Axis
a. 4, 8	12	6	0/6
3, 9	12	6	0/6
b. 0,10	10	5	5/11
3, 7	10	5	5/11
c. 5,10	15	7.5	1.5/7.5
0, 3	3	1.5	1.5/7.5

To compute the inversional axis for a pair of I-related pitches or pitch classes, add the two numbers and divide the sum by two.

Analysis Projects

A. Bartók, "Chromatic Invention" (Mikrokosmos, III/91) (WenAMSS)
(See Analysis Project of Chapter Three.)

1. Locate points of imitation in which the *dux* is answered by an inverted *comes*. For each point answer the following questions:
   a. Is the *comes* an exact inversion of the *dux,* or have some pitches been altered?
   b. What is the interval of transposition between the *dux* and *comes?*
   c. What is the inversional axis for each pair of lines?
2. Locate a point of imitation where an inverted *dux* is answered by *its own* transposition. Compute the interval of transposition between *dux* and *comes.*

So far we've been concerned exclusively with "local" T and I relations, that is, those occurring between a *dux* and its *comes*. Now that you are familiar with "Chromatic Invention," we can consider transposition and inversion from the "global" perspective of the entire piece.

3. Where does Bartók consistently answer the prime form of the subject with a transposed inversion? In view of the overall form of the piece, and especially the treatment of the subject in mm. 6–11, what is the significance of this practice?
4. In Analysis Project A of Chapter Three you were advised to assign pitch number zero to A_3. Can you now explain why this advice was given?
5. Determine the interval of transposition between the reference pitch, A_3, and the first pitch of each complete or partial *dux* by completing the worksheet below.

Meas. no.	2	3	6	7	7	8	9	9	11	13	15
Pitch	A_4	A_4	$B^\flat_5$	$A^\flat_5$	$F^\sharp_5$	E_5	D_5	C_5	A_4	A_4	A_4
Pitch no.	12										
Reference	0	0	0	0	0	0	0	0	0	0	0
Interval	12										

6. Now consider the question of its tonality. Is Bartók's "Chromatic Invention" tonal, atonal, or neotonal? Write a brief essay in which you state your opinion on this issue and defend it with a few well-chosen examples. You may wish to review the definitions of tonality, atonality, and neotonality that were given in Chapter One.

B. Webern, Five Pieces for String Quartet, Op. 5; Piece No. 3
(see Ex. 14–11, pp. 264–65)

1. Locate an example of imitation by inversion. What type of inversion is used (pitch or pitch class)? What is the interval of transposition? What is the inversional axis between the *dux* and *comes?*
2. Locate at least one example where I-related lines are presented simultaneously.

C. Bartók, "Subject and Reflection" (Mikrokosmos, VI/141; see Ex. 7–8, p. 108)

Look carefully at the top and bottom voices. Are they I-related? If so, are they related by pitch inversion or pc inversion? What is the axis pitch or pc?

D. Webern, Concerto for Nine Instruments, Op. 24; first movement
(Ex. 5–1, p. 80)

The motives stated in mm. 1–3 by the oboe, flute, trumpet, and clarinet can be grouped into two I-related pairs.

1. Which pairs state I-related motives? Are these motives related by pitch inversion or by pc inversion?
2. Compute the interval of transposition between each I-related pair. Is it the same for both pairs?
3. Compute the inversional axis between each I-related pair. Is it the same for both pairs?

E. Schoenberg, Piano Piece, Op. 33a (see Ex. 15–3, p. 280)

1. Each chord in m. 1 has an I-related counterpart in m. 2. See if you can locate the I-related pairs by visual scanning, then prove your hypotheses by computation.
2. Determine the axis for each pair of I-related chords. Do all three pairs share the same axis?

QUESTIONS FOR REVIEW

1. Define the following terms: axis of symmetry, commutative operation.
2. Write from memory the formulas for:
   a. pitch inversion
   b. pc inversion
   c. nc inversion
   d. pitch inversion followed by transposition
   e. pc inversion followed by transposition
   f. nc inversion followed by transposition
3. Explain how to invert a pitch about an axis other than middle C.
4. Explain how to compute the axis between two I-related pitches or pitch classes.
5. Explain how to determine whether two lines or chords are related by: a) pitch inversion, b) pc inversion, c) nc inversion.

RECOMMENDED READING

Compare Cogan and Escot's analysis of Schoenberg's "Colors" (in *Sonic Design,* pp. 412–19) with John Rahn's (in *Basic Atonal Theory,* Chapter 3 and Analysis Two). See the Bibliography for full citations.

CHAPTER 5

Basic Operations with Unordered Sets

Normal Form

Consider the problem posed by the following sets:

$$\{7\ 11\ 2\} \quad \{7\ 2\ 11\} \quad \{11\ 2\ 7\}$$
$$\{11\ 7\ 2\} \quad \{2\ 7\ 11\} \quad \{2\ 11\ 7\}.^{[1]}$$

They are equivalent as unordered sets because they contain the same pcs, but problems arise in referring to them collectively. What should we call the entire class? It would be tedious to list all six of its permutations and even more tedious to list those of larger sets. For example, a 4-element set would have 24 permutations.

To solve this problem, music theorists have devised the concept of *normal form*. The normal form of an unordered set is the permutation that has the smallest interval between its first element and each of its succeeding elements. If more than one permutation meets this condition, then the one that begins with the lowest number is arbitrarily designated as the normal form.[2]

Computing Normal Form

To compute the normal form of an unordered set, first arrange its pcs in *canonical order*. Canonical order includes any listing that requires less than one full revolution around the pc clock (see Fig. 2–2, p. 40). As a rule, it is best to begin by sorting the pcs into ascending numerical order. Thus, we begin with {0 2 6 9}.

Next, list the clockwise rotations of the set. A set is rotated in a clockwise direction by placing its first pc at the end. Sets have as many rotations as they have elements. The four rotations of our specimen set are:

{0 2 6 9}
{2 6 9 0}
{6 9 0 2}
{9 0 2 6}

---

[1] In keeping with the convention established by Rahn, curly braces will be used to denote unordered pc sets.

[2] Allen Forte has coined the term "normal order" to denote essentially the same concept. His procedure for determining the normal order of an unordered pc set differs slightly from Rahn's method of determining normal form. See *The Structure of Atonal Music* (New Haven: Yale University Press, 1973), pp. 3–5.

Next, find the rotation that has the smallest ordered interval between its first and last pcs. (The pcs that form the relevant interval are underlined.)

Rotations	ipc\<a,b>
{<u>0</u> 2 6 <u>9</u>}	9
{<u>2</u> 6 9 <u>0</u>}	10
{<u>6</u> 9 0 <u>2</u>}	8
{<u>9</u> 0 2 <u>6</u>}	9

In this case, {6 9 0 2} has the smallest interval, so it is the normal form, or representative, of this class of six unordered pc sets.

Some sets require additional computation. Consider, for example, {0 1 3 4 8}.

Rotations	ipc\<a,b>
{<u>0</u> 1 3 4 <u>8</u>}	8
{<u>1</u> 3 4 8 <u>0</u>}	11
{<u>3</u> 4 8 0 <u>1</u>}	10
{<u>4</u> 8 0 1 <u>3</u>}	11
{<u>8</u> 0 1 3 <u>4</u>}	8

In this case *two* rotations share the smallest outside interval. To break the tie, we must compute the interval between the *first* and *next-to-last* pcs of those two rotations.

Rotations	ipc\<a,b>
{<u>0</u> 1 3 <u>4</u> 8}	4
{<u>8</u> 0 1 <u>3</u> 4}	7

Here we have a clear "winner" after the second round of computation. {0 1 3 4 8} is the normal form of this class.

There are a few cases, however, where the problem is not solved so easily. Consider, for example, {0 3 6 9}, the set that corresponds to a diminished-seventh chord.

Round 1		Round 2		Round 3	
Rotations	ipc\<a,b>	Rotations	ipc\<a,b>	Rotations	ipc\<a,b>
{<u>0</u> 3 6 <u>9</u>}	9	{<u>0</u> 3 6 <u>9</u>}	6	{<u>0</u> 3 <u>6</u> 9}	3
{<u>3</u> 6 9 <u>0</u>}	9	{<u>3</u> 6 <u>9</u> 0}	6	{<u>3</u> <u>6</u> 9 0}	3
{<u>6</u> 9 0 <u>3</u>}	9	{<u>6</u> 9 <u>0</u> 3}	6	{<u>6</u> 9 <u>0</u> 3}	3
{<u>9</u> 0 3 <u>6</u>}	9	{<u>9</u> 0 <u>3</u> 6}	6	{<u>9</u> <u>0</u> 3 6}	3

In this case, each round has ended in a four-way tie; we are no closer to finding the normal form than when we began. Such problems occur only with certain "symmetrical" set types such as the augmented triad {0 4 8}, the diminished-seventh chord {0 3 6 9}, and the whole-tone scale {0 2 4 6 8 10}.[3] In these cases, it is conventional to designate as the normal form the rotation that begins with the lowest pc number. Thus, {0 3 6 9} was already in normal form. In the same manner, {0 4 8} and {0 2 4 6 8 10} are in their respective normal forms.

To find the **normal form** of an unordered pc set:

1. Arrange the pcs in canonical order, preferably in ascending numerical order.
2. List all of the set's rotations.
3. Compute the ordered pc interval between the first and last pcs of each rotation. Compare these intervals. If one rotation has the smallest outside interval, it is the normal form.
4. If the smallest outside interval is shared by more than one rotation, compute and compare the interval between the first and next-to-last pcs for *only* those rotations.
5. If a tie still exists, compute and compare the interval between the first and next-to-next-to-last pcs of *only* those rotations that are still in contention.
6. Continue this process as long as necessary to break a tie. If you have computed all possible intervals and a tie still exists, select the rotation that begins with the lowest pc number.

A Short Cut

The rotations and ordered interval patterns of {3 5 6 0} are shown below.

Rotations	{3 5 6 0}	{5 6 0 3}	{6 0 3 5}	{0 3 5 6}
Interval patterns	2 1 6	1 6 3	6 3 2	3 2 1

Comparison reveals that 6 is the largest interval. It occurs in the patterns of the first three rotations, but not of the fourth rotation, where it is formed by the first and last pcs. The shortcut, therefore, is to look for a *single largest interval* that occurs in all but one of the rotations. If such an interval can be found (and, in some cases, one cannot), then the rotation whose interval pattern does *not* contain that interval is the normal form.

EXERCISE 5–1

Represent each segment as an unordered pc set, then determine the normal form of that set. The first example has been done for you.

---

[3]Symmetrical sets are discussed in Chapter 11.

a.

pc nos.:   5   9   4   1   1   3   3   6

asc. order: { 1   3   4   5   6   9 }

normal form: { 1   3   4   5   6   9 }

b.

pc nos.: _____

asc. order: _____

normal form: _____

c.

pc nos.: _____

asc. order: _____

normal form: _____

d.

pc nos.: _____

asc. order: _____

normal form: _____

Recognizing T$_n$-Related Unordered Sets

In order to compare unordered sets for T$_n$-relations, it is essential that each set be in its normal form. Consider the first three measures of Webern's Concerto for Nine Instruments, Op. 24 (Ex. 5–1). We explored the relationship between these trichordal motives as *ordered pitch sets* in the previous chapter (see Chapter Four, Analysis Project D). Now we want to know whether they are T$_n$-related as *unordered pc sets*. To answer this question, we must find the normal form of each set, then compare the normal forms for T$_n$-relatedness. There are two options:

Example 5–1. Webern, Concerto for Nine Instruments, Op. 24, I, mm. 1–10 (all instruments are notated at sounding pitch)

1. Compare the interval patterns

   The rightmost column of Table 5–1 shows that there are two T_n-related pairs: the flute and clarinet motives, and the oboe and trumpet motives.

2. Compute the differences between corresponding pcs

   This strategy not only reveals whether two sets are T_n-related. It also yields n, the interval of transposition.

Oboe	{11 0 3}	Flute	{ 4 7 8}
Trpt.	{ 5 6 9}	Clar.	{10 1 2}
n	6 6 6	n	6 6 6

T_n-Type

We can also transpose each normal form so that it begins with pc zero. This produces the *T_n-type* of a set. The transposition can be done in either of two ways:

1. Add the complement of the first pc to each element of the set.

Oboe	**Trumpet**
{11 0 3}	{5 6 9}
1 1 1	7 7 7
(0 1 4)	(0 1 4)

2. Subtract the first pc from each element.

Flute	**Clarinet**
{ 4 7 8}	{ 10 1 2}
−4 −4 −4	−10 −10 −10
(0 3 4)	(0 3 4)

Both methods produce the same result. We have shown that these two sets are T_n-related because they share the same T_n-type.

TABLE 5–1. Unordered pc sets in Webern, Op. 24, I, mm. 1–10
Reference pc: B = 0

	Ordered pcs	Canonical order	Normal form	Interval pattern
Flute	<4 8 7>	{4 7 8}	(4 7 8)	3 1
Oboe	<0 11 3>	{0 3 11}	(11 0 3)	1 3
Clarinet	<1 2 10>	{1 2 10}	(10 1 2)	3 1
Trumpet	<9 5 6>	{5 6 9}	(5 6 9)	1 3

TABLE 5-2.   Classes of sets related to (0 1 4) and (0 3 4) by T$_n$

Interval of Transposition	T$_n$-type (0 1 4)	T$_n$-type (0 3 4)
0	{0 1 4}	{0 3 4}
1	{1 2 5}	{1 4 5}
2	{2 3 6}	{2 5 6}
3	{3 4 7}	{3 6 7}
4	{4 5 8}	{4 7 8}
5	{5 6 9}	{5 8 9}
6	{6 7 10}	{6 9 10}
7	{7 8 11}	{7 10 11}
8	{8 9 0}	{8 11 0}
9	{9 10 1}	{9 0 1}
10	{10 11 2}	{10 1 2}
11	{11 0 3}	{11 2 3}

The *T$_n$-type* represents all twelve of a set's transpositions. Thus, (0 1 4) represents a class of twelve T$_n$-related sets, and (0 3 4) represents another such class.[4] These two set classes are listed in the second and third columns in Table 5–2. The first column lists the interval that produces the set listed on a given row.

Since each set in Table 5–2 is in normal form, it represents not only itself, but all of its other permutations, as well. For example, {3 4 7} represents itself as well as {3 7 4}, {4 3 7}, {4 7 3}, {7 3 4}, and {7 4 3}. Each T$_n$-type represents twelve transpositions, and each transposition represents six permutations. Furthermore, each integer within a set represents a class of pitches that are related by octave and/or enharmonic equivalence. As you can see, a great deal of power is being wielded here. Integers represent classes of pitches, normal forms represent classes of content-equivalent sets, and T$_n$-types represent classes of T$_n$-equivalent sets.

To determine whether two **unordered pc sets** are **T$_n$-related**, arrange both sets in normal form. Then do at least one of the following:

1. Compute and compare the interval patterns of the two sets. If the patterns are identical, the sets are T$_n$-related.
2. Subtract (mod 12) the corresponding pcs of one set from those of the other. If the differences are constant, the sets are T$_n$-related, and the constant difference is the interval of transposition.
3. Find the T$_n$-type of each set by subtracting its first pc from each of the pcs (including the first). If the sets have identical T$_n$-types, they are T$_n$-related.

---

[4]Parentheses will be used to denote Tn-types, and TnI-types.

EXERCISE 5-2

Notate a realization of each set on the staff provided. Then determine the normal form and T_n-type of each set. If both sets share the same T_n-type, compute the interval of transposition by subtracting the normal form of the first set from that of the second.

a.

(staff)

	{7 10 6 11}	{7 6 2 3}
asc. order:	_____	_____
normal form:	_____	_____
T_n-type:	_____	_____
Interval (if T_n-related)	_____	

b.

(staff)

	{3 5 10 4 9}	{5 6 0 1 11}
asc. order:	_____	_____
normal form:	_____	_____
T_n-type:	_____	_____
Interval (if T_n-related)	_____	

c.

(staff)

	{2 4 7 9 5 0}	{10 9 7 5 2 0}
asc. order:	_____	_____
normal form:	_____	_____
T_n-type:	_____	_____
Interval (if T_n-related)	_____	

Recognizing T_nI-Related Unordered Sets

The Effect of Inversion upon Normal Form

Before learning to recognize unordered sets related by inversion, we must investigate the effect that inverting a set has upon its normal form. To do so, we'll invert {0 1 4}, a set that is already in normal form. As you know, a set can be inverted either by negating its pcs or by complementing them with respect to 12, the modulus of the pc system:

Negation method

Prime negation   **mod12 Inversion**

$$\{0\ 1\ 4\} \longrightarrow \{0\ -1\ -4\} \longrightarrow \{0\ 11\ 8\}$$

Complementation method

modulus	0 12 12
Prime	{0 1 4}
Inversion	{0 11 8}

Both methods produce {0 11 8}, a set that cannot be in normal form because it is not in canonical order. It appears that we'll have to recompute the normal form for this set.

Rotations	**ipc<a,b>**
{0 8 11}	11
{8 11 0}	4
{11 0 8}	9

Upon doing so, we discover that {8 11 0} is the normal form of {0 11 8}. These two sets are retrogrades of each other; {8 11 0} is {0 11 8} read backwards, and vice versa. Have we discovered a general principle? If we invert a set in normal form, can we find the normal form of that inversion by retrograding the result? The answer is, yes, in all but a relatively few cases. This greatly simplifies the process.

Negation method

Prime	negation		mod12	Inversion		retrograde	Normal form
{0 1 4}	$\longrightarrow$		{0 –1 –4}	$\longrightarrow$	{0 11 8} $\longrightarrow$	$\longrightarrow$	{8 11 0}

Complementation method

modulus	0 12 12		
Prime	{ 0 1 4	retrograde	Normal form
Inversion	{ 0 11 8}	$\longrightarrow$	{8 11 0}

Having discovered that {8 11 0} is the normal form of the inversion of {0 1 4}, we can now determine *its* T_n-type.

Normal form	{8 11 0}
	4 4 4
T_n-type	(0 3 4)

Recognizing T_nI-Related Unordered Sets

(0 3 4) is the T_n-type of the class of twelve sets listed in the rightmost column of Table 5–2. Any set in that column can be mapped onto any other set in the same column by pc transposition (T_n). Furthermore, any set in one column can be mapped onto any set in the other column by inversion followed by transposition (T_nI), assuming, of course, that the inverted set is restored to its normal form before it is transposed. Rahn has coined the term T_nI-*type* to refer to the T_n-type of the inversion of a set.[5] In the present case, (0 3 4) is the T_nI-type of any set in the left column of Table 5–2, and conversely, (0 1 4) is the T_nI-type of any set in the right column.

Comparing Unordered Sets for Inversional Equivalence

We can now learn two methods for determining whether unordered pc sets are related by inversion.

1. Compare their interval patterns What is the relationship between the interval patterns of T_nI-related sets in normal form? To discover this, let's compute and compare the interval patterns of two sets that we know to be T_nI-related.

T_n-type	(0 1 4)	(0 3 4)
pattern	1 3	3 1

From this we discover that T_nI-related sets in normal form have R-related interval patterns. We can use this discovery to devise a test for inversional equivalence. To determine whether two unordered sets are T_nI-related, arrange the sets in normal form, then compute and compare their ordered interval patterns. If the patterns are R-related, then the sets are T_nI-related. Referring back to Table 5–1, we can now see that the two pairs of motives (flute and oboe, clarinet and trumpet) share R-related interval patterns and are, therefore, T_nI-related as unordered sets.

2. Add their corresponding pcs If two T_nI-related sets in normal form have R-related interval patterns, we can retrograde one of the sets, so that their interval patterns match, and then add the corresponding pcs of both sets. If they sum to the same number, then the original sets are T_nI-related. To illustrate:

$$\{0\ 3\ 4\} \xrightarrow{\text{retrograde}} \begin{array}{c} \{0\ 1\ 4\} \\ \{4\ 3\ 0\} \\ \hline 4\ 4\ 4 \end{array}$$

From this we can predict that {0 1 4} will map onto {0 3 4} when inverted and transposed by interval 4. To validate this prediction, let's perform the operations:

---

[5] *Basic Atonal Theory*, Chapter 4.

$$\{0\ 1\ 4\} \xrightarrow{\text{negate}} \{0\ -1\ -4\} \xrightarrow{\text{mod12}} \{0\ 11\ 8\} \xrightarrow{\text{retrograde}} \xrightarrow{} \{8\ 11\ 0\} \xrightarrow{\text{T}_4} \{0\ 3\ 4\}$$

Summing the corresponding pcs is the most efficient method because it also yields the interval of transposition.

To determine whether two **unordered pc sets** are **T$_n$I-related**:

1. Arrange both sets in normal form.
2. Retrograde the pcs of one set, the one presumed to be the inversion.
3. Add the corresponding pcs of both sets. If the sums are constant, the sets are T$_n$I-related, and the constant sum is the interval of transposition.

EXERCISE 5–3

Notate a realization of each set on the staff provided. Determine the normal form and T$_n$-type of each set. Then use the method described above to determine whether the sets are T$_n$I-related. If so, compute the interval of transposition.

a.

{0 3 7 1 4 6}   {1 8 2 7 4 5}

normal form: _____   _____
T$_n$-type: _____   _____
Interval (if T$_n$I-related) _____

b.

{0 5 7 2 3}   {9 7 2 4 6}

normal form: _____   _____
T$_n$-type: _____   _____
Interval (if T$_n$I-related) _____

c.

$$\{2\ 5\ 4\ 0\ 6\ 10\}\qquad \{4\ 1\ 2\ 6\ 0\ 8\}$$

normal form: _____   _____

T_n-type: _____   _____

Interval (if T_nI-related) _____

Analysis Projects

Schoenberg, Piano Piece, Op. 33a (see Ex. 15–3, p. 280)

1. Determine the normal form, T_n-type, and T_nI-type of each chord in mm. 1–2. List these in the table below.

Meas./Beat	Unordered set	Normal form	T_n-type	T_nI-type
1/2	_____	_____	_____	_____
1/3	_____	_____	_____	_____
1/4	_____	_____	_____	_____
2/1	_____	_____	_____	_____
2/2	_____	_____	_____	_____
2/3	_____	_____	_____	_____

2. Find other instances of these T_n-types or T_nI-types in subsequent measures.

SUMMARY

Analysis procedures for tonal music involve eliminating octave doublings, revoicing chords in close and/or root position, and identifying their sonority type. The analysis of atonal music involves comparable tasks. These include determining a set's normal form, its T_n-type, and its T_nI-type. Sets that share the same normal form are content-equivalent, that is, they contain the same pcs. Sets that share the same T_n-type are T_n-equivalent, that is, they can be transposed onto each other.

QUESTIONS FOR REVIEW

1. Define the following terms: permutation, canonical order, rotation, normal form, T_n-type, T_nI-type.
2. Describe from memory the procedure for finding the normal form of an unordered pc set.
3. Explain how to find a set's T_n-type and T_nI-type.
4. Explain how to determine whether two unordered sets are related by transposition (T_n) or by inversion followed by transposition (T_nI).

CHAPTER 6

The Universe of Set-Types

T_n/T_nI-Type

Analysis procedures for atonal music are comparable in many respects to those for tonal music. But there is at least one significant difference. Metonymy is used more often in the analysis of atonal music.

Metonymy is the practice of referring to a class of objects by citing one instance of that class.[1] For example, we might refer to the category *symphony* by citing Beethoven's Fifth, or to *sports car* by citing a Porsche. In atonal theory we refer to a class of content-equivalent sets by citing one of those sets, the normal form. We also refer to a class of T_n-equivalent sets by citing one of *those* sets, the T_n-type. We can go one step further by considering a single set as the representative of a superclass of 24 T_n- and T_nI-related sets.

To illustrate, the sets listed in Table 6–1 comprise two classes of T_n-related sets. Each class is represented by its T_n-type at the head of its column. The sets within a column are related by transposition (T_n). Any set in one column is related to any set in the other column by inversion followed by transposition (T_nI). Thus, the T_n-type of a set in one column is the T_nI-type of a set in the other column. The T_n/T_nI-type, the representative of this superclass, is centered on the top row of the table.

The T_n/T_nI-type of a set will always be either its T_n-type or its T_nI-type. To find the T_n/T_nI-type, we compare the two types to determine which is in the "best" normal form. Since both of these sets begin with pc zero, we can start with the last pc and work toward the first.

first comparison   **second comparison**

(0 3 <u>7</u>)   (0 <u>3</u> 7)
(0 4 <u>7</u>)   (0 <u>4</u> 7)

Both sets have 7 as their last pc, but (0 3 7) has a smaller number as its next-to-last pc. Thus, [0 3 7] is the T_n/T_nI-type of this superclass of twenty-four T_n- and T_nI-related sets.[2]

---

[1] See George Lakoff, *Women, Fire, and Dangerous Things: What Categories Reveal About the Mind* (Chicago: University of Chicago Press, 1987).

[2] Forte uses the term "prime form" instead of T_n/T_nI-type. See *The Structure of Atonal Music* (New Haven: Yale University Press, 1973), pp. 3–13.

TABLE 6–1.   The superclass of T_n/T_nI-type [0 3 7]

T_n/T_nI-type [0 3 7]	
T_n-type (0 3 7)	**T_n-type (0 4 7)**
{0 3 7}	{0 4 7}
{1 4 8}	{1 5 8}
{2 5 9}	{2 6 9}
{3 6 10}	{3 7 10}
{4 7 11}	{4 8 11}
{5 8 0}	{5 9 0}
{6 9 1}	{6 10 1}
{7 10 2}	{7 11 2}
{8 11 3}	{8 0 3}
{9 0 4}	{9 1 4}
{10 1 5}	{10 2 5}
{11 2 6}	{11 3 6}

To find the **T_n/T_nI-type** of an unordered pc set:

1. Determine its T_n-type and its T_nI-type (the T_n-type of its inversion).
2. Compare the T_n-type and T_nI-type beginning with the last pcs and working backward toward the first pcs. When you find that one set has a lower number in a given place than the other set, that set is the T_n/T_nI-type.
3. If the T_n-type and T_nI-type are identical, then comparison is pointless. The T_n/T_nI-type is identical to both of these types.

EXERCISE 6–1

1. Several pairs of T_n- and T_nI-types are listed below. The T_n/T_nI-type of the first three pairs of sets is marked with an asterisk and the critical pc (i.e., the pc with the lower number in a given position) is underlined. Determine the T_n/T_nI-type of the remaining pairs by marking the appropriate set(s) with an asterisk and underlining the critical pc (if there is one).

a. (0 1 2 4 6 9)*   f. (0 1 4 6 8)
   (0 3 5 7 8 9)   (0 2 4 7 8)
b. (0 1 3 4 6 8 9)*   g. (0 3 6 8)
   (0 1 3 5 6 8 9)   (0 2 5 8)
c. (0 2 6 8)*   h. (0 1 3 6 8)
   (0 2 6 8)*   (0 2 5 7 8)
d. (0 3 7)   i. (0 1 2 4 5 6 7 9)
   (0 4 7)   (0 2 3 4 5 7 8 9)
e. (0 1 3 5 6)   j. (0 1 2 6 7 8)
   (0 1 3 5 6)   (0 1 2 6 7 8)

> 2. Determine the T_n/T_nI-type of each chord in mm. 1–2 of Schoenberg's Piano Piece, Op. 33a. (Use the T_n- and T_nI-types that you listed the Analysis Project of Chapter 5.)

Interval-Class Content

A set's interval-class content is one of its most distinctive features. To determine it, we must compute the *unordered* interval formed between each pair of pcs. This has been done below for the T_n-types from Table 6–1:

pcs	ipc(a,b)	pcs	ipc(a,b)
(0 3 7)	3	(0 4 7)	4
(0 3 7)	5	(0 4 7)	5
(0 3 7)	4	(0 4 7)	3

Notice that both sets contain the same unordered pc intervals (interval classes). (Would this be true if their pcs were reordered, transposed, and/or inverted?)

Interval-Class Vector

An *interval-class vector* is a miniature table that tells how many times each interval class occurs in a pc set. To illustrate, let's use the ic vector for T_n/T_nI-type [0 3 7]. For ease of reading, we'll superimpose column headings for the six interval classes:

interval class	1 2 3 4 5 6
multiplicity	<0 0 1 1 1 0>

Here we can see that [0 3 7], or any other set in its superclass, contains zero instances of ics 1, 2, and 6, and one instance of ics 3, 4, and 5.

The number of interval classes contained within a pc set depends on that set's *cardinality*. Table 6–2 shows that an arithmetic increase in cardinality produces a

TABLE 6–2.   Cardinality and the number of intervals in unordered pc sets

No. of pcs (cardinality)	No. of intervals
3	3
4	6
5	10
6	15
7	21
8	28
9	36

geometric increase in the number of unordered intervals. We can compute this number with the formula

$$\Sigma \ (1 \ ... \ (k-1))$$

where k indicates the cardinality of the set, and Σ represents the sum of a range of numbers. Thus, a set of five pcs has $\Sigma \ (1 \ ... \ (5-1)) = \Sigma \ (1 \ ... \ 4) = (1 + 2 + 3 + 4) = 10$ intervals.[3]

A set's ic vector can be determined by computing all of its unordered intervals and then tabulating the results. This is a rather involved task, so it is important to be methodical. We'll begin by computing the intervals formed by the first pc and each of *its* succeeding pcs, then the intervals formed by the second pc and each of *its* succeeding pcs, then the third pc and *its* successors, etc. When we reach the last pc, we will have computed all of the unordered intervals for the set.

To illustrate, let's use (3 5 6 8 11), a set that is in normal form but is not a T_n-type. The relevant pcs have been underlined so that you may follow the process of isolating each pair. Remember that we are computing *unordered* pc intervals.

Pitch class pair	ipc(a,b)
{3 5 6 8 11}	2
{3 5 6 8 11}	3
{3 5 6 8 11}	5
{3 5 6 8 11}	4
{3 5 6 8 11}	1
{3 5 6 8 11}	3
{3 5 6 8 11}	6
{3 5 6 8 11}	2
{3 5 6 8 11}	5
{3 5 6 8 11}	3

Now we can count the instances of each interval class and display the results in an ic vector:

interval class	1 2 3 4 5 6
multiplicity	<1 2 3 1 2 1>

To verify, we can add the entries to see whether they sum to the correct number of intervals for a set of this cardinality (see Table 6–2). In this case, we can see that

$$1 + 2 + 3 + 1 + 2 + 1 = 10 = \Sigma \ (1 \ ... \ (5 - 1))$$

---

[3] Forte, *The Structure of Atonal Music,* p. 19.

To determine the **interval-class vector** of an unordered pc set:

1. Arrange the pcs in ascending order, preferably normal form.
2. Compute the unordered pc interval between the first pc and each of its succeeding pcs, the second pc and each of *its* succeeding pcs, etc.
3. Count the instances of each interval class and record these in an interval-class vector.

The Table of T_n/T_nI-Types

By invoking the concepts of enharmonic equivalence, content equivalence, transpositional equivalence, and inversional equivalence, music theorists have reduced a seemingly infinite number of possible pitch combinations to 220 distinct T_n/T_nI-types. Table 6–3 shows the symmetrical relationship between set cardinality and the number of unique T_n/T_nI-types.

Books about atonal music often provide a table that lists these T_n/T_nI-types (also called set classes or prime forms), the ic vector of each type, and some additional information. An excerpt from Rahn's table is shown in Table 6–4. Column headings have been added to enhance interpretation.

The outermost columns list the T_n/T_nI-types for trichordal (3-pc) and nonachordal (9-pc) sets. Although some entries have been left blank, it is obvious that for every trichordal type there is a nonachordal type, and vice versa. In moving toward the center, we find two columns labeled *D.S.*, an abbreviation for Degrees of Symmetry. That property will be explored in a later chapter. The next pair of columns lists the ic vector for each set-type. Finally, the center column contains the labels that Allen Forte assigned to each set-type.[4] Each label has a number, a dash, and another

TABLE 6–3.   Cardinality and the number of unique T_n/T_nI-types

Cardinality (name)	No. of T_n/T_nI types
2 (dyad)	6
3 (trichord)	12
4 (tetrachord)	29
5 (pentachord)	38
6 (hexachord)	50
7 (septachord)	38
8 (octachord)	29
9 (nonachord)	12
10 (decachord)	6
Total:	220

---

[4]*The Structure of Atonal Music,* Section 1.5 and Appendix 1.

TABLE 6–4.   **Table of trichordal and nonachordal T_n/T_nI-types (to be completed)***

TRICHORDS					NONACHORDS	
T_n/T_nI-type	DS •	IC vector	Forte's label	IC vector	DS •	T_n/T_nI-type
[0,1,2]	2	<2,1,0,0,0,0>	3-1/9-1	<8,7,6,6,6,3>	2	[0,1,2,3,4,5,6,7,8]
[0,1,3]	1	<1,1,1,0,0,0>	3-2/9-2	<7,7,7,6,6,3>	1	[0,1,2,3,4,5,6,7,9]
[0,1,4]	1	<1,0,1,1,0,0>	3-3/9-3	<7,6,7,7,6,3>	1	[0,1,2,3,4,5,6,8,9]
[0,1,5]	1	<1,0,0,1,1,0>	3-4/9-4	<7,6,6,7,7,3>	1	[0,1,2,3,4,5,7,8,9]
[0,1,6]	1		3-5/9-5	<7,6,6,6,7,4>	1	[0,1,2,3,4,6,7,8,9]
[0,2,4]	2		3-6/9-6	<6,8,6,7,6,3>	2	[0,1,2,3,4,5,6,8,10]
	1		3-7/9-7	<6,7,7,6,7,3>	1	[0,1,2,3,4,5,7,8,10]
[0,2,6]	1		3-8/9-8	<6,7,6,7,6,4>	1	
	2		3-9/9-9		2	
[0,3,6]	2		3-10/9-10		2	
	1		3-11/9-11		1	
	6		3-12/9-12	<6,6,6,9,6,3>	6	

*Adapted from John Rahn, *Basic Atonal Theory* (New York: Longman, 1980) Table II, pp. 140–43.

number. The first number indicates the cardinality of the set. The second tells the position of that set-type in Forte's list of sets of that cardinality. For example, the label 3–3 indicates that the set is a trichord (has three pcs) and its T_n/T_nI-type is third in Forte's list of trichordal set-types.[5]

Set Complementation

Table 6–4 shows that there is a one-to-one relationship between trichordal (3-pc) and nonachordal (9-pc) set-types. The same relation holds for the other complementary cardinalities, as well. Thus, for every tetrachord (4 pcs) there is an octachord (8 pcs), for every pentachord (5 pcs) there is a septachord (7 pcs), and for every hexachord (6 pcs) there is a hexachord. Understanding this relationship, which is called *set complementation,* can help in comprehending the universe of pc sets.

To explain, notice that set-types 3–1 and 9–1 are listed on the first row of the table. Set 3–1 has (0, 1, 2) as its T_n/T_nI-type. The *literal complement* of [0, 1, 2] consists of the remaining nine pcs of the chromatic collection, {3, 4, 5, 6, 7, 8, 9, 10, 11}. The *abstract complement* is the T_n/T_nI-type of the literal complement, or [0, 1, 2, 3, 4, 5, 6, 7, 8].

Finding the abstract complement for this example was easy because {3, 4, 5, 6, 7, 8, 9, 10, 11} is in normal form, and its T_n- and T_nI-types are identical. Doing so for other types may require more computation, but the basic procedure remains the same.

---

[5]Rahn's order does not always coincide with Forte's. This is because Rahn lists complementary set-types opposite each other.

To determine the **abstract complement** of a pc set:

1. Determine its T_n/T_nI-type.
2. Determine the literal complement of *that* set.
3. Find the normal form of *that* set.
4. Determine its T_n- and T_nI-types. From these, select the T_n/T_nI-type. It will be the abstract complement of the original set.

Abstract complementation is the key to completing Table 6–4. For example, set-types 3–5, 3–6, and 3–7 are the abstract complements of 9–5, 9–6, and 9–7, respectively. Conversely, set-types 9–8 and 9–10 are the abstract complements of 3–8 and 3–10, respectively. When you have found these types, there will be only three more remaining for each cardinality.

A bit of thought should reveal that it would be easier to find the trichordal types (since they have fewer pcs) and then derive the nonachordal types by abstract complementation. You'll have to go through a bit of trial and error, but some logical reasoning should help, as well. For instance, set-type 3–9 will have to lie somewhere between {0, 2, 6} and {0, 3, 6}. Thus, it must be the T_n/T_nI-*type* of {0, 2, 7}, {0, 2, 8}, {0, 2, 9}, {0, 2, 10}, {0, 2, 11}, {0, 3, 4}, or {0, 3, 5}.

All of these sets begin with pc zero, but they *may* not be in normal form. Therefore, begin your search by finding the normal form of each, then the T_n-type and T_nI-type, then the T_n/T_nI-type. When you have found a type that is not listed in Table 6–4, you may assume that it is set-type 3–9. Use the same strategy to discover set-types 3–11 and 3–12, then derive 9–11 and 9–12 from these by abstract complementation. Finally, compute the missing ic vectors, and you will have a complete table of trichordal and nonachordal set-types.

SUMMARY

Unordered pc sets are normalized by finding their T_n-, T_nI-, and T_n/T_nI-types. Doing so may reveal sets that are related by transposition or transposed inversion. A set's T_n/T_nI-type (set type, set class, or prime form) can serve as the key for referencing other information in a set-class table that typically includes the Forte name, the interval-class vector, and the degrees of symmetry for that set-type and its abstract complement.[6]

An ic vector is a compact listing of the number of times that each interval class occurs within a set. A set's ic vector can be determined by computation, or by

---

[6]See Forte, *The Structure of Atonal Music,* Appendix 1, pp. 179–181; Joseph N. Straus, *Introduction to Post-Tonal Theory* (Englewood Cliffs, NJ: Prentice-Hall, 1990), Appendix 1, pp. 180–183; John Rahn, *Basic Atonal Theory* (New York: Longman, 1980), Table II, pp. 140–143; Robert D. Morris, *Composition with Pitch Classes* (New Haven, Yale University Press, 1987), Appendix One, pp. 313–319.

using its T_n/T_nI-type as the key to referencing its ic vector in a table of set-types. Transposition and inversion may change a set's pc content, but these operations do not affect a set's ic content. An ic vector applies not only to a given set, but also to any other set of the same superclass.

EXERCISE 6–2

The following three exercises should be answered by consulting the Table of T_n/T_nI-types given in Appendix A.

1. Does each trichordal set-type have a unique ic vector? Is the same true of each nonachordal set-type?
2. Does each tetrachordal set-type have a unique ic vector? Does each octachordal type? How is this reflected in the Forte names for these types?
3. How are the ic vectors of complementary set-types related? If you knew the vector of one set-type, could you derive that of the other?

QUESTIONS FOR REVIEW

1. Define the following terms: metonymy, inversional equivalence, T_n/T_nI-type, multiplicity, interval-class vector, cardinality, literal complement, abstract complement.
2. Explain the meaning of each column in Table 6–4.
3. Locate in Table 6–4 the T_n/T_nI-types for the following pitch combinations: major triad, minor triad, diminished triad, augmented triad.

Part III

OTHER ASPECTS

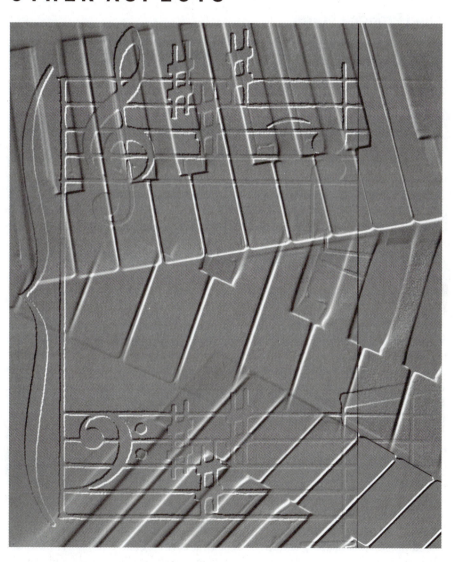

CHAPTER 7

Rhythm and Meter

Common-Practice Meter

The most basic concept for musical rhythm is that of *pulse.* A pulse may be defined as any sound that recurs in close succession. Most pulses recur regularly and establish a steady *tempo,* which is the rate or speed of a pulse. In active listening our mind correlates the various pulse rates of a musical passage and constructs an aural framework called *meter.*

To illustrate, consider the beginning of Ravel's Menuet from *Le tombeau de Couperin* (Ex. 7–1a). Immediately below the score (Ex. 7–1b) is a table of pulses that can be discerned from listening. The quarter-note level is labeled the *Beat* because it is moderate in tempo and prominent. Immediately below is a series of eighth notes labeled D1 (for division level 1). Eighth notes do not appear as consistently as quarter notes, but their presence in mm. 1, 2, 3, 5, and 6 implies their availability throughout. As the underlying bracket shows, the eighth notes are grouped in twos by the slower quarter-note pulse.

Above the Beat are levels labeled G1, G2, and G3 (for grouping levels 1, 2, and 3). Brackets show that the quarter-note pulses are grouped into threes by the slower pulses of level G1. G1 does not exist merely because the melody contains dotted half notes, for there is only one such note. Rather, G1 prevails because two rhythmic patterns (labeled *x* and *y*) recur.

G2 represents a slower pulse that organizes the G1 pulses into units of two. Again, G2 is not obvious; it must be inferred by listening for significant events: the recurrence of rhythmic pattern *x,* the introduction of a true bass voice in m. 3, the V–I cadence in mm. 3–4, the recurrence of durational patterns *y* and *x* in mm. 5–6, and the cadential harmonic progression in mm. 7–8.

G3 shows that these four 2-measure units combine to form two 4-measure units. The pulses of G2 and G3 are not marked as accented or unaccented because it is doubtful that accents can be perceived over such long time spans.

The above discussion might be termed a "bottom-up" approach, since we were concerned with grouping shorter, faster pulses to form longer, slower pulses. Ex. 7–1 can also be viewed from a "top-down" perspective in which longer, slower pulses are *divided* by shorter, faster ones.

To summarize, meter is a mental image of the way that various pulse levels are correlated in a musical passage. In this respect, it is analogous to tonality. Both are multi-leveled frameworks that the mind constructs from hearing music and that, in turn, influence our perception of music. Meter is the framework for perceiving

Example 7-1.

a. Ravel Menuet from *Le tombeau de Couperin*, **mm. 1–8**

b. Metric framework for Menuet, mm. 1–8

G3

G2

G1

Beat
   etc.

D1
   etc.

temporal organization; tonality is the framework for perceiving pitch organization. Although we are considering them separately, meter and tonality are highly interrelated. Our perception of meter is influenced by the tonal function of pitches, and our perception of tonality is influenced by their metric placement.

Ravel's Menuet was chosen as an introductory example because it exhibits a type of meter that has characterized most of Western music composed between about 1650 and 1900, a type that Allen Winold has termed "common practice" metric structure. Winold has summarized the general characteristics of such structures as follows:

1. *Pulses are clearly enunciated or implied on all levels, and they are isochronal or equal-timed; that is, they are heard at regularly recurring intervals of time. Pulses on the fastest or division levels rarely approach extremely fast rates of speed.*
2. *Pulse groups on the beat level, the first division level [our D1], and the first multiple level [our G1] may be in either two-pulse or three-pulse groups. On faster and slower levels they tend to be in two-pulse groups.*
3. *Pulse groups on the beat level, all division levels, and usually the first multiple level are unvaried; that is, once two-pulse or three-pulse groups are established on particular levels they are maintained throughout the composition or section.*
4. *Pulse groups on various levels are synchronous; that is, all pulses on slower levels coincide in time with stronger pulses on faster levels.*
5. *Metric structures tend to remain consistent in tempo throughout a composition or section.*
6. *In terms of notational practice, it is customary for composers to choose a beat value and measure length which enable them to write whole compositions or sections without changing meter signature.*[1]

Metric Change in Common-Practice Music

Having defined the basic attributes of common-practice metric structures, let's now consider various ways that metric structures can change.

Variable Division of the Beat-Level Pulse   Simultaneous duple and triple division of the beat-level pulse can be seen in Ex. 7–2a where the bass *ostinato* beginning in m. 3 implies four pulse levels (see Ex. 7–2b). (Can you explain how each level can be inferred from listening?) Eighth-note triplets are introduced in mm. 9–10 and 17–18, then additional variation occurs in mm. 11, 13–14, and 16 as thirty-second notes emerge with the coloratura figures. Notice how these moments of "metric dissonance" reinforce the harmonic dissonances that occur between melody and accompaniment.

The contribution of the habanera bass to Debussy's "very expressive" melody can be appreciated by hearing the melody without it. Doing so should convince you that it is difficult to infer a metric framework from the melody alone. (Can you explain why?) The habanera bass serves, therefore, as an aural "ruler" for measuring

[1]Allen Winold "Rhythm in Twentieth-Century Music," In *Aspects of Twentieth-Century Music,* ed. Gary E. Wittlich (Englewood Cliffs, NJ: Prentice-Hall, 1975), pp. 216–17.

Example 7–2.

a. Debussy, "La puerta del Vino," mm. 1–20

Example 7–2.   *Continued*

b. Metric framework for "La puerta"

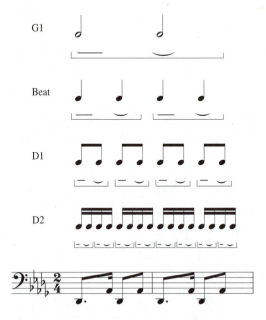

the longer and shorter notes of Debussy's melody. Much of this melody's expressive quality depends on the presence of pulse rates that *do not* appear in the melody itself.

Variable Grouping of the Beat-Level Pulse   Composers of tonal music were less inclined to vary the meter by regrouping the beat-level pulse, but examples can be found. The most familiar case, *hemiola,* is common in Baroque music. Example 7–3a shows how the grouping of the eighth-note pulse changes from triple to duple immediately before the cadence and then reverts to triple as the cadence occurs. As the brackets indicate, the three groups of two eighth notes form a single $\frac{3}{4}$ measure. The same procedure occurs in Ex. 7–3b, but there the beat-level pulse is the half note.

Berg's 1907 setting of "Schliesse mir" (see Ex. 1–1, p. 3) contains a more extensive example of regrouping. Its meter signature is $\frac{4}{4}$, but the melodic subphrases are only four quarter notes in length. This discrepancy is not too apparent in mm. 1–4 where the piano accompaniment provides an "extra" beat at the beginning (mm. 1–3) or end (m. 4) of each subphrase. It becomes more obvious, however, in mm. 5–8 where the phrasing in both voice and piano is clearly "out of sync" with the bar lines.[2]

---

[2]See Exercise 7 at the end of this chapter.

Example 7–3.

a. J. S. Bach, Fugue 11 in F major, BWV 856 (WTC I), ending

b. Debussy, "La cathédrale engloutie" ("The Engulfed Cathedral"), (Preludes, Book I), mm. 28–32, melodic line. (For the full texture see Example 8–7, p. 139)

Meter in 20th-Century Music

Some 20th-century composers have retained much of the common-practice structure described above; others have extended or departed from that practice in significant ways. For the remainder of this chapter we'll be concerned with the contributions of the latter group. Our concern, however, is not meant to devalue the music of the former group. For ultimately any piece of music must be judged on its own merits; rhythmic innovation is only one criterion of quality.

Meter with Unequal Pulses

Some 20th-century works have pulses that are unequal in length and, hence, irregularly paced. These typically occur at only one pulse level, usually the Beat level or the G1 level. Pulses at higher and lower levels remain equal-timed and regularly paced.

Typical are many pieces inspired by asymmetrical dance rhythms of Eastern Europe and the Near East. The first seventeen measures of Bartók's Bulgarian Rhythm are shown along with their metric framework in Ex. 7–4. The beaming in mm. 1–8 indicates a 3 + 2 grouping of the eighth-note pulse. The beat-level pulses are unequal; the first is longer. This arrangement changes in mm. 9–16 where beaming indicates 2 + 3 grouping. There the second beat-level pulse is longer than the first.

Example 7–4. Bartók, Bulgarian Rhythm (*Mikrokosmos*, IV/115), mm. 1–17

a. score

Example 7–5 has a more complex arrangement of unequal beat-level pulses. Its meter signature indicates a grouping of 4 + 2 + 3 rather than the usual 3 + 3 + 3. Note values that correspond to these groups are shown in Ex. 7–5b where brackets reveal that the half-note pulse can be subdivided into two quarter notes which, in turn, can be divided into two eighth notes. When the basic pulse is grouped as 2 + 2 + 2 + 3, grouping by threes occurs at both the beat level and the D1 level.

Olivier Messiaen achieved a comparable effect by adding short time values (either a dot, tie, or rest) to certain notes. Example 7–6 shows a melody from his

Example 7–4. *Continued*

b. metric framework

G2   2 measure phrases

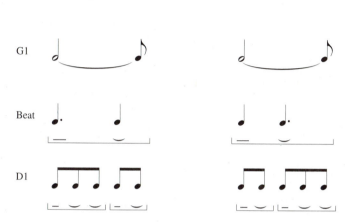

G1

Beat

D1

Quartet for the End of Time, one which Messiaen cited in his treatise entitled *The Technique of My Musical Language.* Notice that Messiaen marked the notes with "added values" with a plus sign.

It is interesting to compare Examples 7–5 and 7–6. The beat-level pulse of Bartók's dance is irregular, but its measure-level pulse is regular, since each measure contains nine eighth notes. In contrast, the pulses of the Messiaen excerpt are irregular at both the beat and measure levels, since some measures contain more than one note with an added value. The eighth-note, or D1, pulse of the Bartók is constant and prominent. The comparable sixteenth-note pulse of the Messiaen is less prominent because it occurs only briefly and at irregular intervals. Messiaen apparently intended that these irregular rhythms be perceived in terms of an implied sixteenth-note pulse, but recent experiments have shown that listeners are not inclined to hear such relationships.[3] His technique of adding short values to irregularly placed beats has a more disruptive effect than Bartók's unusual grouping of eighth notes within the measure.

Changing Meter

Bartók could have written Dance No. 1 as shown in Ex. 7–7, but that solution would have required more bar lines and a separate meter signature for each measure. He

---

[3]Elizabeth West Marvin, "The Perception of Rhythm in Non-Tonal Music: Rhythmic Contours in the Music of Edgard Varèse." *Music Theory Spectrum* 13 (Spring 1991): 62–63.

Example 7–5.

a. Bartók, Dance No. 1 in Bulgarian Rhythm (*Mikrokosmos*, **VI/148), mm. 1–8**

b. Metric framework for Dance No. 1

apparently decided to subsume the entire 2 + 2 + 2 + 3 pattern within one measure and to indicate the grouping of the eighth-note pulse by the meter signature and the beaming of eighth notes. (How does this grouping compare with the Baroque hemiola shown in Ex. 7–3a?)

Example 7–8, the beginning of another piece from *Mikrokosmos,* shows that Bartók *did* provide separate meter signatures when the measures do not form a

Example 7–6. Messiaen, Quartet for the End of Time, Dance of Fury, for the Seven Trumpets, mm. 1–6*

*As cited in Olivier Messiaen, *The Technique of My Musical Language*, Eng. trans. John Satterfield (Paris: Alphonse Leduc, 1956), Example 13.

Example 7–7. Alternate notation for Ex. 7–5

consistent higher-level pattern. Notice that the eighth-note pulse is constant, but the beat-level pulse varies between quarter notes (two eighths) and dotted quarter notes (three eighths).

The practice of grouping a prominent D1-level pulse irregularly into twos and threes, often termed *additive rhythm,* can be found in early 20th-century works of other composers. Example 7–9, from one of Stravinsky's "Russian" works, exhibits the same "additive" principle as Bartók's "Subject and Reflection." Notice, however, that Stravinsky used vocal notation (flagged instead of beamed eighth notes) and shorter measures. It is interesting to speculate on the reasoning behind Stravinsky's decisions. Why, for example, did he write a $\frac{4}{8}$ measure in some places and consecutive $\frac{2}{8}$ measures in others?

Paul Hindemith achieved virtually the same effect in his String Quartet No. 3, but he omitted meter signatures altogether and wrote measures of variable length (see Ex. 7–10). An eighth-note pulse prevails throughout the movement and provides a constant reference for other pulses. The same approach can be seen in Exx. 8–1 (p. 131) and 18–1 (p. 324).

To summarize, Exx. 7–4 through 7–10 show that essentially the same musical effect can be obtained in various ways. A composer's approach to rhythmic notation

Example 7–8. Bartók, Subject and Reflection (*Mikrokosmos,* VI/141), mm. 1–14

is often a highly personal and idiosyncratic matter. Passages that look different in score notation may sound quite similar when performed.

Metric Modulation

Some composers have used pulse levels to link passages with different meters and tempos. This technique has been developed most extensively by Elliott Carter, although it was used by Alban Berg earlier in the century.[4] Carter's term, *metric modulation,* implies an analogy with harmonic modulation, the technique of linking two key centers with a common chord or pitch class.[5] Other writers have suggested that *beat modulation* might be a more appropriate term.[6]

Example 7–11 contains the first section of "Canaries," one of Carter's *Eight Pieces for Four Timpani.* The piece begins in $\frac{6}{8}$ with the dotted quarter note as the

[4]Douglas Jarman, *The Music of Alban Berg* (Berkeley and Los Angeles: University of California Press, 1979), Chapter 4, pp. 169–172.

[5]Carter has developed this analogy in his lecture "The Time Dimension in Music" (1965) reprinted in *The Writings of Elliott Carter,* ed. Else and Kurt Stone (Bloomington: Indiana University Press, 1977) and in Allen Edwards, *Flawed Words and Stubborn Sounds: A Conversation with Elliott Carter* (New York: W. W. Norton, 1971).

[6]Robert Cogan and Pozzi Escot, *Sonic Design* (Englewood Cliffs, NJ: Prentice-Hall, 1976, reprint Cambridge, MA: Publication Contact International, 1985), pp. 284–89.

Example 7–9. Stravinsky, *Les Noces* (*The Wedding*), Reh. 12–14 (reduced score)

beat-level pulse. Measures 1–2 contain rhythmic patterns that confirm this meter, but the second half of m. 3 has four notes in the time span of the usual three. Duple division appears again in mm. 7–9, but the accents in mm. 9–10 group these dotted sixteenths in threes. This implication is realized in m. 11 where the meter changes back to $\frac{6}{8}$ but with a faster beat-level pulse. As indicated in m. 10, the "modulation" occurs as the previous dotted sixteenth-note pulse is reinterpreted as the ensuing eighth-note pulse.

Example 7–10. **Hindemith, String Quartet No. 3, Op. 22, II, mm. 1–6**

Schnelle Achtel. Sehr energisch (♪ = 176–184)

Another, more complex, metric modulation begins in m. 15 where the $\frac{6}{8}$ measures are shortened to $\frac{5}{8}$. With this grouping of eighth notes, Carter introduced a new quarter-note pulse. He changed the meter signature to $\frac{3}{4}$ in m. 18, but in the very next measure introduced eighth-note triplets that divide the quarter-note pulse into threes. After interpolating a single $\frac{3}{8}$ measure, he regrouped the eighth notes in m. 21 to form the quarter-note pulse of the new $\frac{3}{4}$ meter. The net effect is shown by the metronome indications above the score. The passage begins in m. 11 with a beat-level tempo of 120. That tempo is increased by a ratio of 3:2 during the modulation in mm. 15–18, and *that* tempo is increased by the same ratio in mm. 19–21.

As these two examples show, a metric (beat) modulation begins with the clear establishment of a metric framework. Soon one of the prevailing pulses is divided

Example 7–11. Carter, "Canaries," mm. 1–24

or grouped in an unusual manner. This generates a new pulse level that eventually "takes over" with its own tempo and metric framework.

Polymeter

Polymeter is a term that denotes the simultaneous presence of more than one meter. It occurs in polyphonic textures where each layer has its own metric structure. Although the variations on this idea are limited only by a composer's imagination, there are essentially three possibilities.

Differing Division-Level Pulses   In the simplest type the metric frameworks are congruent at the beat and grouping levels, but non-congruent at the first (and, perhaps, the second) division level. The most typical case involves simultaneous duple and triple division of the beat-level pulse. We have already seen one instance in the opening of Debussy's "La puerta del Vino" (see Ex. 7–2, mm. 9–10 and 17–18). More pronounced contrast can be seen in a passage from *Prelude to the "Afternoon of a Faun"* (see Ex. 7–12, mm. 79–85), which illustrates Debussy's conviction that

"It is nonsense to speak of 'simple' and 'compound' time. There should be an interminable flow of both."[7]

Differing Grouping-Level Pulses   A more disruptive type of polymeter occurs when textural layers are *not* congruent at one or more of their grouping, or super-primary, levels. In such cases, there is often a pronounced discrepancy between the perceived and notated meter. A good example can be found in the "Dirge" from Benjamin Britten's *Serenade,* Op. 31.

The movement is based on a vocal melody that serves as an ostinato with varied text. This melody is notated without bar lines in Ex. 7–13. Sing the melody several times until you are familiar with it. Then insert bar lines where they seem most appropriate. Remember that bar lines occur *before* notes that sound like strong beats. When you feel confident of your placement, count the number of beats in each measure, and write in appropriate meter signatures. Finally, compare your rebarred score with those of your classmates and discuss points of agreement and disagreement. Then follow the same procedure with the fugue subject shown in Ex. 7–14.

Now look at Britten's score (Simms, WenAMSS). As you can see, the composer did not change meter in either the vocal melody or the instrumental fugue subject. But this does not mean that such changes cannot be *heard;* perhaps other factors are involved. Notice, for example, that the low strings begin the fugue subject just as the voice completes the first statement of its ostinato melody in m. 6. The second statement of the vocal ostinato is, thus, superimposed over the first statement of the fugue subject. This layering process continues as the violas take up the subject in m. 10, the vocal line continues its second statement, and the low strings continue with other melodic material related to the fugue subject.

Britten's decision to notate the entire Dirge in $\frac{4}{4}$ can be understood if we consider the alternative. Ex. 7–15 is a revised score with each textural layer barred separately. This revision may reveal the metric structure of the various lines, but it would probably not serve a conductor's needs. To accommodate a conductor, composers often notate polymetric passages in a "neutral" meter, one that is minimally disruptive for the performers.[8]

Differing Beat-Level Pulses   A final category of polymeter includes passages having textural layers with different tempi. Example 7–16 shows the ending of a well-known work by Charles Ives with instrumentation and texture similar to those of Britten's Dirge. Both works require a string orchestra and a solo brass instrument: French horn for the Britten, trumpet for the Ives. Britten, however, included a solo voice as the third textural component, whereas Ives used a quartet of flutes.

---

[7] As quoted in Edward Lockspeiser, *Debussy: Life and Mind,* I (London: Cassell, 1962), 207. Reprinted in Piero Weiss and Richard Taruskin, eds., *Music in the Western World: A History in Documents* (New York: Schirmer Books, 1984), p. 417.

[8] A brief discussion of various solutions to this problem can be found in Chapter 7 of Messiaen's *The Technique of My Musical Language.* Eng. trans. John Satterfield (Paris, Alphonse Leduc, 1956).

Example 7-12. Debussy, Prelude to "The Afternoon of a Faun" mm. 79-85, piano reduction

Example 7–13.   Britten, "Dirge" from Serenade for Tenor, Horn, and String Orchestra, vocal ostinato, unbarred

Example 7–14.   Britten, "Dirge" from Serenade for Tenor, Horn, and String Orchestra, instrumental fugue subject, unbarred

To depict the work's literary program, which concerns the philosophical quest for the meaning of life, Ives assigned a different meter and tempo to each component of the ensemble. The music for off-stage string orchestra, which symbolizes the "silence of the druids," is notated in a $\frac{4}{4}$ meter with a tempo indication of "Largo molto sempre (about ♩ = 50.)" It is difficult to perceive this duple-compound meter because of its very slow beat-level pulse and the prevalence of sustained notes.

The trumpet part is actually in triple-compound meter, but Ives notated it as three groups of quarter-note triplets. Ex. 7–17 shows the trumpet's "question" motive rewritten in $\frac{9}{4}$ without the bracketed groups. Each measure of the trumpet solo is equal to one measure of the string music, but the trumpet part has only three beats per measure versus the strings' four. Since the temporal ratio between trumpet and strings is 3:4, the tempo of the trumpet part is $\frac{3}{4}$ times 50, or about 37.5 dotted half-note beats per minute.

The flutes are usually led by a second conductor who must ensure that their enigmatic responses to the trumpet's incessant questions are played at gradually faster tempi. Ives' tempo indications for the successive flute responses—Adagio, Andante, Allegretto, Allegro, Allegro molto, Allegro accel. to Presto, and Molto

Example 7–15. Rebarred score for Britten, "Dirge," mm. 1–11

agitando—reveal a pattern of increasingly frantic and chaotic answers to the "perennial question of existence."

Ametric Music

Some composers have achieved an ametric (without meter) effect by juxtaposing highly contrasting note values and by placing notes and rests at irregular intervals. The opening of *Density 21.5,* a famous piece for solo flute by Edgar Varèse, can serve as an introduction. Before studying Ex. 7–18, listen to the complete piece without following the score and try to capture some sense of an underlying pulse.

Example 7–16. Ives, *The Unanswered Question*, mm. 46-end

Example 7–16. *Continued*

Example 7–17. **Alternate notation of the Question motive**

Example 7–18. Varèse, *Density 21.5*, A section (mm. 1–23)

* Written in January, 1936, at the request of Georges Barrere for the inauguration of his platinum flute. Revised April, 1946. 21.5 is the density of platinum.
** Always strictly in time – follow metronomic indications.
*** Notes marked + to be played softly, hitting the keys at the same time to produce a percussive effect.

Varèse directed the flute soloist to play strictly in time and to follow the metronome indication, but he apparently did so to control the degree of rhythmic freedom and to ensure the ametric character. The other alternative, writing more traditional, on-the-beat rhythms and allowing the performer to "bend" the tempo through the use of rubato, would surely have produced a less consistent result.

Webern's Concerto for Nine Instruments, Op. 24 (see Ex. 5–1, p. 80) is another work in which the sense of regular pulse has been intentionally obscured. Listen to the entire first movement and try to detect a constant underlying pulse. Then study the score (Turek) and account for the effects that you heard. Notice that Webern was rather precise in his tempo indications, and that he called at several points for a brief slackening and then a resumption of the prevailing tempo. Are these changes audible? Can you follow a pulse throughout, or only the general effects of speeding up and slowing down?

It is difficult, if not impossible, to perceive the notated meter in the Varèse or the Webern passages because note and rest values do not coincide regularly with the stronger pulses of the notated meter. Thus, we have a paradox. A performer must maintain a strong sense of the notated meter in order to render the rhythms accurately, but doing so will not guarantee that a listener will perceive that meter. Indeed, it might guarantee that the notated meter will *not* be perceived. It is likely, therefore, that the rhythmic patterns of ametric music are perceived somewhat differently by performers and listeners.

Rhythm

Rhythm in Metric Contexts

Listeners tend to perceive durational patterns in one of two ways: as clusters of notes, or as time points along a metric framework (see Ex. 7–19). Jeanne Bamberger has termed these two modes *figural* and *formal*.[9] She has found that figural perception is characteristic of younger children and some adults who do not read music. Formal, or durational, hearing is practiced by older children and most adults, especially those who do read music.

Example 7–19. Depiction of figural vs. formal hearing

---

[9]Jeanne Bamberger, "Cognitive Structuring in the Apprehension and Description of Simple Rhythms," *Archives de Psychologie* 48 (1980): 171–199.

TABLE 7-1. Basic patterns of rhythmic grouping

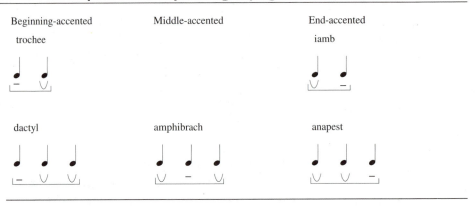

Particularly interesting is Bamberger's discovery that one mode often precludes the other. It seems that we all begin as figural listeners, but most of us make the transition to formal hearing sometime during late childhood or early adolescence. The transition is facilitated by learning to read music. But once the threshold is crossed, formal listeners often become so accustomed to that mode of perception that they ignore the benefits of figural hearing.

Figural hearing is especially valuable for performers who must grasp the essence of a musical passage and project that understanding through a voice or instrument. Doing so requires an understanding of rhythm, which Cooper and Meyer have defined as "the way in which one or more unaccented beats are grouped in relation to an accented one."[10] To represent rhythmic grouping these authors have used three basic symbols:

- the breve (‿) indicates an accented beat.
- the macron (–) indicates an unaccented beat.
- the bracket shows how weaker beats are grouped around a stronger beat.

Table 7–1 shows five basic patterns that result from combining one or two unaccented beats with a single accented beat.

Rhythmic grouping can best be understood in contrast to that of meter. Example 7–20 shows a table of four pulse levels for $\frac{2}{4}$ meter. In addition to the beat-level, quarter-note pulse, there are two division levels and one grouping level. Brackets show how the pulses group at each level. Each bracket encloses a trochee (see Table 7–1), one of the two beginning-accented patterns. Trochaic patterns tend to prevail when note values are even and the meter is easily perceived.

Now let's examine the passage from which this framework was derived. Example 7–21 shows the opening snare drum solo from the second movement of Bartók's Concerto for Orchestra. Notice that accent and unaccent marks are placed under

[10]Grosvenor Cooper and Leonard B. Meyer, *The Rhythmic Structure of Music* (Chicago: University of Chicago Press, 1960), p. 6.

Example 7–20. Metric framework for Ex. 7–21

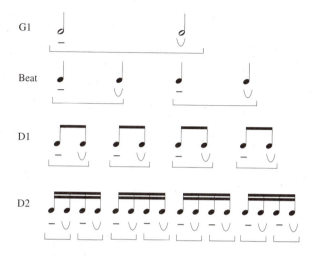

the very same beats (compare Ex. 7–20), but some marks have an acute accent (′)
to indicate that they are stressed. A summary of analysis symbols is provided in
Table 7–2.

What has changed most in Ex. 7–21 is the rhythmic grouping as indicated by
the underlying brackets. The change is most apparent at level D1 where unaccented
eighth-note beats now combine with the *following* accented beat to form *end*-accented
or *middle*-accented patterns. The rests in mm. 1–6 also affect the grouping by
suppressing the normal metric accents. They cause the sixteenth notes to join with
the *next* beat-level pulse rather than the preceding one. In a few instances patterns
overlap as indicated by the overlapping brackets (see mm. 3–4). The grouping at
the Beat level is decidedly more trochaic, but several quarter-note pulses are suppressed as indicated by the enclosing parentheses.

Most significantly, the analysis reveals the overall shape of this brief solo. Bartók
built the passage around the first beats of mm. 1–3 and, especially, the climactic
first beat of m. 7. He began by suppressing the second beats of mm. 1–3. This, in
turn, strengthened the first beats of mm. 2–4. Instead of continuing in this manner,
however, he surprised us in m. 4 by doing the opposite—suppressing the first beat
and stressing the second beat. He did the same thing in m. 5 and then suppressed
both of the beat-level pulses in m. 6. As a result, mm. 4–6 combine to form an
extended anacrusis (upbeat) to the first beat of m. 7 where this pent-up energy
is released.

As you can see from this brief analysis, the issue of rhythmic grouping can be
fascinating. Cooper and Meyer have noted that

> *Rhythmic grouping is a mental fact, not a physical one. There are no hard and fast rules*
> *for calculating what in any particular instance the grouping is. Sensitive, well-trained*
> *musicians may differ. Indeed, it is this that makes performance an art—that makes different*

TABLE 7-2. Analysis symbols used by Cooper and Meyer*

‒	Accent
⌣	Weak beat or group
(‒)(⌣)	Felt but unperformed beats or groups; or a parenthetical beat or group
▽	Beat or group at first presumed to be accented, but retrospectively understood to be weak
⊻	Beat or group at first presumed to be weak but retrospectively understood to be accented
‿⌣	Accent fused to a weak beat or group
⌣‿	Weak beat or group fused to an accent
⌣‿⌣	Fused weak beats or groups
⌣-------	Extended anacrusis
▽-------	Extended anacrusis at first presumed to be an accent
/	Stress (stressed accent or group ⟋ ; stressed weak beat or group ⌣̸)
└──┘	Grouping, manifest or dominant; except where the analysis is above the example, when it indicates the latent grouping
┌──┐	Grouping, latent; except where the analysis is above the example, when it indicates the manifest grouping
└───	Grouping without a definite conclusion or which blends into another grouping
───┘	Grouping without a definite beginning point
└─└─┘	Overlapping or pivoted rhythmic groups
└─↗└─┘	Splitting of one rhythmic level into two

*Grosvenor Cooper and Leonard B. Meyer, *The Rhythmic Structure of Music* (Chicago: University of Chicago Press, 1960), p. 204.

phrasings and different interpretations of a piece of music possible. Furthermore, grouping may at times be purposefully ambiguous and must be thus understood rather than forced into a clear decisive pattern. In brief, the interpretation of music—and this is what analysis should be—is an art requiring experience, understanding, and sensitivity.[11]

Syncopation

Example 7–22 presents the first eight measures of "Summertime," the familiar lullaby from George Gershwin's opera *Porgy and Bess.* Immediately below is a transcription of a classic performance by Miles Davis, the famous jazz trumpeter.[12] Davis obtained

---

[11]*The Rhythmic Structure of Music,* p. 9.

[12]Miles Davis and Gil Evans, *Porgy and Bess,* (Columbia CL 1274, 1958). "Summertime" has been reissued on the *Smithsonian Collection of Classic Jazz* (Washington, DC: Smithsonian Institution, 1973).

Example 7–21. Analysis of rhythmic grouping in the opening snare drum solo from Bartók, Concerto for Orchestra, second movement*

*Pulse levels are arranged and labeled in a manner consistent with the examples in this text, but opposite from the Cooper-Meyer text.

most of his syncopations by placing notes slightly ahead of their "normal" metric position, but in a couple of places, he delayed the first note of a phrase. Here we can regard the vocal melody (composed in 1934) as the "normal" version and Davis's performance (recorded in 1958) as a syncopated variation. In other cases, a "normal" version may not predate a syncopated melody, but one can usually be derived through a technique known as *normalization*.[13]

Example 7–23 shows a phrase from Gunther Schuller's "Little Blue Devil," a piece inspired by a painting of Paul Klee and by Schuller's high regard for the music of Miles Davis and other jazz artists. We can validate the normalization process by

---

[13]See J. Kent Williams, "A Method for the Computer-Aided Analysis of Jazz Melody in the Small Dimensions," *Annual Review of Jazz Studies* 3 (1985): 41–70; and William Rothstein, "Rhythmic Displacement and Rhythmic Normalization," in *Trends in Schenkerian Analysis,* ed. Allen Cadwallader (New York: Schirmer Books, 1990), pp. 87–113.

Example 7–22. Gershwin, *Porgy and Bess,* "Summertime" mm. 1–8. Top staff: original melody; bottom staff, Miles Davis's interpretation

Example 7–23. Schuller, *Seven Studies on Themes of Paul Klee,* III. Little Blue Devil, reh. B; original and normalized versions of a syncopated melodic line

listening carefully to the two melodies. In this case, the normalized version sounds correct, but more "square" than the original.

Syncopation has an effect in the temporal domain that is comparable to dissonance in the tonal domain.[14] Both depend upon normative backgrounds to achieve their intended effect. If a metric framework or tonal center cannot be perceived, then syncopated notes or dissonant pitches will lose much of their intended meaning.

---

[14]This point is developed more fully in William Rothstein, "Rhythmic Displacement and Rhythmic Normalization," p. 89.

Rhythm in Ametric Contexts

When music is ametric, rhythmic patterns are perceived in their local durational context instead of a global metric framework. Elizabeth West Marvin has shown how such patterns can be represented generally enough to facilitate wide and meaningful comparisons.[15] Her method involves isolating a pattern from its surrounding context, ranking its notes in terms of their duration, and then constructing a *duration segment,* an ordered set in which the durational rank of each note is represented by an integer.

As an illustration consider the first phrase of *Density 21.5* (see Ex. 7–18, mm. 1–3). The phrase contains seven notes but only six different durations. These can be ranked on a scale from 0 to 5, with 0 representing the shortest and 5 representing the longest. The duration segment (abbreviated as dseg) for this pattern would, therefore, be <0 0 4 2 1 3 5>. *Durational subsegments* (abbreviated as dsubsegs) can be represented in a similar manner. For example, the dsubseg for the first four notes of this phrase would be <0 0 2 1>, and that for the first five notes would be <0 0 3 2 1>. Notice that the integers always indicate the durational rank of a note *within its segment or subsegment.* If a segment has n different durations, then the integers will range from 0 to n–1.

Using this method, Marvin has shown that most phrases of the A section (mm. 1–23) of *Density 21.5* begin with a recurring rhythmic figure that can be represented as dsubseg <0 0 1>. This fact is apparent for the phrases that begin with two sixteenth notes followed by a longer note. It is less obvious, however, when durational values change but the rhythmic contour remains the same. For example, the phrase in mm. 13–14 also begins with a dsubseg of <0 0 1>, but the actual note values there are different—two eighths followed by a dotted quarter.

Spatial Notation of Duration

To attain greater flexibility some composers have invented alternative forms of rhythmic notation. These may differ in appearance, but they are usually based on a common underlying notion, that distance along the horizontal axis represents time.

The score of Bruce Saylor's Psalm 13 (see Ex. 7–24) is particularly interesting; its flute part is notated traditionally, but its voice part is represented spatially. The performance directions tell the singer to watch the flute part and align her part approximately with it. This frees the singer from having to discern a steady pulse from the flutist's ametric music, but it still enables the two performers to synchronize their parts. Another approach to spatial notation can be seen in Ex. 8–14 (p. 146).

As a final observation, note that these examples of ametric music (Exx. 7–18 and 7–24) are set in an atonal idiom. Composers who have avoided tonality in the pitch domain have often avoided perceptible meter in the temporal domain. Charles Wuorinen, a spokesman for this group, has remarked that these two idioms have traditionally been, and ought to remain, closely associated:

---

[15]Marvin, "The Perception of Rhythm in Non-Tonal Music," pp. 65–73.

Example 7–24. Bruce Saylor, Psalm 13, mm. 1–15

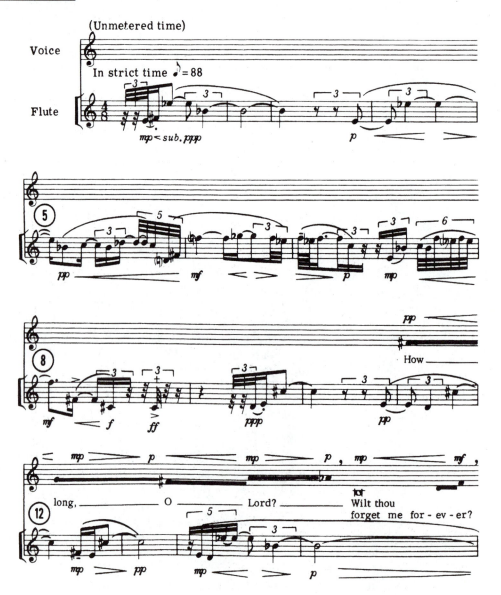

the rhythmic structure of most such music features aperiodicity and irregularity in its unfolding. The intuitive sense of composers of increasingly chromatic music from Wagner onward has been to complement homogeneity within the pitch class hierarchy with rhythmic irregularity. . . . We advise a general use of rhythmic aperiodicity, whether of meter, beat subdivision, foreground rhythm, or all of these in combination.[16]

---

[16]Charles Wuorinen, *Simple Composition* (New York and London: Longman, 1979), pp. 42–43.

Example 7–25. Berg, *Wozzeck,* Act III, Scene 2. Initial statement of the Murder motive

Motivic Uses of Rhythm

Composers of the 20th century have continued to emphasize rhythm as a constructive element in music, often with a corresponding deemphasis of pitch. Alban Berg, Igor Stravinsky, and Charles Ives pioneered this practice during the early decades. Oliver Messiaen, Edgar Varèse, and others continued it during succeeding decades.

The term *constructive rhythm* has been used in connection with Berg's music "to denote any recurrent rhythmic pattern which operates independently of harmonic or melodic material."[17] A most vivid and extensive example occurs in the final act of Berg's opera *Wozzeck.* The dramatic climax occurs in Act III, Scene 2 when Wozzeck, a poor, downtrodden soldier gone insane, murders Marie, his mistress and the mother of his child. Berg associated the rhythmic motive (Ex. 7–25) with Wozzeck's crime during the brief instrumental interlude that follows the murder scene. To emphasize the rhythmic component of this motive and to stamp it upon our memory, Berg had the initial statement played *fff* on the bass drum.

Act III, Scene 3 takes place in a tavern. Berg repeated and developed the motive incessantly to depict Wozzeck's overwhelming sense of guilt and fear. It is easy to locate various statements of the motive in the score because Berg marked them with the symbol H¬, an abbreviation for the German word *Hauptrhythmus* (principal rhythm). In addition to repeating the motive, Berg developed and varied it using several standard techniques. These include:[18]

1. Exact augmentation—multiplying the durations by a constant factor greater than 1.
2. Inexact augmentation—multiplying the durations by a variable factor greater than 1.
3. Exact diminution—multiplying the durations by a constant factor less than 1 but greater than zero.
4. Metric displacement—shifting an entire pattern forward or backward with respect to the metric framework.
5. Rhythmic canon—repeating the motive in different voices at staggered time intervals.

---

[17]Jarman, *The Music of Alban Berg,* p. 147. The following discussion of the *Wozzeck* example is abstracted from this source.

[18]Ibid., p. 163.

6. Paraphrase—inserting or deleting notes while preserving the essential rhythmic contour of the motive.

Listen to a recording of Act III, Scenes 2 and 3 of *Wozzeck*. Then study the score of Scene 3 (Palisca) locating as many examples of the Murder motive as you can find. Classify each example as either a literal repetition or a variant. Explain how each of the variants was derived from the original by one or more of the techniques listed above.

QUESTIONS FOR REVIEW

1. Define the following terms: pulse, tempo, meter, isochronal, synchronous, additive rhythm, syncopation, polymeter, ametric, constructive rhythm.
2. Explain in your own words how tonality and meter are analogous concepts in the domains of pitch and time.
3. List five characteristics of common-practice metric structures.
4. Describe the three stages of a metric modulation. Compose one or two to illustrate your point.
5. Explain the difference between figural and formal hearing.
6. List three ways that syncopation can be expressed.

EXERCISES

A. Rhythmic Analysis

1. Using Exx. 7–1b, 7–2b, 7–4b, and 7–5b as your models, construct the metric framework for Exx. 7–12, 7–13, and 7–23.
2. Analyze Ex. 7–9 for aspects of polymeter. Then rewrite the voice parts to conform to the duple meter of the piano part. Use beams instead of flags so that the grouping of the eighth-note pulse is more apparent. A beginning is shown below. When you have completed your score, compare it to Stravinsky's. Why do you think Stravinsky used changing meters instead of syncopation? Would a performance from either version produce the same effect? Which version seems easier to read?

3. Isolate several short rhythmic figures in Exx. 7–18 and 7–24. Determine the duration segment (dseg) of each figure and compare these dsegs to discover any equivalent patterns within each excerpt and between two excerpts.

4. The term isorhythm is associated with the music of 14th century, but it has also been applied to some 20th-century music. Study the score of Messiaen's "Liturgie de cristal" from his *Quatuor pour la fin du temps (Quartet for the End of Time)* (Turek). Which part is isorhythmic? How long is the recurring rhythmic pattern? How does it relate to the notated meter?

5. Rebar the following melody to reflect how you hear the meter. Then compare your version with Berg's (see Ex. 1–1 on p. 3).

"Schliesse mir die Augen beide" mm. 5–9 (unbarred)

6. The final section of Debussy's "The Engulfed Cathedral" can be rebarred and rebeamed to reveal its polymeter. A beginning is given below. Continue it through m. 83. Because this passage is a restatement of mm. 28–40, you should remember to account for the hemiola at the end of each phrase (see Ex. 7–3b). What happens to the meter of the right hand part in mm. 82–83? How is this implied by Debussy's beaming of the eighth notes in the left hand?

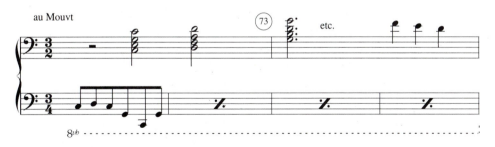

RECOMMENDED LISTENING AND ANALYSIS

Bartók, from *Mikrokosmos:* II/59, Major and Minor (Turek), V/126, Change of Time (Wen20), V/128, Peasant Dance (Turek), V/133. Syncopation (Burkhart), VI/140, Free Variations (Morgan), VI/148, Six Dances in Bulgarian Rhythm, No. 1 (Morgan, Wen20)
———, Forty-Four Violin Duets: Song of the Harvest (Turek)
Bernstein, Symphonic Dances from *West Side Story,* "Cool" and "Rumble" (Kamien)
Boulez, *Le marteau sans maître,* No. 3 (DeLio-Smith)

Britten, Serenade, Op. 31; Prologue (Turek), "Dirge" (Simms, Turek, WenAMSS), "Sonnet" and Epilogue (Burkhart)

Carter, *Eight Etudes and a Fantasy for Woodwind Quartet,* No. 9 Fantasy (Wen 20)

Copland, *Appalachian Spring* (excerpt) (Wen20)

———, *Rodeo,* "Hoedown" (Morgan)

Dallapiccola, Goethe-Lieder, Nos. 1 and 3 (Wen20)

Debussy, *Prelude à "L'après-midi d'un faune"* (Burkhart)

———, from Preludes, Book I: "Les sons et les parfums tournent dans l'air du soir" from Preludes (Turek); "La cathédrale engloutie" (Burkhart)

———, from Preludes, Book II: "La puerta del Vino" (WenAMSS)

———, *Syrinx* (DeLio-Smith)

Hindemith, String Quartet No. 3, Op. 22, second movement (Wen20)

Ives, Piano Sonata No. 2 ("Concord"), third movement "The Alcotts" (Turek)

———, "General William Booth Enters into Heaven" (Burkhart, Morgan)

Messiaen, *Quatuor pour la fin du temps (Quartet for the End of Time),* (I in Turek, III in DeLio-Smith, VI in Wen20)

Prokofiev, Seventh Piano Sonata, third movement (Simms)

Reich, Clapping Music for Two Performers (DeLio-Smith, Simms, Wen20)

———, Music for Pieces of Wood (Morgan)

Schuller, *Seven Studies on Themes of Paul Klee,* "Little Blue Devil" (Wen20)

Stravinsky, *Petroushka* (Second Tableau in Simms, Third Tableau in Wen20)

———, from *The Rite of Spring*; Augurs of Spring: Dances of the Young Girls (Morgan, Turek, WenAMSS)

———, from *L'Histoire du Soldat (The Soldier's Tale)* The Soldier's March (Burkhart, Turek, Wen20), Triumphal March of the Devil (Turek, Wen20), Three Dances (WenAMSS)

Varèse, *Hyperprism* (Morgan, excerpt in Wen20)

———, *Octandre,* first movement (Simms)

Webern, Concerto for Nine Instruments (I in Turek)

———, Six Pieces for Orchestra, Op. 6, No. 1 (Wen20)

CHAPTER 8

Texture

Traditional Categories

Monophonic Texture

Several 20th-century composers have written for unaccompanied wind instrument or voice (see Ex. 7–18, p. 118). Monophonic textures also occur in recitatives or cadenzas of instrumental works. They are less common in music for keyboard instruments, but they can be found. Alan Hovhaness wrote his *Visionary Landscape No. 1* (see Ex. 8–1) for solo piano but drew upon performance techniques for the Hungarian *cimbalom* and other instruments of the dulcimer family. The music on

Example 8–1. Alan Hovhaness, *Visionary Landscape No. 1,* opening

the lower staff consists of a reiterated pitch while that on the upper staff moves around an exotic scale.

The Hovhaness excerpt illustrates two important facts about musical textures. First, texture is often closely associated with performance technique. Composers have devised novel textures by trying to imitate one instrument with another. Second, textures can be conceived in various ways. Since the present example divides into two strands that exhibit oblique motion, its texture is actually polyphonic.

The term *compound* (or *polyphonic) melody* is often used to describe a melodic line that can be separated into two or more textural strands. Compound melody was typical of instrumental music of the Baroque era, but it can also be found in 20th-century works, especially those in the neotonal idiom (see Chapters 12 and 13).[1]

Homophonic Texture

Homophonic texture is characterized by a clear delineation between melody and accompaniment. The accompaniment provides the harmonic and rhythmic background for the "main event" presented in the melodic foreground.

Maurice Ravel used conventional accompaniment figures in *Le tombeau de Couperin,* his tribute to François Couperin (1668–1733) and other composers of the French *clavecin* school. Example 8–2a can be parsed into melody and accompaniment, but the melodic line is not always the highest voice. In addition, the accompaniment has linear motion that endows it with some melodic interest. Example 8–2b, a textural reduction, reveals three components: a melodic line in the treble staff, harmonic filler in the middle, and a bass line that descends by step (mm. 3–5) and then by perfect fifth (mm. 6–7). Compare this reduction to the score and describe how it both simplifies and distorts Ravel's music.

The piano accompaniment of Berg's 1907 setting of "Schliesse mir" (see Ex. 1–1, p. 3) contains motives from the vocal melody. This tendency to integrate melody and accompaniment is more evident in Berg's Four Songs, Op. 2 (1908–09). The third song (Ex. 8–3a) has a piano part that competes with the voice for the listener's attention. The vocal melody is built around four distinct motives (Ex. 8–3b), three of which (x, y, and z) appear in the piano "accompaniment." Berg reserved a more neutral accompaniment figure, the syncopated, reiterated-chord pattern, for the few brief moments of repose.

Polyphonic Texture

To be perceived as polyphonic, the strands of a musical fabric must be delineated by contrasts in duration, pitch contour, register, and/or tone color. If they are not sufficiently delineated, they will tend to fuse into a single percept.[2]

---

[1]See Allen Forte and Steven D. Gilbert, *Introduction to Schenkerian Analysis* (New York: W. W. Norton, 1982), Chapter 3; Leonard B. Meyer, *Explaining Music* (Chicago: University of Chicago Press, 1973), Part Two; David Butler, *The Musician's Guide to Perception and Cognition* (New York: Schirmer Books, 1992), pp. 104–114.

[2]David Butler, *The Musician's Guide to Cognition and Perception,* pp. 104–110.

Example 8–2.

Ravel, *Le tombeau de Couperin,* **Rigaudon, (a) mm. 3–7, (b) textural reduction**

The second movement of Bartók's *Concerto for Orchestra* is a virtual study in two-voice, note-against-note, parallel motion. Bartók presented various themes in homogeneous pairs of instruments and harmonized each pair at a different interval. Example 8–4 quotes the first few measures of successive statements, but the full effect can only be experienced by listening to the entire movement. Doing so should convince you that persistent parallel, note-against-note motion makes two lines (with similar timbres) sound like one.

It is interesting to compare these excerpts with the Hovhaness passage. Example 8–1 is ostensibly monophonic but is actually polyphonic. The texture of Bartók's duets is ostensibly polyphonic but is really monophonic, since the two parts tend to fuse into a single, thickened line.

Contrapuntal textures are often classified as *free* or *imitative*. Free counterpoint has lines that complement each other but do not share the same melodic idea. Imitative counterpoint presents the same melodic motive(s) successively in different voices.

Igor Stravinsky referred to the outer movements of his *In Memoriam Dylan Thomas* as "dirge-canons." The Prelude of the work opens (see Ex. 8–5) with a point of imitation for four trombones. The opening motive stated by Trombone II is answered an octave lower by Trombone IV and then less literally by the other two instruments. This excerpt is followed by a shorter imitative passage for string quartet.

Example 8–3a. Alban Berg, Four Songs, Op. 2, Song No. 3

*) Diese Stellen nicht hastig, sondern im Tempo des gesprochenen Wortes.

Example 8–3b. **Motives in Berg's Op. 2, No. 3**

The first movement of Norman Dello Joio's Piano Sonata No. 3 is a theme and variations based on a fragment of Gregorian chant. Instead of a typical 16-measure theme in binary form, the composer presented a two-phrase, four-and-one-half measure idea three times (Ex. 8–6). The initial statement (mm. 1–5) contains some free imitation between the two voices. The melody is presented again in the soprano voice of a chorale-style setting (mm. 5–10). In the third statement (mm. 10–15), the texture is only slightly imitative, and the number of voices has been reduced to three. Since each statement has its own distinctive texture, Dello Joio's *Theme* may be regarded as a miniature set of textural variations on the chant melody.

Chordal Texture

The middle section (mm. 5–10) of Ex. 8–6 could also be regarded as chordal rather than contrapuntal. The tendency to see and hear chords, rather than lines, depends on one's analytical perspective. When chordal textures are conceived from a melodic point of view, *voice leading* is emphasized. When one's perspective is harmonic, matters of chord spacing, doubling, and registration are given higher priority.

Claude Debussy (1862–1918) was one of the first composers to use parallel motion extensively. Example 8–7 evokes an image of ancient and massive grandeur through extensive octave doubling, parallel fifths, and low registration. *Parallel voice leading* (also called *harmonic parallelism* or *planing*) is also evident in Ex. 8–6, but the voices there move more independently and the chord types are more varied.

Example 8–8, from a piano work by William Schuman, features both parallel and contrary motion. The texture could be termed *compound* because it consists of six voices divided into two groups of three. Within each group the motion is highly parallel; between the two groups it is contrary. How do the individual chords compare in terms of vertical density? Does each chord contain six unique pitch classes, or do some have fewer than six?

Example 13–1a (p. 236) shows Paul Hindemith emulating the texture of the madrigal and chanson, two vocal genres of the late Renaissance. The opening of the first phrase is notable for the use of oblique motion; the soprano reiterates B_4 while the lower three voices move in parallel perfect fourths. (How does this compare to Ex. 8–1?)

Example 8–4. Bartók, *Concerto for Orchestra,* second movement ("Game of the Couples") excerpts

a. Bassoons in minor sixths

b. Oboes in minor thirds

c. Trumpets in major seconds

Innovative Approaches

Heterophony

Heterophony, the simultaneous presentation of nearly identical melodic lines, is characteristic of folk music, but it can also be found in art music, especially in works that are modeled upon folk sources. The opening of Bartók's Dance in Bulgarian Rhythm No. 2 (Ex. 13–2a, pp. 240–42) exhibits heterophonic texture in mm. 4–7. What musical qualities would have been lost if Bartók had written the right-hand part to conform exactly to the left-hand part?

Example 8–5. Igor Stravinsky, *In Memoriam Dylan Thomas*, Prelude, mm. 1–10

Ostinato

An *ostinato* is a short melodic or rhythmic pattern that is repeated in one component of a musical texture. Its repetitions impose a primitive kind of unity upon the music. Variety is achieved by activity and processes in the other layers.

Example 8–6. Norman Dello Joio. Piano Sonata No. 3, I, Theme

Example 8–9 shows the opening of a Bartók piece titled "Ostinato" because of the reiterated trichord in the left hand. In contrast to a typical example of ostinato-based Baroque music,[3] this passage exhibits no sense of harmonic progression or bass-line motion. Instead, Bartók established D as the tonic pc by reiterating the D_3-A_3 perfect fifth and the low D_2 of mm. 5–7 (upper staff), and by delimiting the

---

[3]For example, Dido's Lament from Purcell's *Dido and Aeneas,* or the "Crucifixus" from Bach's Mass in B Minor (both in Burkhart)).

Example 8–7. Claude Debussy, *The Engulfed Cathedral*, mm. 26–42

melody of mm. 8–16 with pitches D_4 and D_5. How does this excerpt compare with Ex. 7–2a (p. 101)?

Layered Textures

Stravinsky also explored the technique of superimposing layers of melodic and rhythmic activity. His *Le Sacre du Printemps* (*The Rite of Spring*) was seminal in this respect. Example 8–10 shows one of numerous passages constructed according to

Example 8–8. William Schuman, *Three-Score Set,* II

Example 8–9. Bela Bartók, "Ostinato" (*Mikrokosmos,* VI/146), mm. 1–16

the layering principle. The texture is comprised of three layers, or *strata:* strings reiterate a dense, low-register chord in eighth notes; oboes, bassoons, and trombone imitate each other with a simple melodic phrase; and the flute reinforces weak-beat notes with its more brilliant timbre. Here we can see several of the devices discussed

Example 8–10. Stravinsky, *The Rite of Spring,* reh. 21–22

above: *ostinato* in the strings, overlapping imitation, or *stretto,* in the double reeds and trombone, and *heterophony* between the flute and oboes.

Stratified textures have been developed more extensively by certain European composers, notably Krzysztof Penderecki, György Ligeti, and Karlheinz Stockhausen. Ligeti has written of the "permeability" of his music where "structures of different textures can run concurrently, penetrate each other and even merge into one another completely."[4] To achieve such novel effects, these composers developed various textural "structures," the simplest of which is the *sustained cluster* or *sound band.* In Ex. 8–11 a low-register flute is combined with cello and bass harmonics to provide a sound band background for a horn cadenza.

A *sound complex* is a more dynamic combination in which several parts have active, but usually brief and repetitive, musical patterns. When the pitch range is narrow and the vertical density is high, the aural effect can be compared to a "swarm of bees."[5]

Example 8–12 from Part One of Penderecki's *St. Luke Passion* illustrates the combined use of sustained clusters and sound complexes. Here we find several clusters (indicated by horizontal lines of various thicknesses) and two sound complexes. One complex is played by the cellos and double basses with each section divided into three strands. Each strand repeats a harmonic second (either major or minor) in sixteenth notes. Penderecki's differential beaming of each part implies

---

[4]György Ligeti, "Metamorphoses of Musical Form," *Die Reihe* 7 (1965): 8.; my translation.
[5]Robin Maconie, *The Works of Karlheinz Stockhausen,* 2nd ed. (Oxford: Clarendon Press, 1990), pp. 4 and 44.

Example 8–11. Ligeti, *Nouvelles Aventures,* I, mm. 13–14

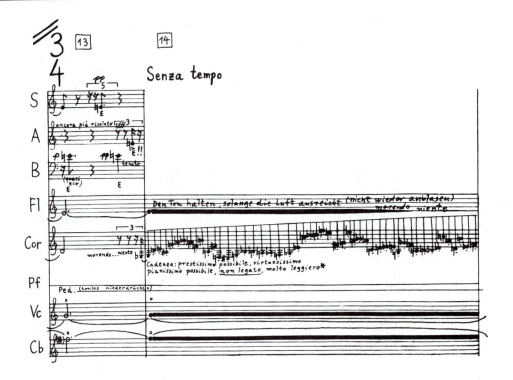

that the aural effect should not be entirely homogeneous. The other sound complex is assigned to a group of percussion instruments. Here again, each strand has the same type of melodic material, but the pitches were assigned at random, presumably to avoid an ostinato effect. Penderecki also varied the *horizontal density,* the number of notes that each percussionist plays during a given span of time.

Fragmented Textures

During the decade following World War II a number of younger European composers became fascinated with a novel type of texture that Anton Webern had used in some of his later works, one characterized by the deliberate avoidance of melody in the traditional sense. Webern achieved this effect by using wide and highly dissonant melodic intervals, as well as short motives. The opening of his Concerto, Op. 24 (Ex. 5–1, p. 80) is exemplary; each instrument plays a three-note motive, and each motive contains a minor ninth (unordered pitch interval 13). Observe how Webern isolated the various motives by timbral contrast and the pitches within each motive by registral contrast.

Example 8–12. Penderecki, *St. Luke Passion*, I, excerpt

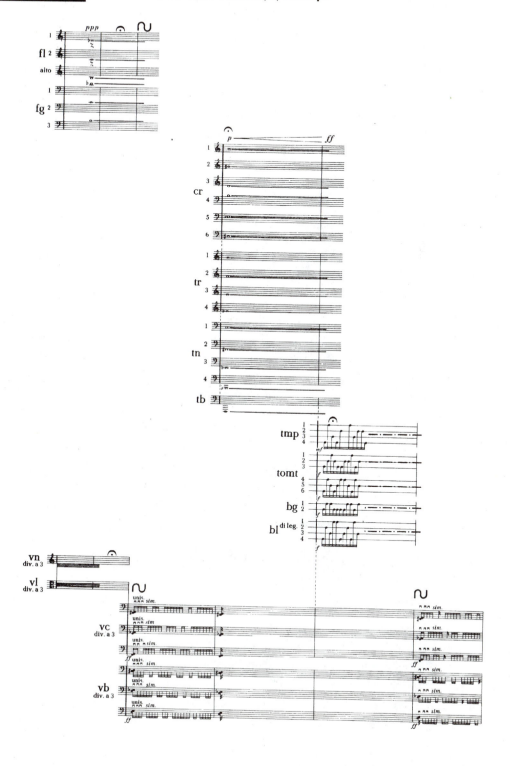

Example 8–12. *Continued*

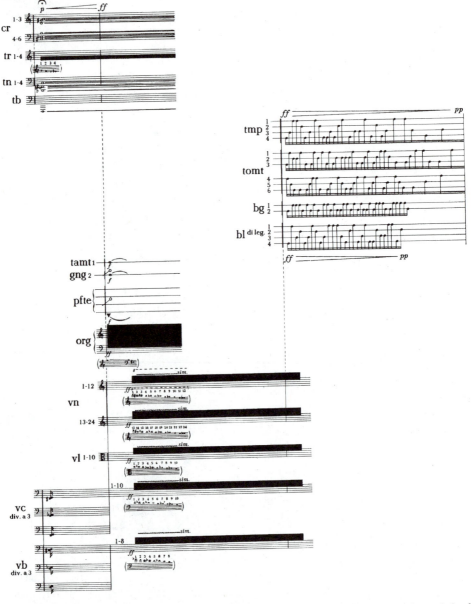

The term *pointillism* has been adapted to describe this effect. In its original sense, this term denoted a technique of painting perfected by certain neoimpressionists, notably the Frenchman Georges Seurat (1859–1891). A standard art reference work states that the technique

consisted in juxtaposing small dots, strokes, or "points" of pure color on the canvas in such a manner that these strokes would blend in the eye to produce, through optical mixture, the

Example 8–13. Stockhausen, Piano Piece No. 3

effect of another color. For instance, many small dots of blue and of yellow intermingled would appear at some distance as a shade of green. By breaking down colors into their prismatic components and then fusing them by juxtaposition, artists discovered that they could achieve a shimmering or luminous quality not possible with mixed colors.[6]

Music theorists have used *pointillism* in a rather different sense, to describe a texture in which notes are widely separated in registral space and often by durational and dynamic contrasts, as well. This can be seen Ex. 8–13 where every note has a separate dynamic marking and durational value. Notice that Stockhausen even wrote

---

[6]*McGraw-Hill Dictionary of Art,* Bernard S. Myers, editor (New York: McGraw-Hill, 1969), vol 4, s.v. "pointillism," by Robert Reiff.

Example 8–14. Ligeti, *Nouvelles Aventures*, I, mm. 28–29

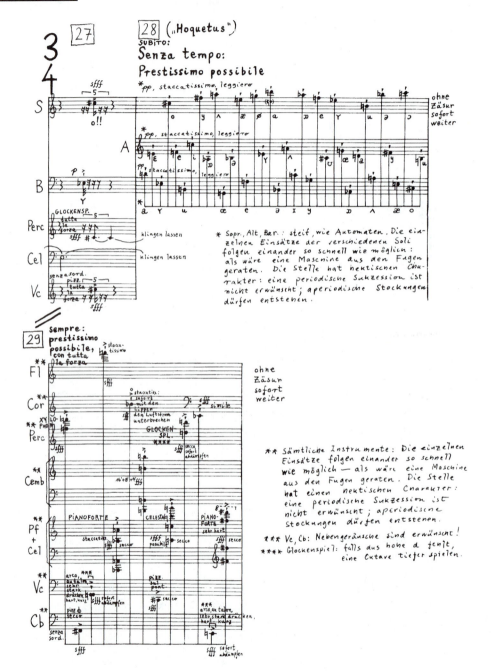

contrasting durations for notes that are struck together. In comparing the Webern and Stockhausen examples, note that Webern's motives are distinctive in terms of sound color, or timbre, whereas Stockhausen's notes are isolated in terms of dynamics and duration.

Pointillistic textures are similar in certain respects to *hocket,* a device whereby performers sound single notes, or short groups of notes, in alternation. The origins of hocket have been traced back to the medieval polyphony of the 13th and 14th centuries, and ethnomusicologists have accounted for it in the music of various indigenous cultures. The most familiar example is the modern-day handbell choir.

Example 8–14 shows hocket in a theater piece by Ligeti. This passage comes immediately after two violent crashes in the percussion. The soprano, alto, and baritone react to these events by singing isolated vowel sounds in rapid alternation at a low dynamic level (see m. 28). That vocalism is followed in m. 29 by instrumentalists exchanging isolated notes as rapidly and as loudly as possible. In both cases the performers are directed to sing, act, and play like automatons, but to sound their notes at irregular time intervals.

SUMMARY

Many composers of the 20th century have utilized textural arrangements that they inherited from the past. Some have explored other possibilities. Ideas for novel textures have come from expanded instrumental techniques, music of other cultures and/or historical eras, and other art forms (e.g., painting, dance, theater, cinema).

Texture is an aspect that requires careful study. Critical examination of musical excerpts often reveals a fabric that is more complex and subtle than it appears to be at first glance. In analyzing texture one should try to identify the number and type of textural components and to describe how they relate to each other and how they combine to achieve their effect.

Analysis Exercises

1. Ravel, *Le tombeau de Couperin,* Sarabande (WenAMSS)
   Using Ex. 8–2 as your model, make a textural reduction of mm. 25–30 and 37–53. Verticalize the accompaniment patterns to reveal the underlying harmony and use stem direction to show linear voice leading.
2. Debussy, Prelude to "The Afternoon of a Faun" (Burkhart)
   Listen with and without the score. Locate as many examples of parallel motion as possible. For each, identify the prevailing harmonic interval or chord type and the extent of octave doubling. Indicate whether the voices move exactly in parallel, or whether their melodic and harmonic intervals have been adjusted to remain within the prevailing scale.

3. Webern, Song and Bagatelles (Morgan)
   How many different types of texture can you find in these short pieces? Write a brief description of each type.
4. Hindemith, "A Swan" from *Six Chansons* (Ex. 13–1a, p. 236)
   a. How many different types of texture can you find?
   b. Locate several examples of parallel motion. For each describe the number of voices that move in parallel and the harmonic interval(s) between those voices.

QUESTIONS FOR REVIEW

1. Briefly describe each of the following types of textures: monophonic, homophonic, polyphonic, heterophonic, pointillistic, hocket.
2. What are the minimum requirements for polyphonic texture?
3. Compose short two-voice examples that illustrate each of the following types of relative voice motion: parallel, contrary, oblique, and similar.

RECOMMENDED LISTENING AND ANALYSIS

Bartók, *Mikrokosmos;* III/91 "Chromatic Invention" (Turek, WenAMSS), IV/109 "From the Island of Bali" (WenAMSS), IV/115 "Bulgarian Rhythm" (Burkhart), V/128 "Peasant Dance" (Turek), V/133 "Syncopation" (Burkhart)

———, Music for String Instruments, Percussion, and Celesta, first movement (Burkhart)

Berg, Four Songs, Op. 2, Nos. 3 and 4 (Wen20)

Britten, Serenade, Op. 31; "Prologue" (Turek); "Dirge" (Turek, WenAMSS) "Sonnet" and "Epilogue" (Burkhart)

Ruth Crawford, String Quartet 1931, third movement (Burkhart)

Debussy, *Prelude to "The Afternoon of a Faun"* (Burkhart)

———, *Nocturnes,* "Nuages" (Turek)

Ligeti, Three Fantasies, No. 2, *Wenn aus der Ferne* (Morgan)

———, Ten Pieces for Wind Quintet, No. 1 (DeLio-Smith)

Messiaen, from *Quatour pour la fin du temps (Quartet for the End of Time)* I. "Liturgie de cristal" (Turek); III. "Abîme des oiseaux" (DeLio-Smith); IV. "Danse de la fureur, pour les sept trompettes" (Wen20)

Penderecki, *Threnody for the Victims of Hiroshima* (Morgan, Turek)

Schoenberg, Three Piano Pieces, Op. 11, No. 1 (Burkhart)

———, Five Pieces for Orchestra, Op. 16, No. 3, "Summer Morning by a Lake (Colors)" (Burkhart); Nos. 1 and 5, *Vorgefühle* and *Das obligate Rezitativ* (Morgan)

Stockhausen, *Kreuzspiel,* first movement (Morgan)

Stravinsky, *Le sacre du printemps,* Introduction to Part II (Burkhart)

Webern, Five Pieces for String Quartet, Op. 5, No. 3 (Turek, WenAMSS); No. 4, (Burkhart)

———, Bagatelles for String Quartet, Nos. 4 and 5 (Morgan)

———, Concerto for Nine Instruments, Op. 24; I. (Turek); III. (WenAMSS)

CHAPTER 9

Form, Process, and Time

Analysis of Form and Conformance

In seeking to comprehend the form of a musical work we try to locate events that articulate the temporal flow and divide the work into formal units. These may include:

- cadence patterns
- temporary pauses (caesurae) due to longer notes and/or rests
- abrupt changes of tempo and/or meter
- abrupt changes of texture and/or timbre
- introduction of new melodic ideas or patterns of figuration

Major divisions are often articulated by several events working in combination. Minor divisions typically involve fewer events.

The term *closure* is often used to describe the sense of momentary pause evoked by articulative events. Analyzing form requires evaluating the degree of closure at each event.

Once units have been isolated they may be compared for *conformance,* the degree to which they resemble each other. Conformant relations can range from absolute identity (exactly the same) to total disparity (nothing in common). These two extremes are the easiest to recognize but often the least interesting. More rewarding comparisons involve passages that are alike in some respects but different in others.

Meyer has noted that our perception of conformant relationships is influenced by several factors as summarized in the formula below.[1] Notice that conformance is strengthened by factors above the line and weakened by those below it.

$$
\text{Strength of perceived conformance} = \frac{\text{regularity of pattern (schemata)}}{\text{variety of intervening events}} \quad \text{individuality of profile} \quad \frac{\text{similarity of patterning}}{\text{temporal distance between events}}
$$

Analysis of "Marie's Lullaby"

To illustrate, let's consider "Marie's Lullaby" from Act I, Scene 3 of Berg's opera, *Wozzeck.* The piano-vocal score for the first major section is given in Ex. 9-1.

---

[1]Leonard B. Meyer, *Explaining Music: Essays and Explorations* (Chicago: University of Chicago Press, 1973), p. 49.

Example 9–1. Berg, *Wozzeck*, Act I, Scene 3, Marie's Lullaby; first strophe

Example 9–2. **Phrase-structure diagram of the first strophe (compare Ex. 1–2, p. 4)**

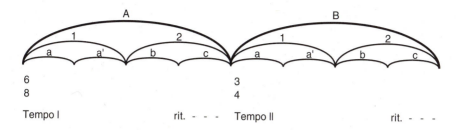

Form and Conformance of Larger Units The lullaby consists of two strophes, or verses, that are set to essentially the same music. Example 9–2 shows that the first strophe is divided into two units of equal length (labeled A and B in the diagram) by the introduction of a new melodic idea in m. 9. The divisive function of that event is corroborated by a change of meter, a textural contrast in the accompaniment, and a somewhat slower tempo.

Each section divides into four-measure units (labeled 1 and 2), which, in turn, divide into a pair of two-measure phrases. (Can you explain the basis for each division?) Phrase group A.1 has parallel design, while the phrases of A.2 are contrasting. The same pattern prevails in section B. Sections A and B are based on contrasting melodic ideas, and while they share the same formal scheme, their corresponding units differ somewhat. B.1 is a four-measure phrase, while A.1 is a pair of two-measure phrases.

The phrase structure of "Marie's Lullaby" resembles that of functionally tonal works (compare Exx. 1–2, p. 4 and 9–2). Its segments are articulated by longer notes and rests as well as by melodic contrast and changes of meter, texture, and tempo. This piece is an exception, however, both within the opera *Wozzeck* and the repertoire of atonal music. Berg composed this number and certain others in the opera to have *Volkstümlichkeit,* a folksy character. To achieve that effect he deliberately used symmetrical phrasing, a harmonic language that emphasizes thirds and fourths, and a melodic style based on perfect fourths and whole-tone scales.[2]

Motivic Development and Variation Motivic relations are usually revealed by bracketing and labeling motives on the score. Example 9–3 illustrates this approach. As the brackets show, the passage can be parsed in various ways. The units marked *a* and *a′* are easily isolated because each ends with a longer note. For that reason, and because of their length, they were called phrases in the discussion above. George Perle has identified motive *a* as one of nineteen *Leitmotive* (leading motives)

[2]George Perle, *The Operas of Alban Berg,* Vol. I. *Wozzeck* (Berkeley and Los Angeles: University of California Press, 1980), p. 99.

Example 9–3. Analysis of motivic development in mm. 1–8 (compare Ex. 1–3, p. 4)

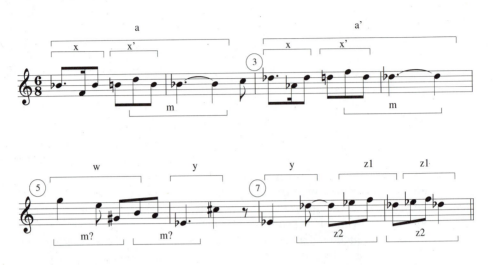

Example 9–4. Derivation of motive *x'* from *x*

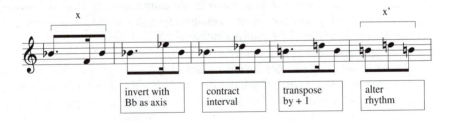

that appear throughout the opera *Wozzeck*.[3] Perle notes, however, that this "Cradle Song" *Leitmotiv* can be parsed into two smaller units that also play prominent musical and symbolic roles. Motive *x* is identified as the "Folk Song" motive, and motive *m* represents "Marie as Mother."

Motive *x* is easily isolated, even without the benefit of Perle's wisdom, because it is followed immediately by one of its variants, *x'*. Example 9–4 shows how *x'* may be derived from *x*. Motive *m* is more difficult to isolate because it overlaps with *x'*. To grasp its full significance, one would have to know that it is an important motive throughout the opera. Motive *w* is first heard as the opening figure of the aria that

---

[3]Perle, *The Operas of Alban Berg:* Vol. I. *Wozzeck,* Chapter 4.

Example 9–5. "Wir arme Leut!" motive from *Wozzeck*

Wozzeck, the main character, sings in Act I, Scene 1 (see Ex. 9–5). At that point, and at the climax of that scene, it is associated with the phrase "Wir arme Leut!" ("We poor folk!"), which Perle calls the "verbal keynote of the work."[4] By using motive *w* in the lullaby, Berg achieves two objectives: melodic contrast and the subtle characterization of Marie and her child as "poor folk." Motive *z* appears in two versions, *z1* and *z2*. It can be heard as either beginning or ending on D$^\flat$.

Analysis of Schoenberg's Op. 19, No. 4

Example 9–6 is clearly not modeled upon folksong, but it does have three distinct phrases of approximately equal length. Notice how Schoenberg used register, tempo, and dynamics to articulate and delineate these units. This usage is typical in the atonal idiom, where tonality is no longer a binding force. The piece has a certain consistency of pitch organization, melodic structure, and texture, but it lacks the hierarchical structure and conformant relations found in Berg's lullaby. Conformance can be found, but it involves motives rather than entire phrases or sections.

Example 9–7 shows how motives that share the same pitch contour can be aligned vertically.[5] Notice, for instance, that m. 10 has virtually the same contour as mm. 1–2 in spite of their rhythmic dissimilarity. Motive tables such as this are useful for acknowledging conformant relations between smaller units.

Additive Structures

Claude Debussy often created "additive" structures, formal schemes whose segments are presented in an order that precludes the possibility of elaborate higher-level grouping. Robert Morgan has noted that

> *The basic formal technique involves subtle variations of repeated musical units, often by means of apparently insubstantial transformations, and the mediation of contrasting units through the retention of common elements. The structure of Debussy's music often resembles a mosaic: seemingly separate and self-enclosed units combining into larger configurations, the individual discontinuities thereby being dissolved into a continuous, unbroken flow. The dynamic thrust toward points of climactic emphasis, typical of German music of the time,*

---

[4] *The Operas of Alban Berg, Wozzeck*, p. 97.

[5] For another such table, see Ex. 14–12 (p. 267).

Example 9–6. Schoenberg, Six Little Piano Pieces, Op. 19, No. 4

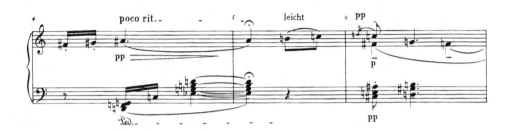

Example 9–7. **Classification of motives in terms of pitch contour**

is replaced by a sort of floating balance among subtly interconnected musical entities, giving rise to wavelike motions characterized by extremely fine gradations of color, pacing, and intensity.[6]

To account for these qualities, let's look briefly at Debussy's "Canope" (Ex. 9–8). Example 9–9 reveals six musical ideas, which have been labeled a–f. No idea is longer than two measures, and several are only one measure long.

Even more significant is Debussy's manner of presentation. This can be seen most vividly by comparing Ex. 9–9 with Ex. 9–2. The first strophe of "Marie's Lullaby" contains less than half as many measures as "Canope," but it has a more intricate phrase structure. Few of Debussy's ideas combine to form higher-level units, and most of those that do are repeated immediately. Only two ideas, *a* and *c*, recur after contrasting material has intervened. The return of the A unit at m. 26ff implies an overall A B A form, but other aspects of ternary form are missing. The result is a relatively "flat" hierarchy, but one that is "subtly interconnected" and balanced.

To account for these connections, we might note that *a* and *f* are the most distinctive of the six ideas, and that A is preceded by the presentation and repetition of *f*. The remaining four ideas are related in various ways:

- *b, c,* and *d* have triplets on the fourth beat of the measure
- *b* and *c* have a rest on the first beat
- *b* and *c* exhibit chromatic motion but in opposite directions
- *d* arpeggiates a D minor triad (mm. 14–15, top staff), which makes it a relative of *a*

---

[6]Robert P. Morgan, *Twentieth-Century Music* (New York: W. W. Norton, 1991), p. 48. See also the discussions and analyses of moment form in Jonathan D. Kramer, *The Time of Music* (New York: Schirmer Books, 1988).

Example 9–8. Debussy "Canope" (Preludes, Book II)

Example 9–8. *Continued*

Example 9–9. Phrase-structure diagram and tonal plan of "Canope"

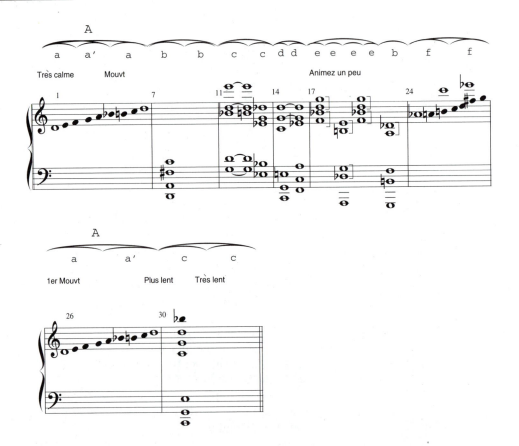

- the harmonic fourths of *e* evolve from the graced half notes in m. 16, but they also relate to the melodic fourths of *a*

"Canope" 's mosaic quality also results from its harmonic, textural, and tonal variety. Instead of basing the piece on one type of scale, chord, or set, Debussy used several as shown by the staff notation in Ex. 9–9. The A material of mm. 1–5 is primarily in D Aeolian/Dorian [D-E-F-G-A-B♭/B-C-D],[7] but Debussy reached beyond B♭ in m. 4 to include E♭, A♭, D♭, and G♭. By doing so, he was able to compose a strong cadence (m. 5) without using the familiar V-I chord progression.

Debussy's contributions to musical form have been extended by Stravinsky, Bartók, Webern, Varèse, Stockhausen, Boulez, and Crumb, composers who have continued to emphasize additive, as opposed to hierarchical, structures.

---

[7] The diatonic modes are discussed in Chapter 10.

Analysis of Process

Introduction

The perceived sense of continuity within formal units, and of connections between them, can be acknowledged by the term *process,* which refers to graduated and perceptible change in one musical element or combination of elements. To analyze a musical process we attempt to trace its steps.

Crucial to the notion of process are the ideas of *implication* and *realization.* Meyer has defined an implicative relationship as

> *one in which an event—be it a motive, a phrase, and so on—is patterned in such a way that reasonable inferences can be made both about its connection with preceding events and about how the event itself might be continued and perhaps reach closure and stability.*[8]

A realization is an expected continuation or completion of an implication.

Melodic, Harmonic, and Contrapuntal Processes

The second phrase of "Marie's Lullaby" (see Ex. 9–1, mm. 3–4) fits these definitions perfectly. It conforms to the first phrase (mm. 1–2) but is transposed three semitones higher. After hearing these two phrases one might predict that the third phrase will rhyme with the second and be pitched another three semitones higher as shown in Ex. 9–10. Perhaps the sequence will even continue to the fourth phrase. The melodic process that would result is shown on the lower staff of Ex. 9–10. Arrows on the underlying beams symbolize implicative events.

The third and fourth phrases of Ex. 9–10 are, of course, only hypothetical (see Ex. 9–1). Berg did not realize the latent implication of the first and second phrases. Instead of sequential repetition, he chose contrast and introduced a new melodic idea for the third phrase.

Schoenberg's "Farben" movement (Burkhart) is based on a longer and more complex process whereby the initial chord is gradually transformed into a transposition of itself four semitones higher (T_4^8) and then back to the original pitch level (T_0^8).[9] This process is more difficult to trace because the melodic motion is staggered among the various voices.

Processes that occur in electro-acoustic and computer music can be even more difficult to follow. Kaija Saariaho based her computer-generated study *Vers le blanc* on the idea of moving very gradually from one chord to another. As Ex. 9–11 indicates, the entire piece lasts fifteen minutes. Because the pitches move through

---

[8]Meyer, *Explaining Music,* p. 110. Meyer admits the necessity of having a "competent, experienced listener—one familiar with and sensitive to the particular style." This condition may not prevail when inexperienced listeners encounter novel styles of 20th-century music.

[9]John Rahn, *Basic Atonal Theory* (New York: Longman, 1980), Analysis Two.

Example 9–10.   Analysis of melodic process in "Marie's Lullaby," mm. 1–8

Example 9–11.   Harmonic process in Kaija Saariaho's *Vers le blanc* for electronic tape*

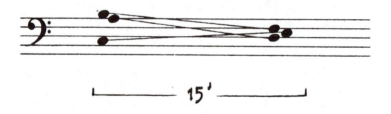

*Kaija Saariaho, "Timbre and Harmony: Interpolations of Timbral Structures," *Contemporary Music Review* 2/1 (1987) figure 6, p. 104.

glissandi, this "harmonic" progression is almost imperceptible both aurally and visually.[10]

Processes in Other Parameters

Graduated change can occur in other parameters, as well. The most familiar processes in the temporal domain include accelerandos and ritardandos. Traditional

---

[10]Kaija Saariaho, "Timbre and Harmony: Interpolations of Timbral Structures," *Contemporary Music Review* 2/1 (1987): 104.

Example 9–12. **Accelerando in traditional and contemporary notation**

notation with its discrete note values is inadequate for representing truly graduated changes of duration, so contemporary composers have devised new symbols. Example 9–12 shows how an accelerando might be notated using traditional and contemporary symbology.

Metric modulations can also be considered temporal processes because they effect a graduated change from one tempo to another. Two examples were discussed in Chapter 7 (see pp. 108–111).

Timbral and textural processes are significant in music composed during the past few decades. Unfortunately, they are not easily revealed by brief examples that are suitable for textbooks.

Methodological Problems

When analysis is done with the aid of a score, music is often evaluated retrospectively, by identifying a significant event and then trying to locate earlier events that *could have* implied it. If one or more such events can be found, it is tempting to claim that the later event *was* implied by the earlier one(s).

To illustrate, consider Ex. 9–13. The analysis underneath m. 13 (stems down) indicates that after hearing C–D we expect continued stepwise ascent, and the E♭ fulfills this expectation. There are good musical reasons for making this statement. It is not just that E♭ comes after C and D; the linear ascent C-D-E♭ is also evenly paced, and a similar melodic figure (D♭-E♭-F) occurs in mm. 7 and 8.

Now consider mm. 1–4 of Ex. 9–13. The underlying analysis (stems down) reveals a chromatically ascending line in those measures. It is tempting to regard E♭5 in m. 13 as the logical continuation of that process, but there are several reasons why the connection is quite weak. These are summarized by the formula below.

$$
\begin{array}{lcl}
\text{Strength of} & & \text{regularity of implicative} \qquad \text{strength of} \\
\text{perceived} & & \text{pattern} \qquad\qquad\qquad\qquad \text{implication} \\
\text{process} & = & \overline{\qquad\qquad\qquad\qquad\qquad\qquad\qquad\qquad} \\
& & \text{variety of intervening} \qquad \text{temporal distance} \\
& & \text{events} \qquad\qquad\qquad\quad \text{between implication} \\
& & \qquad\qquad\qquad\qquad\quad\ \text{and realization}
\end{array}
$$

Example 9–13.   **Analysis of melodic processes in "Marie's Lullaby," mm. 1–14**

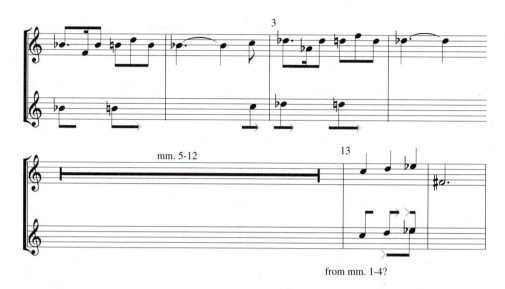

from mm. 1-4?

New Conceptions of Musical Time

Background

In a recent book[11] Jonathan Kramer has described various ways that 20th-century composers have conceived and structured spans of time. Kramer begins by establishing two main categories: *linear* and *nonlinear* time. Music that imparts a sense of linear time seems to move toward goals. This quality, which permeates virtually all of Western music from the Baroque, Classical, and Romantic eras, can be attributed to processes that occur simultaneously within tonal and metrical frameworks on various structural levels. Music that evokes a sense of nonlinear time appears to stand still or evolve very slowly. It is more concerned with the eternal present than with the foreseeable future, with stasis than with motion, with being than with becoming.[12]

It appears that Western musicians first became aware of nonlinear conceptions of time during the late 19th century. Debussy's encounter with Javanese gamelan music at the 1889 Paris Exhibition has often been cited as a seminal event. Kramer notes that

> *Other composers attended the Exhibition but failed to appreciate the potential of what they heard. Debussy, on the other hand, was ready for an exotic influence and was looking for*

[11]Jonathan Kramer, *The Time of Music* (New York: Schirmer Books, 1988).

[12]Ibid., pp. 62–63.

an alternative to Wagnerian harmonies. He understood that the strange sounds he was hearing were unfolding in a different time world. He heard sonorities that were allowed to be themselves, that did not exist primarily in functional relationships to other sounds, that were not participants in an upbeat-downbeat compositional world. The Javanese influence on the French composer was enormous. His music is really the first in the West to contain extended moments of pure sonority, events that are to be appreciated more for themselves than for their role in a linear progression.[13]

These qualities are apparent in Debussy's piano prelude "Canope" (Ex. 9–9). Since Debussy, composers have realized nonlinear conceptions of time in a variety of ways. We'll consider two of them briefly.

Moment Form

Some composers have broken down connections between musical events in order to create a series of more or less discrete moments. The terms *moment time* and *moment form* refer to music composed in this manner. Certain works of Stravinsky, Webern, Messiaen, and Stockhausen exemplify this approach.[14]

Vertical Time

At the other extreme of the nonlinear continuum is music that maximizes consistency and minimizes articulation. Here a virtually static moment is often expanded to encompass an entire piece. A highly processive work such as Saariaho's *Vers le blanc* (Ex. 9–11) resists division into standard formal units: motives, phrases, periods, and sections.

Kramer has coined the term *vertical time* to denote this category because "whatever structure is in the music exists between simultaneous layers of sound, not between successive gestures."[15] He goes on to observe that

> *A vertically conceived piece . . . does not exhibit large-scale closure. It does not begin, but merely starts. It does not build to a climax, does not purposefully set up internal expectations, does not seek to fulfill any expectations that might arise accidentally, does not build or release tension, and does not end but simply ceases.*[16]

The musical style known as *minimalism, process music, pattern music,* or *trance music* also exemplifies vertical time but in a slightly different way. Instead of absolute stasis, it generates constant motion. The sense of movement is, however, so evenly paced and the goals are so vague that we usually lose our sense of perspective.[17] Specific examples of process music are analyzed in Chapter 17.

---

[13]Ibid., p. 44.

[14]See Exx. 5–1 (p. 80), 8–5 (p. 137), 8–11 (p. 142), 8–13 (p. 145), and 15–8 (p. 290).

[15]Kramer, *The Time of Music,* pp. 54–55.

[16]Ibid., p. 55.

[17]Ibid., p. 57.

SUMMARY

Art music of the 20th century is quite diverse in its formal structure, process, and time sense. In some works articulation and continuity are rather balanced, but in others one aspect is accorded higher priority. The result, which can be termed *nonlinear* time, usually takes two forms. *Moment forms* result from a high degree of articulation and discontinuity. *Vertical time* denotes music that seems to stand still or move very slowly.

Analysis Exercises

A. Berg, "Marie's Lullaby" (Ex. 9–1)

1. Construct a musical example showing how phrase B.1.a′ can be derived from B.1.a. Do the same for phrase B.2.b from B.1.a′. Use Ex. 9–4 as your model.
2. Locate two brief passages where the harmony is based on parallel motion.
3. What is the T_n/T_nI-type of the set formed by all of the pitches in m. 8? By what other name do you know this set-type?
4. How does the meter change in mm. 5–7 of the accompaniment? Rewrite these measures so that the beaming and barring conform to the actual meter.
5. Locate at least one instance of imitation between the vocal melody and the accompaniment.
6. Study the ending of the complete lullaby. How is it related to the beginning? Would you describe it as tonal or atonal? If it is tonal, how would you describe the final sonority in terms of traditional harmonic analysis?

B. Schoenberg, Op. 19, No. 4 (Ex. 9–6)

1. Schoenberg's first phrase contains a transposition of Berg's "Wir arme Leut!" motive (Ex. 9–5). Locate the pitches that form this ordered set and determine the interval of transposition between the two sets.
2. Locate and label at least one instance of T_n/T_nI-types [0 1 4], [0 1 3], and [0 1 2 3].
3. What relationship can you discover between the two trichords in the left hand of m. 6?

C. Debussy, "Canope" from Preludes, Book II (Ex. 9–8)

1. Identify the chords, scales, or pc sets shown in Ex. 9–9. (See Appendix B for chord symbols.)
2. Form a pc set from the pitches in mm. 24–25. Determine its normal form, T_n-type, and T_n/T_nI-type.
3. Compare mm. 1–5 and 26–30 for conformance. How are these passages alike? How do they differ? What types of root motion are involved? Is the ending of either phrase implied in its preceding measures?
4. Why do you think Debussy used enharmonic spelling in m. 18? Hint: What do the vertical brackets in Ex. 9–9 reveal about the intervallic structure of the chords?

RECOMMENDED LISTENING AND ANALYSIS

Bartók, Fourteen Bagatelles for Piano, Op. 6, Nos. 1, 4, 8, and 14 (Simms)

Berg, Four Songs, Op. 2 (No. 4 in Simms and Turek)

Copland, Appalachian Spring (excerpt) (Wen20)

Crumb, Black Angels, sections 6 and 7 (Simms)

———, "Los muertos" from Madrigals, Book I (Turek)

Debussy, La Soirée dans Grenade (Evening in Granada), No. 2 of *Estampes* (Morgan; see Analytical Comments)

———, from Preludes, Book I, No. 4 "Les sons et les parfums" (Turek); No. 6 "Des pas sur la neige" (Wen20)

Terry Riley, In C (Burkhart, Godwin)

Schoenberg, *Vorgefühle (Premonitions)* and *Das obligate Rezitativ (The Obligatory Recitative)*, Nos. 1 and 5 of Five Orchestral Pieces, Op. 16 (Morgan)

———, Six Little Piano Pieces, Op. 19, Nos. 2, 4, & 6 (Wen20), No. 6 (DeLio-Smith)

Sessions, *From My Diary,* Nos. 2 and 3 (Morgan)

Stockhausen, Piano Piece No. 3 (DeLio-Smith)

Stravinsky, from Le Sacre du Printemps (The Rite of Spring) Augurs of Spring; Dances of the Young Girls (Morgan, Turek, WenAMSS); Rounds of Spring (Morgan, Turek)

Varèse, Hyperprism (Morgan)

———, Octandre, first movement (Simms)

Webern, Five Movements for String Quartet, Op. 5, No. 3 (WenAMSS), No. 4 (Burkhart)

———, Bagatelles for String Quartet, Op. 9, Nos. 4 and 5 (Morgan)

Part IV

PITCH ORGANIZATION:
A CLOSER LOOK

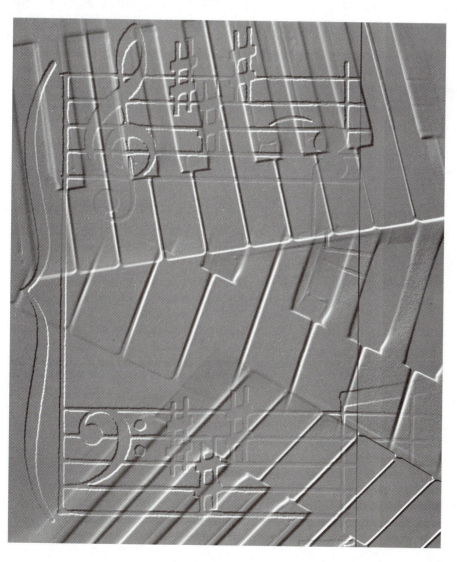

CHAPTER 10

Diatonicism and Pentatonicism

Diatonic Modes

The diatonic modes that can be formed from the natural pcs (the white keys of the piano) are shown along with their interval patterns in Ex. 10–1. Notice that each pattern contains two instances of interval 1 and five of interval 2. The differences among these patterns can be acknowledged by completing Table 10–1.

Constructing Modal Scales

Since the advent of equal-tempered tuning, musicians have been able to construct any mode on any chromatic scale degree. Various ways to do this are described below.

Example 10–1. Modes of the "white-key" collection

Ionian (Major)

ipc<a,b> 2 2 1 2 2 2 1

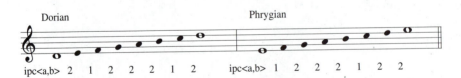

Dorian

ipc<a,b> 2 1 2 2 2 1 2

Phrygian

ipc<a,b> 1 2 2 2 1 2 2

Lydian

ipc<a,b> 2 2 2 1 2 2 1

Mixolydian

ipc<a,b> 2 2 1 2 2 1 2

Aeolian (Natural Minor)

ipc<a,b> 2 1 2 2 1 2 2

Locrian

ipc<a,b> 1 2 2 1 2 2 2

TABLE 10–1.   Location of half steps within modes of the diatonic collection (to be completed)

Begin by numbering the degrees of the modes shown in Ex. 10–1. Use the integers 1–8 in keeping with the traditional numbering system for scale degrees. Then record the locations of the half steps (interval 1) in the table below.

Mode	Half steps formed by scale degrees	
Dorian	2–3	6–7
Phrygian	_____	_____
Lydian	_____	_____
Mixolydian	_____	_____
Aeolian	_____	_____
Locrian	_____	_____
Ionian (Major)	_____	_____

Interval Pattern   One method is to locate the half steps, the two instances of interval 1, in the mode's interval pattern. Once the positions of these intervals are fixed, the mode can be replicated easily, since the remaining intervals are whole steps (interval 2).

Example 10–2 illustrates this procedure. Suppose that we wish to notate the Lydian mode on E♭. We can begin by placing the tonic pc at the upper and lower ends of the sale (see Ex. 10–2a), continue by filling in the octave so that the scale includes the remaining six name classes (Ex. 10–2b), and finish by providing accidentals to form the appropriate interval pattern (10–2c). As a rule, we should not add accidentals to the tonic scale degree, since it is the point of reference. In some cases, however, it may be easier to notate the enharmonically equivalent mode. For example, seven flats are needed to notate E♭ Phrygian, but only five sharps are required for D♯ Phrygian (see Ex. 10–3).

Example 10–2.   Procedure for notating a diatonic mode (E♭ Lydian)

Example 10–3. Enharmonically equivalent modes

Eb Phrygian   D# Phrygian

ipc<a,b> 1 2 2 2 1 2 2   ipc<a,b> 1 2 2 2 1 2 2

Relative Modes The modes shown in Ex. 10–1 share the same pc collection and, thus, the same scale signature. These pcs can be rearranged to form a continuous segment on the circle of perfect fourths/fifths (see Ex. 10–4a). Other diatonic collections can be formed by similar segments (see Ex. 10–4b). In fact, we will define a *diatonic collection* as a set of seven pcs and ncs that forms such a segment. This means that a diatonic collection may contain only one instance of each name class. For example, it would be wrong to spell the fifth degree of Eb Lydian as A# (see Ex. 10–2), since the scale would then have two instances of nc A and none of B.

Modes that share a diatonic collection are related in the same way as relative major and minor scales. We can say, for example, that D is the relative Dorian of C major, or that E is the relative Phrygian of A Aeolian. This concept of relative scales is useful for determining the scale signature of a mode. Suppose, for example, that we wish to find the signature of C Dorian. To do so, we could identify its relative major scale. Since the Dorian mode begins on the second degree of its relative major scale, we would regard C as scale degree 2 and count down to scale degree 1, which is Bb.

Parallel Modes Modes can also be conceived as parallel scales that have the same tonic but different signatures. Example 10–5 illustrates the seven parallel modes on E. A given mode can be notated by inflecting the appropriate degrees of its parallel major or minor scale as summarized below. Sharps and flats are used generically in this summary to denote raising or lowering a tone by a chromatic half step. This operation preserves the nc but changes the pc (e.g., C to C#, or B to Bb). In certain cases, a natural sign may be the appropriate accidental; in others, a double sharp or double flat may be required.

Beginning with the major scale

Mode	Scale-degree inflections				
Lydian	#4				
Major					
Mixolydian	b7				
Dorian	b7	b3			
Aeolian	b7	b3	b6		
Phrygian	b7	b3	b6	b2	
Locrian	b7	b3	b6	b2	b5

Example 10–4. Two diatonic collections represented as segments of the circle of perfect fourths/fifths

a.

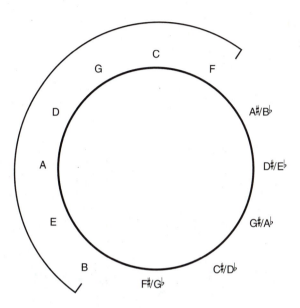

b.

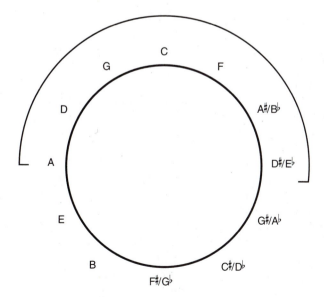

Example 10–5. **Parallel diatonic modes on E**

Ionian (Major)

ipc⟨a,b⟩ 2   2   1   2   2   2   1

Dorian

ipc⟨a,b⟩ 2   1   2   2   2   1   2

Phrygian

ipc⟨a,b⟩ 1   2   2   2   1   2   2

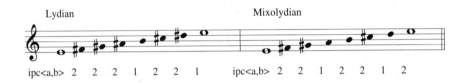

Lydian

ipc⟨a,b⟩ 2   2   2   1   2   2   1

Mixolydian

ipc⟨a,b⟩ 2   2   1   2   2   1   2

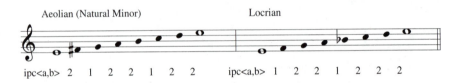

Aeolian (Natural Minor)

ipc⟨a,b⟩ 2   1   2   2   1   2   2

Locrian

ipc⟨a,b⟩ 1   2   2   1   2   2   2

Beginning with the natural minor scale

Mode	Scale-degree inflections			
Lydian	♯6	♯3	♯7	♯4
Major	♯6	♯3	♯7	
Mixolydian	♯6	♯3		
Dorian	♯6			
Aeolian				
Phrygian	♭2			
Locrian	♭2	♭5		

It is often instructive to compare modes with their parallel major or minor scale, whichever is the closest relative. In doing so, we acknowledge the *characteristic tone*, the scale degree that distinguishes a given mode from its parallel major or minor. For example, using the summary above, we can see that:

Lydian is	major with a ♯4
Mixolydian is	major with a ♭7
Dorian is	natural minor with a ♯6
Phrygian is	natural minor with a ♭2

Transposition A mode can also be constructed by transposing another instance of the same mode. Transposition may be done in the traditional manner or with integers using binomial representation to retain the correct spelling. Suppose, for example, that we wish to construct B Mixolydian by transposing G Mixolydian. We would first compute the ordered br interval between the two tonics, G and B, then transpose each br of G Mixolydian by that interval. The resulting brs could then be converted into letter-name or staff notation as needed.

br of B	<11, 6>
br of G	< 7, 4>
ibr of M3	< 4, 2>

	G	A	B	C	D	E	F	G
G Mixolydian	< 7, 4>	<9, 5>	<11, 6>	<0, 0>	<2, 1>	<4, 2>	<5, 3>	< 7, 4>
ibr of M3	< 4, 2>	<4, 2>	< 4, 2>	<4, 2>	<4, 2>	<4, 2>	<4, 2>	< 4, 2>
B Mixolydian	<11, 6>	<1, 0>	< 3, 1>	<4, 2>	<6, 3>	<8, 4>	<9, 5>	<11, 6>
	B	C♯	D♯	E	F♯	G♯	A	G

EXERCISE 10–1

1. Write the appropriate letter name in each cell. The middle row has been done for you.

Key Sig	Lydian	Major	Mixolydian	Dorian	Aeolian	Phrygian	Locrian
######							
#####							
####							
###							
##							
#							
	F	C	G	D	A	E	B
♭							
♭♭							
♭♭♭							
♭♭♭♭							
♭♭♭♭♭							
♭♭♭♭♭♭							

2. Notate the following modes using accidentals only, no key signatures. Number the scale degrees and show the interval patterns as in Ex. 10–1.

   a. G Lydian (bass clef)

b. F# Dorian (treble clef)

c. B♭ Mixolydian (alto clef)

d. B Phrygian (tenor clef)

e. D# Locrian (treble clef)

3. Notate the following modes using key signatures only, no accidentals. Use the same format as for exercise 2 above.

   a. F Aeolian (tenor clef)

   b. E Mixolydian (alto clef)

   c. G# Dorian (treble clef)

   d. D♭ Lydian (bass clef)

   e. B Phrygian (treble clef)

Identifying Modes

Having learned to notate modes with and without signatures, we can now use this knowledge to identify them. Let's first consider the task of identifying a mode when it is notated as a scale. Example 10–6 shows three modes, one of which is notated without a signature.

Example 10–6. Three diatonic modes for identification

ipc<a,b> _____

ipc<a,b> _____

ipc<a,b> _____

To identify a diatonic mode, do any of the following:

1. Compute its interval pattern, noting in particular the location of the half steps, then compare this pattern to those in Ex. 10–1 to find a match.
2. Use the mode's signature to identify its relative major or minor scale, and from that scale identify the mode itself. If a signature is not provided, it may be formed by tabulating the accidentals.
3. Compare the non-tonic scale degrees to those of the parallel major or minor scale, noting which have been raised or lowered (see Ex. 10–5).

Identifying a mode from a musical excerpt involves two preliminary steps: tabulating the pitch classes and identifying the tonic.

Example 10–7 shows the beginning of a waltz by Francis Poulenc. The scale can be identified by tabulating the pcs in the melody: C, E, and G in m. 1; F♯ and B in m. 2; A in m. 3; and D in m. 6. These produce a diatonic collection that could be oriented around any of its seven pcs. To select one mode, we must identify the tonic pc. That can only be done by analyzing the tonal structure of the passage.

In this case, C is the obvious tonic. The melody begins by arpeggiating the C major triad, continues by embellishing G with neighboring motion (see m. 3), and ends with a stepwise descent (mm. 6–7) and two stepwise ascents, all to C (mm. 7–8). Furthermore, the accompaniment reiterates a root-position C major triad. In light of these facts, we can orient the collection around C, spelling it as [C D E F♯ A G B C] to form the C Lydian mode.

The mode of Ex. 10–8 is not as easily identified because the melody contains only five pcs (A B C D E). It is possible, however, to identify A as the tonic. (Can you explain why?) To determine the mode we must locate the missing sixth and

Example 10–7. Poulenc, *Valse* for piano, mm. 1–8

Example 10–8. Bartók, *Little Pieces for Children*, III

seventh scale degrees; these should be instances of name classes F and G, respectively. F♯, an instance of nc F, appears in m. 2, but an instance of nc G does not appear until mm. 16–17. In fact, the first G natural coincides with the F natural in m. 16, but the F natural is a temporary chromatic inflection. Having gathered the necessary data, we can now orient this collection around A to form [A B C D E F# G A], the A Dorian mode.

Before leaving these two examples, let's make some comparisons. First, both excerpts share the same scale signature (no sharps or flats), but neither is in C major or A minor. Each composer could have provided a signature of one sharp but chose instead to use accidentals. Second, the scale of the Poulenc excerpt can be inferred from the melody alone, but that of the Bartók requires attention to both the melody and accompaniment. Finally, the Poulenc excerpt is entirely diatonic; all of its pcs belong to the C Lydian mode. The Bartók piece, however, contains one chromatic pc, F natural, which appears at a critical point in conjunction with the strongest and most complete harmonic progression (see mm. 15–18).

> ### EXERCISE 10–2
>
> Identify the scale basis of the following musical examples. Explain your decision.
>
> a. Copland, "The World Feels Dusty," mm. 1–10 (see Ex. 1–12, pp. 20–21)
> b. Britten, "Dirge" (fugue subject) (see Ex. 7–14, p. 114)
> c. Gershwin, "Summertime" (Ex. 7–22, p. 124)
> d. Ravel, Rigaudon, (Ex. 8–2a, p. 133)
> e. Bartók, Fourteen Bagatelles, Op. 6, No. 4 (Ex. 10–13, p. 185)

Modes as Sets

When a mode is conceived as a set, one of its tonic scale degrees must be discarded because a set may not contain duplicate elements. Ex. 10–9 shows how G Mixolydian can be represented as a pitch-class set, a name-class set, and a set of brs. To reconvert a set to a mode we can replace the discarded tonic so that the scale spans an octave.

Properties of the Diatonic Collection

Normal Form and Set-Type   It is convenient to represent a class of relative modes, such as those shown in Ex. 10–1, as a class of pc sets that are related to each other by rotation.

Example 10–9. **G Mixolydian represented as a pitch-class set, a name-class set, and a set of brs**

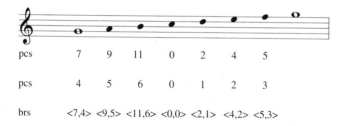

pcs	7	9	11	0	2	4	5
pcs	4	5	6	0	1	2	3
brs	<7,4>	<9,5>	<11,6>	<0,0>	<2,1>	<4,2>	<5,3>

C Major	< 0, 2, 4, 5, 7, 9, 11>
D Dorian	< 2, 4, 5, 7, 9, 11, 0>
E Phrygian	< 4, 5, 7, 9, 11, 0, 2>
F Lydian	< 5, 7, 9, 11, 0, 2, 4>
G Mixolydian	< 7, 9, 11, 0, 2, 4, 5>
A Aeolian	< 9, 11, 0, 2, 4, 5, 7>
B Locrian	<11, 0, 2, 4, 5, 7, 9>

We can use the normal form, the Locrian rotation, to compute the set-types of this collection.

Normal form:	{11,	0,	2,	4,	5,	7,	9}
T_1	1	1	1	1	1	1	1
T_n-type:	(0,	1,	3,	5,	6,	8,	10)
Last pc	10	10	10	10	10	10	10
R of T_n-type:	{10,	8,	6,	5,	3,	1,	0}
T_nI-type:	(0,	2,	4,	5,	7,	9,	10)
T_n/T_nI-type:	[0,	1,	3,	5,	6,	8,	10]

Since any other class of relative modes is T_n-related to this class, the set-types shown above represent not only this class, but any other such class, as well. We could say, therefore, that they represent any transposition of any diatonic mode.

Interval-Class Content   The interval class vector for [0, 1, 3, 5, 6, 8, 10], Forte name 7–35, is <2, 5, 4, 3, 6, 1>. Example 10–10 shows instances of the six interval classes in one instance of this set class. Notice that the ic vector contains no zeros. This means that any diatonic mode contains at least one instance of each interval class; no interval class is missing. Furthermore, the vector has no duplicate entries; each entry is unique. To assess the significance of this finding, we can compare this vector to those of other 7-pc sets. A careful look at the Table of T_n/T_nI-types (in Appendix A) reveals that only one other septachordal set-type has this property of *unique multiplicity*. That is [0, 1, 2, 3, 4, 5, 6], which represents a 7-pc segment of the chromatic scale.

Pentatonic Modes

Bartók based some of his folk melodies on pentatonic (5-tone), rather than septatonic (7-tone), modes. One such melody can be seen in Ex. 13–2 (p. 240). Measures 4–12 contain only five pcs; there is no instance of name classes D or A. Since C is the tonic of mm. 1–7, the scale is [C ( ) E♭ F G ( ) B♭ C]. (The empty parentheses indicate two "missing" degrees.)[1] Later in the excerpt Bartók reoriented this collection

---

[1]This procedure is used in Elliott Antokoletz, *The Music of Béla Bartók* (Berkeley: University of California Press, 1984).

Example 10–10. Instances of the various interval classes in the "white-key" diatonic collection

around B♭ (in mm. 8–10), and then around F (in mm. 11–12). To acknowledge these "modulations" we could rewrite the scale as [B♭ C ( ) E♭ F G ( ) B♭] and [F G ( ) B♭ C ( ) E♭ F], respectively.

Example 10–11 shows Bartók's collection as a 5-pc segment of the circle of perfect fourths/fifths. Indeed, we will define a *pentatonic collection* as any similar segment of that cycle. The modes of this collection are obtained by sorting the pcs into canonical order and rotating the set as shown in Ex. 10–12.[2] Observe that these pentatonic modes are related in the same manner as the diatonic modes in Ex. 10–1. Both classes of modes may be termed *relative* since they share the same pcs.

Constructing Pentatonic Modes

Pentatonic modes can be built using the same procedures as for diatonic modes (see above). It is more convenient, however, to represent pentatonic modes as pc

---

[2]This system of numbering is used in Ray Ricker, *Pentatonic Scales for Jazz Improvisation* (Lebanon, IN: Studio PR, 1975).

Example 10–11. A pentatonic collection as a segment of the circle of perfect fourths/fifths

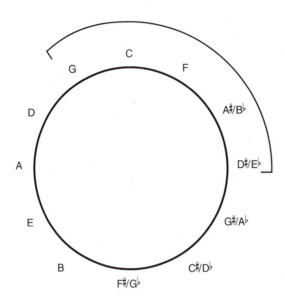

sets. This enables us to derive pentatonic modes from each other by set operations. Several possibilities are discussed below.

Rotation As Ex. 10–12 illustrates, relative modes can be derived from each other by rotation. If the pcs of a pentatonic collection are arranged in canonical order to form an unordered set, the set can be rotated to obtain the four remaining modes of that collection.

Example 10–12. Modes of a pentatonic collection (compare Ex. 10–11)

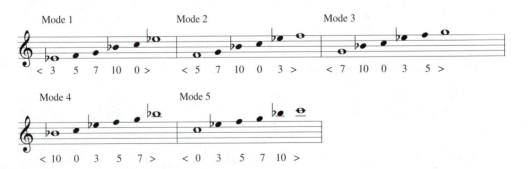

$\{0\ 3\ 5\ 7\ 10\}$
$\quad\{3\ 5\ 7\ 10\ 0\}$
$\quad\quad\{5\ 7\ 10\ 0\ 3\}$
$\quad\quad\quad\{7\ 10\ 0\ 3\ 5\}$
$\quad\quad\quad\quad\{10\ 0\ 3\ 5\ 7\}$

Transposition   Transposition can be used to replicate a mode on a different pc. Assume, for example, that we wish to replicate mode 3 on F$\sharp$. That could be done by transposing another instance of mode 3, for example the one shown in Ex. 10–12. The transposition will be done here using pitch and interval brs.

G pentatonic (mode 3)	<< 7, 4>	<10, 6>	< 0, 0>	< 3, 2>	< 5, 3>>
ibr<G,F$\sharp$>		<11, 6>	<11, 6>	<11, 6>	<11, 6>	<11, 6>
F$\sharp$ pentatonic (mode 3)	<< 6, 3>	< 9, 5>	<11, 6>	< 2, 1>	< 4, 2>>

Transposition can also be used to derive a class of pentatonic sets that have only one pc in common. Such a class would be analogous to the parallel diatonic modes shown in Ex. 10–5. We'll begin with mode 1 of Ex. 10–12 and transpose that set (labeled set A) recursively by ordered pc interval 5 (labeled n). *Recursive transposition* involves transposing a set, transposing the result, transposing that result, etc. After each transposition we'll rotate the result so that it begins with 3, the pc that all five sets have in common.

set A:	3	5	7	10	0		<3 5 7 10 0>
n:	5	5	5	5	5		
T5 (A):	8	10	0	3	5	rotate:	<3 5 8 10 0>
n:	5	5	5	5	5		
T5 (T5 (A)):	1	3	5	8	10	rotate:	<3 5 8 10 1>
n:	5	5	5	5	5		
T5 (T5 (T5 (A))):	6	8	10	1	3	rotate:	<3 6 8 10 1>
n:	5	5	5	5	5		
T5 (T5 (T5 (T5 (A)))):	11	1	3	6	8	rotate:	<3 6 8 11 1>

EXERCISE 10–3

Notate the ordered pc sets in the example above as parallel pentatonic modes using Ex. 10–12 as your model. Be sure to spell each mode so that its pcs could be rearranged to form a series of perfect fourths or fifths.

Inversion   It is also possible to obtain a class of parallel pentatonic modes by inverting and transposing a pentatonic set. This requires five operations. In each operation the interval of transposition will equal one of the pcs in the set. As you will recall, a pc may be transposed and inverted by subtracting that pc from n, the interval of transposition. Thus, T_nI (pc) = mod12 (n − pc). In keeping with the conventions used above, the original set is labeled A in the computations below.

n:	3	3	3	3	3
A:	−3	−5	−7	−10	−0
T_3I (A):	0	10	8	5	3

n:	5	5	5	5	5
A:	−3	−5	−7	−10	−0
T_5I (A):	2	0	10	7	5

n:	7	7	7	7	7
A:	−3	−5	−7	−10	−0
T_7I (A):	4	2	0	9	7

n:	10	10	10	10	10
A:	−3	−5	−7	−10	−0
$T_{10}I$ (A):	7	5	3	0	10

n:	0	0	0	0	0
A:	−3	−5	−7	−10	−0
T_0I (A):	9	7	5	2	0

EXERCISE 10–4

Arrange the pcs of the sets labeled T_nI (A) in the example above in ascending order. Then notate those sets as parallel pentatonic modes using Ex. 10–12 as your model. Be sure to spell each mode so that its pcs could be arranged to form a series of perfect fourths or fifths.

Properties of the Pentatonic Collection

Normal Form and Set-Type   Using the normal form of a pentatonic collection, let's compute its set-types as shown below.

	Normal form:	{3	5	7	10	0}
	T_9	9	9	9	9	9
	T_n-type:	(0	2	4	7	9)

	Last pc:		9	9	9	9	9
	R of T_n-type	{9	7	4	2	0}
	T_nI-type:	(0	2	5	7	9)

$$T_n/T_nI\text{-type:} \qquad [0\ 2\ 4\ 7\ 9]$$

The Table of T_n/T_nI-Types (Appendix A) lists [0, 2, 4, 7, 9] as set-type 5–35, directly opposite 7–35, the set-type of any diatonic collection. This reveals a complementary relationship, one that can be understood by visualizing the piano keyboard. If the white keys form a diatonic collection, then the black keys form its pentatonic complement. The same relationship would hold if these two collections were transposed by the same interval. Thus, for every diatonic set there is a pentatonic complement and vice versa. Any two such sets will always be related as *literal complements*. Note, however, that the set-types listed opposite each other in Appendix A are the T_n/T_nI-types of their respective set classes. Thus, they are *abstract complements*.

EXERCISE 10–5

Notate the diatonic mode and its pentatonic complement. Provide absolute br numbers for each mode and identify the pentatonic mode as to type. Be sure to spell each mode so that it could form a chain of perfect fourth or fifths. The first example has been done for you.

a. G Lydian   Mode 1

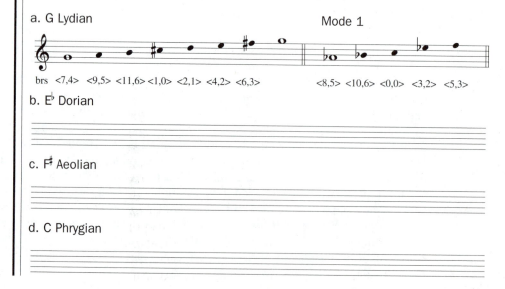

brs <7,4> <9,5> <11,6> <1,0> <2,1> <4,2> <6,3>   <8,5> <10,6> <0,0> <3,2> <5,3>

b. E♭ Dorian

c. F♯ Aeolian

d. C Phrygian

e. C$^\sharp$ Mixolydian

Interval-class content   The ic vector of the pentatonic set-type is <0, 3, 2, 1, 4, 0>. Its zeros indicate that pentatonic sets contain no instances of ics 1 and 6. (What are the traditional names for these intervals?) The entries for the remaining interval classes are unique; ic 5 is the most common, and ic 4 is the least common. The pentatonic collection resembles the diatonic collection, but it lacks ics 1 and 6, the two interval classes that provide tonal orientation. For this reason, music based on a pentatonic collection has a rather static quality.

Aspects of 20th-Century Modality

Modal Harmony

Example 10–13 shows how Bartók harmonized a folk melody whose melodic design can be represented as *a a′ b c b c*. Several points are worth noting:

- All of the chords are tertian and diatonic to the D Aeolian mode except for the penultimate chords in the *c* phrases, which contain the chromatic tones G$^\sharp$ and F$^\sharp$.
- Bartók selected a mode whose seventh degree lies a whole step below the tonic and never raised that degree by writing C$^\sharp$ instead of C natural. He used G$^\sharp$ near the end of the *c* phrases, but he weakened its leading-tone effect with the melodic figure G$^\sharp$-F$^\sharp$-A.
- Parallel voice leading and unprepared harmonic sevenths occur frequently.
- The root motions of this passage differ from those of functional tonality. Notice that root motion by descending fifths is rare; the tonic triad or seventh chord is never approached from its dominant.

Each diatonic mode has one diminished triad and one half-diminished seventh chord. These chords can cause problems because they tend to sound like vii^0 or vii^{0}7 of the relative major scale. To avoid slipping into that more familiar mode composers either shun these chords or apply chromatic alterations. The latter option usually involves lowering the chord's root so that a diminished triad becomes major, and a half-diminished seventh chord becomes a major seventh chord.

Notice how these principles influenced the harmonization in Ex. 10–13. Bartók used five of the seven diatonic triads in the first phrase. He avoided E-G-B$^\flat$ and B-D-F, the two triads that *could* be diminished, depending upon whether B natural or B flat was used. He avoided a dominant (major-minor) seventh sonority in m. 3 but used that chord type (with added ninth) in the following measure. The same is true for the *b* phrases (mm. 5–6 and 9–10). The first B$^\flat$ avoids a tritone; the second B$^\flat$ causes one. Finally, note that Bartók's chromatic alterations in mm. 8 and 12 create tritones with other pitches of the chord (G$^\sharp$ with D, F$^\sharp$ with C). These two-tritone chords function in a manner analogous to cadential dominants of functional tonality.

Example 10–13. Bartók, Fourteen Bagatelles, Op. 6, No. 4

Pandiatonicism

Some passages are clearly based on a diatonic collection, but their tonality remains ambiguous because a tonic scale degree cannot be readily identified. Numerous examples of *pandiatonicism* occur in Stravinsky's music from about 1920 to 1954. Example 10–14 shows an organ interlude that is based on the collection [C D E F G A B], except for the B♭ in m. 39. The passage may be diatonic, but its tonal orientation is vague. For a variety of reasons, no single pc dominates. G can be heard as the root of the final sonority, but is it the tonic for the entire passage? Perhaps G should be the dominant instead. This issue would have to be resolved before the mode could be determined unequivocally.

Example 10–14. Stravinsky, *Canticum Sacrum*, I, mm. 32–40

Modulation and Mixture

You are probably familiar with various techniques of modulation from your study of tonal harmony. Many of the same concepts can be applied to modal and pentatonic passages. The primary difference is the wider range of scale types. Instead of only two types, major and expanded minor, there are now at least twelve: the seven modes of the diatonic collection, plus the five modes of the pentatonic collection. Some possibilities are explored below.

Modulation to the Same Scale Type   In this type of modulation the scale type remains the same, but the pc collection and tonic pc change. The most familiar example is a modulation from one major key to another, such as from C major to F major. Such a modulation can be seen in mm. 4–5 of Ex. 1–1 (p. 3). A modal example might involve a modulation from D Dorian to G Dorian, or E Phrygian to F Phrygian.

Modulation to a Relative Mode   Here the collection remains constant, but the tonal orientation changes. As a result, the scale type changes, as well. This category includes any modulation between the members of a class of seven relative diatonic modes (see Ex. 10–1), or between any of five relative pentatonic modes (see Ex. 10–12). An example from the literature is discussed below.

Mode Mixture (or Interchange)   Here the tonic remains, but one or more of the non-tonic degrees changes, so the scale type changes, as well. An abstract case would involve a modulation between any of seven parallel diatonic modes (see Ex.

10–5), or any of five parallel pentatonic modes (see Exercises 10–3 and 10–4). Mode mixture also occurs in Ex. 13–1a (p. 236).

Modulation to a Different Scale Type with a Change of Tonic and PC Collection

Here all three factors (scale type, tonic and collection) change, as can be seen in Ex. 10–15a, the first section of Debussy's *The Engulfed Cathedral*. As the passage begins, G is established as the focal pc with [G A B ( ) D E ( ) G] as the prevailing collection. Debussy presents the same melodic idea in mm. 3–4 and again in mm. 5–6 but moves the bass from a G/D harmonic dyad through F/C to E/B. The low register of the E/B dyad prompts us to reorient the collection around E as [E ( ) G A B ( ) D ( )]. Because of this we are encouraged to hear the F/C bass notes of mm. 3–4 as large-scale passing tones in an otherwise pentatonic context.

Debussy isolated and repeated E in m. 5 then used it as a link to a new collection. By continuing to repeat E in three different octaves he assured that mm. 8–12 are heard as [E ( ) G♯ A♯ B C♯ D♯ E], which is E Lydian with a missing second degree. The E/B dyad returns in m. 13 and then descends to C/G. Due to the low register of the C/G dyad, we hear mm. 14–15 as [C D E ( ) G A B C]. This could be C Lydian or C major, depending on the missing fourth scale degree. Notice that the pentatonic collection of mm. 1–2 has been reoriented around C, one of the two pcs that was absent from those measures. The tonal plan of this section is summarized in Example 10–15b.[3]

Chromaticism

Example 10–16 (p. 190) shows more extensive chromaticism in a diatonic setting. This little piece exhibits an overall ternary form on the basis of its tonal structure and accompaniment patterns. The first eight measures are dominated by a five-finger pattern based on the D–A pentachord. To create the contrasting B section Stravinsky shifted the pattern up a third in mm. 9–13 to the F–C pentachord and changed the left-hand accompaniment pattern. The tonal focus and texture of the A section return from m. 14 to the end.

The A sections feature a *cross-relation* formed by two instances of name class F: F♯ in the right hand and F natural in the left hand. In functional tonality, where diatonic scales predominate, such problems can usually be resolved by regarding one pitch as diatonic and the other as chromatic. That solution is not possible here because F and F♯ are equally prominent. It is impossible to identify the mode because the right-hand melody has a limited range. We can only note that the tonic is D and the scale is [D E F/F♯ G A ( ) ( ) D].

The B section (mm. 9–13) is based on a complete diatonic collection, but its orientation is more ambiguous. We are tempted to hear F_4 (RH part) as tonic because its analog, D_4, was tonic of the A section. But Stravinsky complicated matters by

---

[3]For another analysis see David Neumeyer and Susan Tepping, *Guide to Schenkerian Analysis* (Englewood Cliffs, NJ: Prentice-Hall, 1991), p. 40.

Example 10–15a.   Debussy, *The Engulfed Cathedral*, mm. 1–15

placing F$_4$ in weak metric and melodic positions until the very end of the section. In addition, he retained D$_3$ as the lowest note in the left-hand accompaniment.

As this example shows, tonal ambiguity can prevail even when music contains a full complement of diatonic pcs. The A sections of this piece are more tonally

Example 10–15b. Analysis of Ex. 10–15a

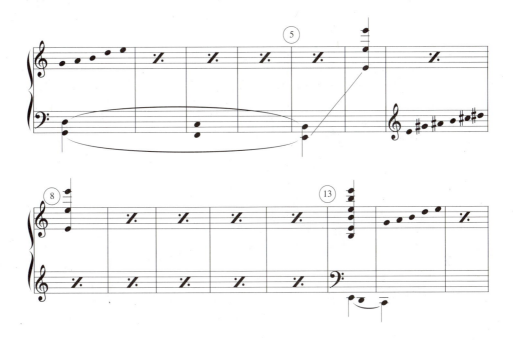

stable than the B section even though they are based on an incomplete scale and feature a prominent cross-relation.

Polymodality

The term *polymodality* denotes the successive or simultaneous use of two (or more) different modes that share the same tonic. This produces cross-relations like those seen in Ex. 10–16 above.

The idea of exploiting cross-relations is carried one step further in Ex. 10–17. Each line is bounded by an F–C fifth that is filled to produce either [F G A B C] or [F G A♭ B♭ C]. Instead of presenting these pentachords successively in ascending or descending form (as in the melodic minor scale), Bartók stated them simultaneously and moved each line in either direction.

Polytonality

The simultaneous use of two or more diatonic scales with different tonics, often termed *polytonality,* was explored by Russian and French composers in the decades following World War I. Example 10–18 shows an excerpt from a Brazilian dance by Darius Milhaud (1892–1974). The texture consists of three layers: a bass that establishes F as its tonic, a tenor melody that repeats a two-measure figure, and a

Example 10–16.   Stravinsky, *Five Fingers*, Lento

Example 10–17. Bartók, Major and Minor (*Mikrokosmos*, II/59)

[42 sec.]

treble melody that projects F♯ minor. The bass and tenor present only five pcs that form the pentachord [F G A♭ B♭ C] (compare Ex. 10–17 above). There are no instances of ncs D and E, but we are encouraged, nevertheless, to assume that the scale is F minor. Particularly interesting is how Milhaud achieves a cadence in m. 13 by resolving the dissonance between the two layers.

Example 10–18. Milhaud, *Saudades do Brazil*, "Botafogo" mm. 1–14

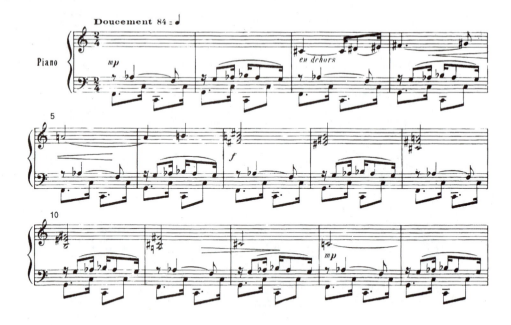

Recent research has demonstrated that listeners were unable to perceive separate major keys in brief excerpts from Stravinsky's *Petroushka*.[4] One of these excerpts is shown in Ex. 10–19. The experimenters tried repeatedly to prove that their subjects were hearing two keys, C major and F♯ major, simultaneously, but they were unable to do so. Instead, they concluded that listeners blended the two triads to form an *octatonic* set (see Chapter 13). Do these findings apply to other bitonal passages, such as Ex. 10–18, as well? The texture of Milhaud's dance differs considerably from that of Stravinsky's fanfare, but are these differences salient enough to enable bitonal hearing in the former while precluding it in the latter?

EXERCISE 10–6

1. Construct the set of seven pcs that form the literal complement to Ex. 10–11 (p. 180). Notate and identify all seven of the relative diatonic modes that can be formed by rotating this set.
2. List the pentachordal set that forms the literal complement of each mode shown in Ex. 10–6. Notate and identify by number the five modes of each of

---

[4]Carol L. Krumhansl, *Cognitive Foundations of Musical Pitch*, Chapter 9, pp. 226–39. The results were originally published in Carol L. Krumhansl and M. L. Schmuckler, "The *Petroushka* Chord," *Music Perception* 4 (1986): 153–84.

Example 10–19. Stravinsky, *Petroushka*, second tableau, reh. 49 (all instruments are notated at sounding pitch)

these pentatonic collections. Be sure to notate the pcs so that they can be arranged to form a segment of the circle of perfect fourths/fifths.

3. Choose a class of relative modes and compose seven short melodies, each one based on a different mode. Play these melodies for your classmates, and see if they can identify the tonic pc and the scale type of each.

4. Using only the five pcs of a pentatonic collection, compose five short melodies, each with a different tonic. Play these melodies for your classmates, and see if they can identify the tonic pc and the mode of each.

QUESTIONS FOR REVIEW

1. Define the following terms: mode, relative modes, parallel modes, diatonic collection, pentatonic collection, subset, pandiatonicism, polymodality, polytonality, synthetic scale.

2. Explain how to form a set from a diatonic or pentatonic mode. Explain how to form a mode from a diatonic or pentatonic set.
3. List the ic vector for the diatonic set-type. Describe its unique multiplicity property.
4. How many pentatonic subsets are contained within a given diatonic set, for example, [0, 2, 4, 5, 7, 9, 11]?
5. Describe the procedure for identifying the diatonic mode of a musical excerpt.

RECOMMENDED LISTENING AND ANALYSIS

Bartók, *Bluebeard's Castle* (opening segment) (Morgan)
—— Mikrokosmos, V/128, "Peasant Dance" (Turek)
Britten, Serenade for Tenor, Horn, and Strings, "Prologue" (Turek) "Dirge" (Simms, Turek, WenAMSS) "Sonnet" and "Epilogue" (Burkhart)
Copland, *Rodeo*, "Hoedown" (Kamien)
Debussy, "The Engulfed Cathedral" (Burkhart)
—— *Pour le Piano*, Sarabande (Turek)
Ives, 114 Songs, No. 2 "Evening" (Turek)
Prokofiev, Classical Symphony, first movement (Godwin)
Ravel, Sonatine, first movement (Burkhart), Mouvement de Menuet (Turek)
—— Le tombeau de Couperin, Menuet (Palisca; WenAMSS)
Satie, *Trois Gymnopedies*, No. 1 (Turek)
Stravinsky, *The Rite of Spring*, "Rounds of Spring" (Morgan)

CHAPTER 11

Symmetrical Sets

Introduction

A *symmetrical* set is one whose content remains unchanged when the set is inverted and/or transposed by some interval. Most of the chords and scales used in functional tonality are *asymmetrical,* but one symmetrical type does occur: the diminished-seventh chord. Locate its set-type in Appendix A, and find the column labeled D.S. (for Degrees of Symmetry). The number 8 in that column indicates that any instance of T_n/T_nI-type [0 3 6 9] can be transposed or inverted eight times without altering its content.

$$T_0 [0 3 6 9] = \{0 3 6 9\}$$
$$T_3 [0 3 6 9] = \{3 6 9 0\}$$
$$T_6 [0 3 6 9] = \{6 9 0 3\}$$
$$T_9 [0 3 6 9] = \{9 0 3 6\}$$

$$T_0I [0 3 6 9] = \{0 9 6 3\}$$
$$T_3I [0 3 6 9] = \{3 0 9 6\}$$
$$T_6I [0 3 6 9] = \{6 3 0 9\}$$
$$T_9I [0 3 6 9] = \{9 6 3 0\}$$

Most set-types have only one degree of symmetry, and thus instances of these types can be replicated under only one operation, T_0. Since that operation is trivial, we'll not consider such sets to be truly symmetrical.

Several set-types have two degrees of symmetry. Their sets map onto themselves under two operations: T_0 and T_nI. Here the subscript n stands for the set's *inversional index(es),* the interval(s) by which it must be transposed, after inversion, to produce another set (or sets) with identical pc content.

Inversional Index

To determine a set's inversional index(es), we must find rotations of its normal form that have palindromic interval patterns. (A *palindrome* is a string of symbols that reads the same in either direction, for example, the words *noon* and *rotor.*) We might begin by testing whether the set's T_n/T_nI-type has such a pattern. Two examples are set-types 4–1 and 4–3:

interval pattern: 1 1 1
set-type 4–1:   [0, 1, 2, 3]

interval pattern: 1 2 1
set-type 4–3:   [0, 1, 3, 4]

In other cases, we may need to rotate the T_n/T_nI-type (or any other transposition of the set's normal form) to find a palindromic interval pattern. If the set has an even number of pcs, these patterns will occur in pairs.

interval pattern: 1 4 4   <u>4 3 4</u>   3 4 1   <u>4 1 4</u>
set-type 4–20:   {0, 1, 5, 8}   {1, 5, 8, 0}   {5, 8, 0, 1}   {8, 0, 1, 5}

In other cases, we may need to append the first pc to the end of each rotation.

interval pattern: 1 1 5 5   <u>1 5 5 1</u>   5 5 1 1   <u>5 1 1 5</u>
set-type 4–6:   {0, 1, 2, 7, 0} {1, 2, 7, 0, 1} {2, 7, 0, 1, 2} {7, 0, 1, 2, 7}

The inversional index(es) are then computed by adding the first and last pcs of the rotations that produced those patterns.

4–1:	{<u>0</u>, 1, 2, <u>3</u>}	0 + 3 = 3
4–3:	{<u>0</u>, 1, 3, <u>4</u>}	0 + 4 = 4
4–20:	{<u>1</u>, 5, 8, <u>0</u>}	1 + 0 = 1
4–20:	{<u>8</u>, 0, 1, <u>5</u>}	8 + 5 = 1
4–6:	{<u>1</u>, 2, 7, 0, <u>1</u>}	1 + 1 = 2
4–6:	{<u>7</u>, 0, 1, 2, <u>7</u>}	7 + 7 = 2

Notice that the index for set-type 4–6 was obtained by adding the first pc to the last pc (which duplicates the first pc). To validate a set's inversional index, we can invert the set and transpose the result by that interval.

4–1:	T_3I [0, 1, 2, 3]	=	{3, 2, 1, 0}
4–3:	T_4I [0, 1, 3, 4]	=	{4, 3, 1, 0}
4–20:	T_1I [0, 1, 5, 8]	=	{1, 0, 8, 5}
4–6:	T_2I [0, 1, 2, 7]	=	{2, 1, 0, 7}

A few set-types have four degrees of symmetry. Sets of these types map onto themselves under T_n for two values of n, and under T_nI for two additional values of n. Their inversional indexes can be determined as described above. The only difference is that two pairs of rotations will have palindromic interval patterns. To illustrate:

interval pattern: 1 5 1   5 1 5   1 5 1   5 1 5
set-type 4–9:   {<u>0</u>, 1, 6, <u>7</u>} {<u>1</u>, 6, 7, <u>0</u>} {<u>6</u>, 7, 0, <u>1</u>} {<u>7</u>, 0, 1, <u>6</u>}

The inversional indexes are, therefore:

$$0 + 7 = 6 + 1 = 7$$
$$1 + 0 = 7 + 6 = 1$$

These indicate that $[0, 1, 6, 7]$ maps onto itself under T_7I and T_1I.

$$T_7I\ [0, 1, 6, 7] = \{7, 6, 1, 0\}$$
$$T_1I\ [0, 1, 6, 7] = \{1, 0, 7, 6\}$$

Transpositional Index

A set's *transpositional index* is the interval by which its pc content can be replicated under transposition. To compute this value, we can subtract the rotations of its normal form from the normal form. For example,

$\{0,\ 1,\ 6,\ 7\}$	$\{0,\ 1,\ 6,\ 7\}$	$\{0,\ 1,\ 6,\ 7\}$	$\{0,\ 1,\ 6,\ 7\}$
$\{0,\ 1,\ 6,\ 7\}$	$\{1,\ 6,\ 7,\ 0\}$	$\{6,\ 7,\ 0,\ 1\}$	$\{7,\ 0,\ 1,\ 6\}$
0 0 0 0	11 7 11 7	6 6 6 6	5 1 5 1

In this case, two operations produce a constant difference. The first is trivial since any set maps onto itself under T_0. The second difference, 6, indicates that any instance of $[0, 1, 6, 7]$ is symmetrical under T_6. Thus, $T_6\ [0, 1, 6, 7] = \{6, 7, 0, 1\}$.

There is a significant difference between these two indexes. Transpositional indexes remain constant for a given set-type, but inversional indexes vary. To illustrate, let's first transpose several instances of $[0, 1, 6, 7]$ by interval 6, the transpositional index for this set-type.

$$T_6\ \{5, 6, 11, 0\} \quad = \quad \{11, 0, 5, 6\}$$
$$T_6\ \{2, 3, 8, 9\} \quad = \quad \{8, 9, 2, 3\}$$
$$T_6\ \{4, 5, 10, 11\} \quad = \quad \{10, 11, 4, 5\}$$

As you can see, the pc content is preserved in each case. Now we'll *invert* the same three sets and transpose the result by 6.

$$T_6I\ \{5, 6, 11, 0\} \quad = \quad \{1, 0, 7, 6\}$$
$$T_6I\ \{2, 3, 8, 9\} \quad = \quad \{4, 3, 10, 9\}$$
$$T_6I\ \{4, 5, 10, 11\} \quad = \quad \{2, 1, 8, 7\}$$

These sets are *not* symmetrical under T_6I. In order to map each set onto itself, we must use the inversional index for that specific set. This value is computed by summing the first and last pcs of *that set,* not of its T_n/T_nI-type. When the value of n is computed in this way, transposed inversion produces a set with identical pc content.

$$T_5I \{\underline{5}, 6, 11, \underline{0}\} \quad = \quad \{0, 11, 6, 5\}$$
$$T_{11}I \{\underline{2}, 3, 8, \underline{9}\} \quad = \quad \{9, 8, 3, 2\}$$
$$T_3I \{\underline{4}, 5, 10, \underline{11}\} \quad = \quad \{11, 10, 5, 4\}$$

Axis of Symmetry

Pitch Sets

Every symmetrical set has a balancing point called its *axis of symmetry*. The axis for a set of *pitches* is the pitch, or pair of adjacent pitches, that lies precisely in the middle of the set. A symmetrical set with an odd number of pitches contains its own axis. A symmetrical set with an even number of pitches has some other pitch, or semitonal dyad, as its axis.

To illustrate, the trichordal set shown in Ex. 11–1a has F_4 as its axis. The other two pitches lie equidistant above and below. If this set were expanded to a tetrachord as shown at *b,* the axis would shift to the semitonal dyad G/A♭. In contrast, the set shown at *c* has a single pitch, D♯₄ (or E♭₄), as its axis.

Locating the axis of a symmetrical pitch set requires finding the pitch, or semitonal dyad, that lies halfway between every I-related pair of pitches. This can be done by adding the numbers of any pair, such as the lowest and highest pitches, and halving that sum. The procedure is illustrated below for the three sets in Ex. 11–1.

Ex. 11–1a
add pitch nos.: $0 + 10 = 10$
halve this value: $10 / 2 = 5$

Ex. 11–1b
add pitch nos.: $0 + 15 = 15$
halve this value: $15 / 2 = 7.5$

Ex. 11–1c
add pitch nos.: $0 + 6 = 6$
halve this value: $6 / 2 = 3$

Example 11–1.   **Symmetrical pitch sets (pitches are numbered using Rahn's system)**

Pitch-Class Sets

Now let's consider the same three examples as *pc* sets. Figure 11–1a represents Ex. 11–1a as a set of pcs. Solid lines point to pcs that are contained within this set; arrows point to the axis pcs. Notice that the line pointing to pc 5 is extended to pc 11, the diametrically opposite pc, but its dotted segment indicates that pc 11 is not a member of this set.

To cope with Ex. 11–1b we must arrange the pcs in normal form, then find a rotation that has a palindromic interval pattern. Fortunately, the set's normal form has such a pattern.

interval pattern: 2 3 2
normal form: {10, 0, 3, 5}

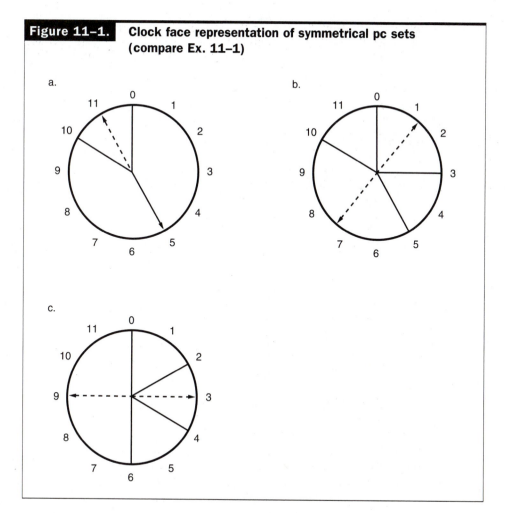

Figure 11–1.   **Clock face representation of symmetrical pc sets (compare Ex. 11–1)**

The pcs that comprise this set are represented by the solid radial lines in Fig. 11—1b. The axis is represented by the dotted, diametric line whose arrows point between two pairs of semitonal dyads, 1/2 and 7/8. Figure 11–1c is a model of the pitch set shown in Ex. 11–1c. Here the axis is a pair of pcs, rather than a pair of pitches.

From these examples we may conclude that the axis of a symmetrical pc set is a *pair* of pcs, or semitonal dyads, that lie opposite each other on the clock face and are, therefore, separated by interval 6.

To compute the **axis of a pc set:**

1. Arrange the pcs in normal form.
2. List the rotations and compute the interval pattern of each.
3. Select a rotation that has a palindromic interval pattern. If more than one rotation has such a pattern, perform steps 4 and 5 for each of these rotations.
4. Add (mod 12) the first and last pcs of the rotation, and divide that number by two.
5. If the result is an integer, the axis is that pc and its diametric opposite on the clock face (e.g., 1 and 7). If the result is not an integer, the axis is the pair of pcs that lie on either side of this number, and the diametrically opposite pair (for example, 1/2 and 7/8).

Interval Cycles

An interval cycle is a circular arrangement of equally spaced pcs. Cycles 1/11 and 5/7 (Fig. 11–2 a and b) are the only ones that include all twelve pcs. Observe that 0, 3, 6, and 9 are located in the same positions on these two cycles, while the other pcs are inverted with respect to either the 0/6 or 3/9 axis.

Each of the other four cycles must be transposed to use up the complete chromatic set. Cycle 2/10 must be transposed twice (Fig. 11–2 c), cycle 3/9 three times (d), cycle 4/8 four times (e), and cycle 6/6 six times (f). We will refer to each transposition as a *collection* of pcs. Thus, there are two collections for cycle 2/10, three for cycle 3/9, four for cycle 4/8, and six for cycle 6. These are shown in standard pitch notation along with their traditional names in Ex. 11–2.

The Whole-Tone Set-Type

The Whole-Tone Scale

Example 11–2a shows how interval cycle 2/10 may be notated as the so-called *whole-tone scale*. Since this scale has only six degrees, all of its intervals cannot be major seconds; one interval must be written as a diminished third. (Locate the diminished thirds in Ex. 11–2a.) It is also possible to represent this scale as a hexachordal pc set. By doing so we avoid the problem of traditional interval spellings.

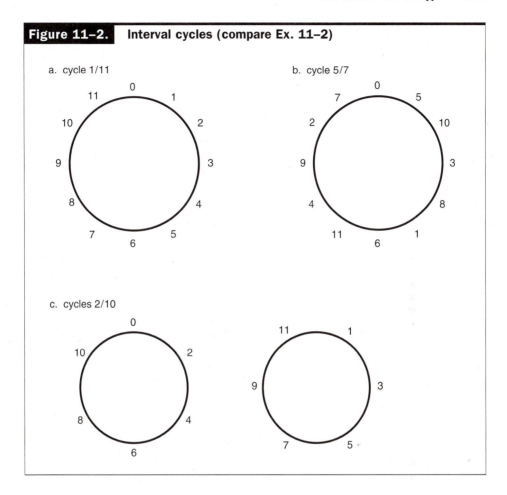

Figure 11–2.   **Interval cycles (compare Ex. 11–2)**

a. cycle 1/11

b. cycle 5/7

c. cycles 2/10

The following exercise will guide you in discovering basic properties of the whole-tone set-type. Analysis projects A and C at the end of this chapter will reveal how composers have used this set-type.

EXERCISE 11–1

Locate the whole-tone set-type in the Table of T_n/T_nI-Types (Appendix A). How many degrees of symmetry does it have? What are its transpositional and inversional indexes? Demonstrate that the set is symmetrical under T_n and T_nI for these indexes. What is its interval-class vector? Which interval classes are present? Which are absent? Give the integer names and traditional names for these intervals.

Figure 11–2. *Continued*

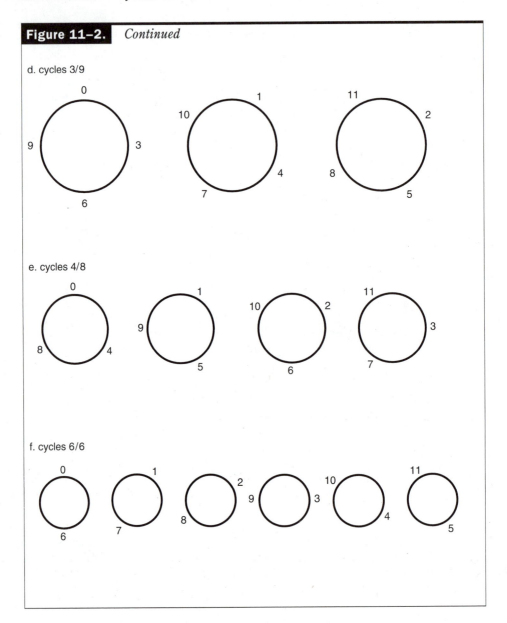

d. cycles 3/9

e. cycles 4/8

f. cycles 6/6

Subsets of the Whole-Tone Set-Type

Composers often imply a whole-tone set by using certain of its subsets. The most familiar subsets can be formed by raising or lowering the fifth of a major triad, a dominant seventh chord, or a dominant ninth chord (see Ex. 11–3). Some of these chords are respelled enharmonically. All are represented as pc sets below the staff.

Example 11–2. Interval cycles in staff notation (compare Figure 11–2 c, d, and e)

a. cycle 2/10 (notated as a whole-tone scale)

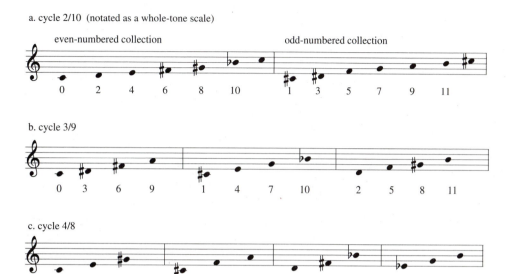

b. cycle 3/9

c. cycle 4/8

Example 11–3. Literal subsets of the even-numbered whole-tone collection

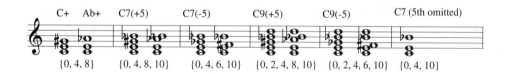

C+   Ab+   C7(+5)   C7(-5)   C9(+5)   C9(-5)   C7 (5th omitted)

{0, 4, 8}   {0, 4, 8, 10}   {0, 4, 6, 10}   {0, 2, 4, 8, 10}   {0, 2, 4, 6, 10}   {0, 4, 10}

The Octatonic Set-Type

A set produced by combining any two of the cycle 3/9 collections (Fig. 11–3) is known as an *octatonic set*. Placement of 8–28, the octatonic set-type opposite 4–28, the diminished-seventh chord (see Appendix A), indicates that these two types are complementary. Any octatonic set includes two of the three 3/9 cycles; the pcs of the remaining 3/9 cycle form its complement.

Set-type 8–28 has eight degrees of symmetry and, therefore, maps onto itself under four levels of T_n and four of T_nI. The set's transpositional indexes can be determined by looking closely at its ic vector.

interval class	1 2 3 4 5 6
multiplicity	<4, 4, 8, 4, 4, 4>

Figure 11–3. **The three octatonic collections in clock face representation**

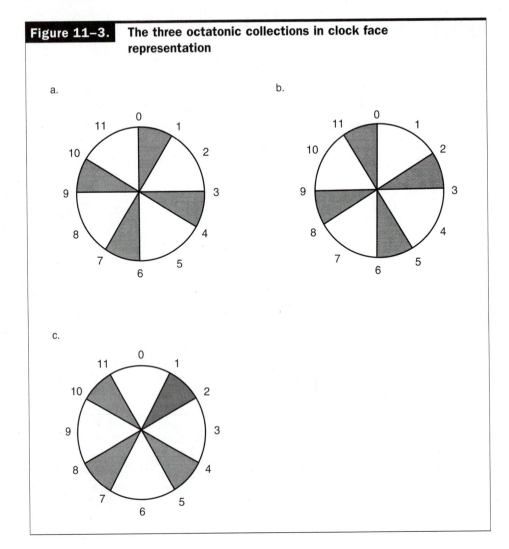

a.

b.

c.

The 8 in the column for ic 3 indicates that all eight pcs are duplicated when any set of this type is transposed by 3 or 9. The 4 in the last column indicates that transposition by interval 6 also produces a set with duplicate content.[1] And of course, an identical set can always be produced by T_0.

To determine the inversional indexes of set-type 8–28 we must find rotations of its normal form that have palindromic interval patterns. As Table 11–1 reveals,

---

[1] The entry for ic 6 is doubled to determine common pcs under T_n. This is because it takes two pcs to form a single instance of ic 6. If those pcs are transposed by ic 6, they will map onto each other, e.g., $T_6(0, 6) = (6, 0)$.

TABLE 11-1.   Computing the inversional indexes of an octatonic set

Interval pattern 1 2 1 2 1 2 1		Sum	Interval pattern 2 1 2 1 2 1 2		Sum
{<u>0</u>, 1, 3, 4, 6, 7, 9, <u>10</u>}		10	{<u>1</u>, 3, 4, 6, 7, 9, 10, <u>0</u>}		1
{<u>3</u>, 4, 6, 7, 9, 10, 0, <u>1</u>}		4	{<u>4</u>, 6, 7, 9, 10, 0, 1, <u>3</u>}		7
{<u>6</u>, 7, 9, 10, 0, 1, 3, <u>4</u>}		10	{<u>7</u>, 9, 10, 0, 1, 3, 4, <u>6</u>}		1
{<u>9</u>, 10, 0, 1, 3, 4, 6, <u>7</u>}		4	{<u>10</u>, 0, 1, 3, 4, 6, 7, <u>9</u>}		7

there are only two distinct patterns both of which are palindromes. We can compute the inversional index for each set by summing the first and last pcs of each rotation.

From the above discussion we may conclude that any instance of set-type 8–28 will map onto itself under T_0, T_3, T_6, T_9, *and* under T_nI for four values of n. These four inversional indexes will, of course, vary with the pc content of each set.

The Octatonic Scale

An octatonic scale may be formed by duplicating the initial pc of an octatonic set at the higher octave (Ex. 11–4). In contrast to a diatonic collection with its seven distinct modes, an octatonic collection has only two modes whose interval patterns alternate intervals 1 and 2. We'll designate these modes as shown in Ex. 11–4.

An octatonic scale has eight degrees, but since there are only seven letters in the musical alphabet, one letter must be used for two adjacent scale degrees. For example, the scale in Ex. 11–4a has an E♭ followed by an E natural, while that in Ex. 11–4b has an F natural followed by an F♯. This feature is also indicated by the name-class numbers and intervals at the bottom of the example. Notice that it is permissible to use sharps and flats within the same octatonic scale. This is often done to avoid double sharps and double flats.

Example 11–4.   **The two forms of the octatonic scale**

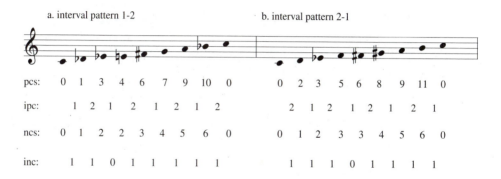

a. interval pattern 1-2   b. interval pattern 2-1

pcs:	0	1	3	4	6	7	9	10	0	0	2	3	5	6	8	9	11	0
ipc:		1	2	1	2	1	2	1	2		2	1	2	1	2	1	2	1
ncs:	0	1	2	2	3	4	5	6	0	0	1	2	3	3	4	5	6	0
inc:		1	1	0	1	1	1	1	1		1	1	0	1	1	1	1	1

Subsets of the Octatonic Set-Type

Interval-Class Content

By superimposing ic vectors, we can see that the property of unique multiplicity of interval classes, a distinctive feature of the diatonic set-type (see below), is noticeably absent from the octatonic set-type.

IC vector of the diatonic set-type   <2, 5, 4, 3, 6, 1>
IC vector of the octatonic set-type   <4, 4, 8, 4, 4, 4>

Instead, the distribution is even. Each interval class occurs four times, and instances of these intervals are evenly spaced within the set (see Ex. 11–4). The sole exception, ic 3, can be formed on each of the eight scale degrees.

Trichordal and Tetrachordal Subsets

Due to its highly symmetrical structure, an octatonic set can be partitioned into numerous instances of the same set-type. To test for a subset-type, one need only look at two locations: the first and second scale degrees. To illustrate, suppose that we wish to know whether an octatonic set contains any instances of [0, 1, 2]. To answer this question, we can try to fit $T_0[0, 1, 2]$ onto the octatonic set-type. If we start on pc 0, the next pc is 1, but the one after that is 3, so this transposition doesn't fit at T_0.

$T_0[0, 1, 2]$ {0 1 2}
Octatonic set-type: [0 1   3 4   6 7   9 10]

Transposing [0, 1, 2] by interval 1 gives us {1, 2, 3}, which doesn't fit either.

$T_1[0, 1, 2]$ {   1 2 3}
Octatonic set-type: [0 1   3 4   6 7   9 10]

Further trials are unnecessary. If a subset-type won't fit at T_0 and T_1, it won't fit at other levels of transposition.

Symmetrical Subsets of the Diatonic Set-Type

Example 11–5 shows symmetrical subsets of the white-key diatonic collection. The T_n/T_nI-type of each group is shown beneath the staff. In some cases, two or more voicings are shown for a given type. In addition to the usual trichords and tetrachords, the listing includes pentachordal and hexachordal subsets. In fact, it even includes the entire diatonic set that is symmetrical in its Aeolian rotation and as the Dorian mode (see the bottom staff).

As noted earlier, symmetrical sets are rare in diatonic modality and functional tonality. Most of the common scale and chord types have an asymmetrical structure.

Example 11–5. **Symmetrical subsets of the white-key diatonic collection**

a. trichords

[0, 2, 4]   [0, 2, 7]   [0, 3, 6]

b. tetrachords

[0, 1, 5, 6]   [0, 1, 5, 8]   [0, 2, 3, 5]   [0, 2, 4, 6]   [0, 2, 5, 7]   [0, 3, 5, 8]

c. pentachords

[0, 1, 3, 5, 6]   [0, 2, 4, 6, 9]   [0, 2, 4, 7, 9]

d. hexachords

[0, 2, 4, 5, 7, 9]

e. entire collection

[0, 1, 3, 5, 6, 8, 10]

Example 11–6 shows how the dominant scale degree divides the octave into two unequal segments, a perfect fifth and perfect fourth, and how the perfect fifth is further subdivided into major and minor thirds. This principle of unequal division characterizes all of the diatonic modes except Locrian.

It is important to note that symmetrical properties may or may not be exploited when pc sets are realized as pitch sets. To illustrate, [0, 1, 3, 5, 6, 8, 10], the diatonic set-type, has two degrees of symmetry; it can be duplicated under T_0 and T_6I. But

Example 11–6. **Asymmetric division of the octave and perfect fifth**

this property pertains to a highly abstract entity, the T_n/T_nI-type of a superclass of unordered pc sets. It does not follow that any mode of any diatonic collection will be symmetrical when its pcs are realized as actual pitches. In fact, most diatonic music emphasizes asymmetrical properties (review Ex. 11–6).

Compositional Uses of Symmetrical Sets

During the latter half of the 19th century, certain composers became interested in using symmetrical sets (although they did not designate them as such). Mikhail Glinka (1804–57), the founder of the Russian nationalist movement, was a pioneer in this regard. Example 11–7 shows an excerpt from the overture to his opera *Russlan and Ludmilla.* Notice that in mm. 357–60 and 365–68 the bass line descends by whole tones through an octave while major triads are outlined on D_4, $B\flat_4$, and $F\sharp_5$, pitches that lie eight semitones apart. As a result, the octave is divided into six

Example 11–7. Glinka, *Russlan and Ludmilla,* Overture, mm. 357–72

Example 11–8. **Melodies that emphasize a tritone**

a. Debussy, Prelude to "The Afternoon of a Faun," mm. 1–4, flute solo

b. Stravinsky, The Firebird, mm. 1–2, cellos and string basses

equal segments by the bass line, and the double octave is divided into three equal segments by the triadic motives.

Glinka's interest in symmetrical pitch collections was taken up by other Russians as well as by composers of other nationalities. Example 11–8 shows how pitch symmetry is emphasized in two familiar melodies by Debussy and Stravinsky. Each theme begins by emphasizing a tritone, the interval that divides the octave into two equal segments. Debussy's theme becomes focused on E for a brief moment in m. 3, but then lapses into ambiguity as it ends on A♯, the pitch that divides the C♯–G tritone into two equal segments and forms a tritone with the implied E tonic of m. 3.

Bartók often used symmetrical subsets of the diatonic collection to harmonize his modal and pentatonic folk melodies. In one of his many essays, he noted that:

> *The simpler the melody the more complex and strange may be the harmonization and accompaniment that go well with it. . . . It is obvious that we are much freer in the invention of an accompaniment than in the case of a melody of a more complex character. These primitive melodies, moreover, show no trace of the stereotyped joining of triads. . . . It allows us to bring out the melody most clearly by building round it harmonies of the widest range varying along different keynotes.*[2]

Example 11–9 shows two excerpts from a Slovakian lullaby as harmonized by Bartók. The melody of 11–9a is clearly based on [F-G-A-B-C], the lower pentachord

---

[2]*Béla Bartók Essays,* ed. Benjamin Suchoff (New York: St. Martin's Press, 1976), p. 342. As quoted in Antokoletz, *The Music of Béla Bartók,* p. 28. For a more critical view see Straus, *Remaking the Past,* pp. 40–42.

Example 11–9. Bartók, *Dorfszenen* (*Village Scenes*), No. 4, *Wiegenlied* (*Lullaby*)

Example 11–9. *Continued*

b. mm. 47–55

of the F Lydian mode, although it cadences on G in mm. 8 and 11. The harmony is comprised of symmetrical chords built exclusively of perfect fifths. Notice that the piano part is not restricted to tones that appear in the F Lydian melody. Bartók expanded the collection to include B♭ and E♭, as well.

Example 11–9b is taken from the middle section of this ternary-form song. Here the melody is based on [B♭-C-D♭-E♭-F], the lower pentachord of B♭-Aeolian (or Dorian), while the harmony is comprised of a symmetrical set [B-E/F-B♭] in the left hand and [B-D♭-( )-F-( )-A], a subset of the odd-numbered whole-tone collection, in the right hand.

SUMMARY

A symmetrical set is one whose pc content can be duplicated by T_nI where n represents the set's *inversional index(es)*, and by T_n where n represents its *transpositional index(es)*. The term *degrees of symmetry* denotes the number of distinct operations that can reproduce a set. For example, $\{0, 1, 6, 7\}$ has four degrees of symmetry, since it can be reproduced under T_1I, T_7I, T_0, and T_6. Transpositional indexes remain constant for any instance of a given set-type; inversional indexes depend on the pc content of a specific set.

Every symmetrical set has axes of symmetry. The axis for a pitch set is the pitch, or semitonal dyad, that lies equidistant from every pitch pair in the set. The axis for a pc set is a pair of pcs that lie diametrically opposite on the pc clock face and equidistant from every pc pair in the set.

Symmetrical sets can be found in functional tonality, but they are relatively rare and usually subordinate to asymmetrical interval, chord, and scale types. Certain composers of the 19th century were fascinated by the tonal ambiguity of symmetrical sets. Their experimental music influenced early 20th-century composers such as Debussy, Stravinsky, and Bartók.

QUESTIONS FOR REVIEW

1. Define the following terms: symmetrical set, palindrome, degrees of symmetry, axis of symmetry, inversional index, transpositional index, interval cycle, subset.
2. Describe how to determine the following characteristics of a pc set:
   a. inversional index(es)
   b. transpositional index(es)
   c. axis of symmetry
3. Notate from memory the interval cycles shown in Fig. 11–2 and Ex. 11–2. Use both clock face and standard musical notation.
4. What are the traditional names for interval cycles 3/9 and 4/8 (see Ex. 11–2)?
5. Example 9–10 (p. 160) is based on one of the interval cycles. Which one?

EXERCISE 11–2

1. Notate a realization of the following symmetrical pc sets. Determine the T_n/T_nI-type of each.

    a. {4, 6, 8, 10, 0, 2}
    b. {1, 4, 7, 10}
    c. {9, 11, 0, 2, 3, 5, 6, 8}
    d. {0, 5, 10, 3}
    e. {2, 5, 6, 7, 8, 11}

2. For each of the sets listed above, demonstrate at least one operation (other than T_0) that maps the set onto itself. For example, T_4 [0, 4, 8] = [4, 8, 0].
3. Set-type 7-35 has two degrees of symmetry. Any set of this type will map onto itself under T_0 and one other operation. Determine that operation including the value of n, the interval of transposition. Compare and contrast the symmetrical properties of the diatonic and octatonic set-types.
4. Locate the axis of symmetry for each of the sets listed in Ex. 11–5.
5. Form a pc set from the clarinet parts of Ex. 10–19 (p. 193). Normalize this set by computing its normal form and T_n/T_nI-type. Locate its set-type in Appendix A. How many degrees of symmetry does it have? What are its inversional and transpositional indexes?
6. Which of the 12 trichordal T_n/T_nI-types are abstract subsets of the octatonic set-type? Which of the 29 tetrachordal types? When you discover a subset-type, notate all of its instances as they occur in Ex. 11–4a.

Analysis Projects

A. Debussy, "Voiles" (Preludes, Bk. I) (Wen20)

This piece is based on two symmetrical sets, which we will term *principal* and *subordinate*. The principal set is used throughout most of the work; the subordinate set is used for only a few consecutive, interior measures. For each of these two sets, answer the following questions:

1. What is its T_n/T_nI-type?
2. What is its ic vector? What does the vector reveal about the set's transpositional symmetry? Is the set transposed during the course of the work or section?
3. What are the set's inversional indexes? Is it possible to find an inversion of this set in the piece?
4. How is the set voiced? Do any of the voicings make it possible to hear one of the pitches or pcs as a focal point? If so, is the music tonal?

B. Bartók, "From the Island of Bali" (Mikrokosmos, IV/109) (WenAMSS)

Section A (mm. 1–11)
1. Form an unordered pc set from the pitches of the left-hand part. Do the same for the right-hand part. How are these two sets related?
2. Determine the T_n-type, T_nI-type, T_n/T_nI-type, ic vector, and degrees of symmetry for each set.
3. What set is formed by combining the right-hand and left-hand parts?
4. How are the two lines related as melodies? What operation could you perform on m. 1 to derive m. 2?

5. Analyze the intervallic structure of RH and LH tetrachordal sets. Do you find any perfect intervals? If so, what is the root of each? Which intervals are emphasized by the melodic patterning? Are any of the intervals given unusual spellings? Why do you think Bartók used these spellings?
6. Consider the ending of this section. In what sense can it be considered a cadence? How does it resemble and differ from traditional tonal cadences?

Section B (mm. 12–30)
1. Can this section be subdivided into smaller units? If so, where and on what criteria?
2. How does the pitch material of this section compare to that of the Section A? Are any new pcs added? If so, where and how? Are any new tetrachordal sets formed? If so, where and of what type?

Section A' (mm. 31–43)
1. In what sense is this section a recapitulation of Section A? How does it differ from Section A?
2. Does the same 8-pc set prevail throughout this section?
3. Describe the final cadence (mm. 40–43) in as much detail as possible. How is it related to the pitch sets used throughout most of the work? How is it related to the cadence at the end of Section A? In what respects is it symmetrical? What pitch is the axis of symmetry? How do the two quarter notes in m. 42 relate to the axis?
4. In view of your answers to the questions in item 3 above, how would you interpret the D that is sustained in two octaves throughout mm. 30–38? Does this pc have a tonal function? If so, what?

C. Bartók, "Diminished Fifth" (Mikrokosmos, IV/101)
(Burkhart: DeLio-Smith)

1. Measures 1–15 have been reduced to unordered pc sets on the worksheet below. Continue this analysis throughout the remainder of the piece. The extent of the next two set combinations is indicated by circled measure numbers. Notice that in the collection for mm. 12–15 one note of each tetrachord is parenthesized. Can you explain why?
2. What scale is formed by combining the treble and bass tetrachords of each passage?
3. Trace the tonal plan by providing a transpositional index for each octachord. Use mm. 1–5 as your reference as shown.
4. Determine the number of common pcs between each 8-pc collection and the succeeding collection.
5. Determine the number of common pcs between the 8-pc collection of mm. 1–5 and each of the other octachords.
6. Can you discern a pattern for Bartók's transposition scheme? Does this piece have a tonal plan? If so, how does it compare to that of Bartók's "Chromatic Invention"? (See Chapter Four, Analysis Project A, questions 5 and 6.)

Worksheet for Bartók, "Diminished Fifth"

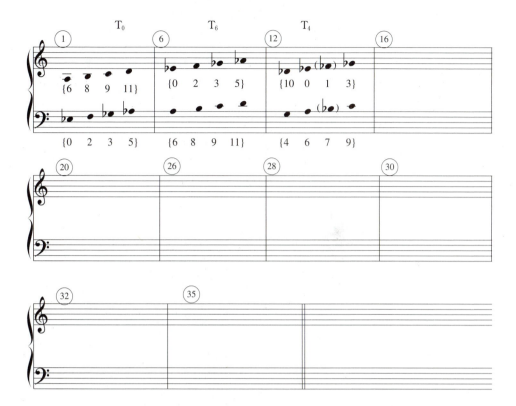

RECOMMENDED LISTENING AND ANALYSIS

Berg, Four Songs, Op. 2, "Schlafend trägt man mich" (Burkhart)

Bartók, *Mikrokosmos* IV/99 "Crossed Hands" (DeLio-Smith), IV/101 "Diminished Fifth" (Burkart; DeLio-Smith), IV/115 "Bulgarian Rhythm (Burkhart), V/133 "Syncopation" (Burkhart), VI/140 "Free Variations" (Morgan), VI/144 "Minor Seconds, Major Sevenths" (Morgan)

Debussy, Prelude to "The Afternoon of a Faun" (Burkhart, Kamien)

Ives, "The Cage" (Burkhart)

Messiaen, *Vingt Regards sur L'enfant Jésus,* No. 2, "Regard de l'étoile" (Kamien)

Scriabin, *Vers la flamme,* Op. 72 (Palisca)

———, Preludes, Op. 74, No. 3 (Morgan), No. 4 (Godwin)

CHAPTER 12

New Concepts of Tonality

Criteria of Tonal Stability

Hindemith's Series I and Series II

In writing his textbook *The Craft of Musical Composition*[1] Paul Hindemith developed two criteria of tonal stability. The first, a continuum called Series I, shows how closely each of the twelve pitch classes is related to a focal pc or tonic. Example 12–1 shows Series I with C as tonic. Like the harmonic overtone series (see Ex. 1–6, p. 9), Series I may be transposed to any other pc level.

Hindemith also devised Series II (see Ex. 12–2) whereby he ranked harmonic intervals and identified their roots. In doing so, he made no attempt to classify intervals as either "consonant" or "dissonant." He merely acknowledged that they vary in terms of sonance and can, therefore, be ranked along a continuum. Be aware that each interval in Ex. 12–2 represents itself as well as its compounds, transpositions, and/or enharmonic equivalents. Bar lines group the intervals in pairs that are complementary with respect to the octave. The intervals within each measure comprise an *interval class*. Note that the octave and the tritone are set off by a double bar to indicate their unique qualities.[2]

Example 12–1. **Hindemith's Series I: A ranking of pitch classes in terms of their kinship to C* (may be transposed)**

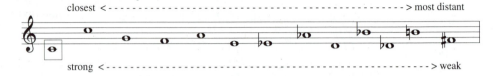

*After Paul Hindemith, *The Craft of Musical Composition* (New York: Associated Music Publishers, 1942), Book I, p. 56.

---

[1]For bibliographical details on the four volumes see David Neumeyer, *The Music of Paul Hindemith* (New Haven: Yale University Press, 1986), p. 287.

[2]This is done in Ex. 54 (p. 81) of *Craft I*.

Example 12–2. Hindemith's Series II: A ranking of interval classes from most consonant to most dissonant. The root of each interval is indicated by an open note head. The numbers indicating harmonic and melodic force are approximations derived from Hindemith's graphic representations of those aspects*

Harmonic force: 5   4   3   2   1   0

Melodic force: 1   2   3   4   5

*Paul Hindemith, *The Craft of Musical Composition* (New York: Associated Music Publishers, 1942), Book I, Example 59, p. 87.

Resolution of Tense Intervals

Example 12–3 shows typical resolutions for intervals that are considered dissonant in two-voice tonal counterpoint. A summary of these tendencies is given below.

- Major and minor sevenths—the lower pitch is more stable, so the upper pitch descends by whole or half step to form a consonant major or minor sixth.
- Major or minor seconds—the upper pitch is more stable, so the lower pitch descends by whole or half step to form a consonant major or minor third.
- Perfect fourths—the upper pitch descends by whole or half step to form a consonant major or minor third whose root is its lower pitch.
- Augmented intervals—neither pitch is more stable; these intervals resolve by *expanding* to a perfect or imperfect consonance.
- Diminished intervals—neither pitch is more stable; these intervals resolve by *contracting* to a perfect or imperfect consonance.

To avoid the negative connotations of the term *dissonant*, some composers have preferred the term *tense*. Example 12–4 is adapted from a composition text by Alvin Etler (1913–1973), one of Hindemith's students and a noted composer in his own right. Etler listed new possibilities for resolving each type of tense interval. Notice, for example, that major and minor sevenths can be resolved by moving the upper pitch down by step or the lower pitch up by step. In either case, the interval of resolution is a sixth, but two intervals are augmented sixths, the enharmonic equivalents to minor sevenths. According to Etler, a minor seventh is still a "tense" interval, but it is less tense than a major seventh.

Here then are two distinctive features of neotonality. Enharmonic equivalence is widely accepted, and distinctions between consonance and dissonance are relative rather than absolute. A tense (dissonant) interval is often considered resolved if one or both of its pitches move (usually by step) to form a less tense interval. Be

Example 12–3. Typical resolutions of dissonant harmonic intervals in two-voice tonal counterpoint

Major and minor 7ths

7 - - - - 6   7 - - - - 6   7 - - - - 6

Major and minor 2nds

2 - - - - - 3   2 - - - - - 3   2 - - - - - 3

Perfect 4ths

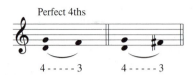

4 - - - - - 3   4 - - - - - 3

Augmented intervals

4 - - - - - 6   4 - - - - - 6   +2 - - - - - 4   +6 - - - 8

Diminished intervals

5 - - - - - 3   5 - - - - 3   o7 - - - - 5

sure to study Exx. 12–4 and 12–5, carefully playing each resolution and listening to the quality of each interval.

Neotonal Melody

Models

Etler approached the study of neotonal melody through an abstract structure that he called a *model*.[3] A model is a short series of pitches, usually seven to twelve, that

---

[3]The ensuing discussion is based on Chapter 3 of Etler's *Making Music*.

Example 12–4. **Resolutions of "tense" intervals in two-voice neotonal counterpoint***

a. All sevenths and all diminished intervals resolve to a tone *within* the interval.

Major and minor 7ths

Diminished 7ths and 8ves

Diminished 4ths and 5ths

b. All seconds and all augmented intervals resolve to a tone *outside* the interval.

Major and minor 2nds

Augmented 4ths and 5ths

Augmented 2nds

Augmented primes and 8ves

*Alvin Etler, *Making Music: An Introduction to Theory* (New York: Harcourt Brace Jovanovich, Inc., 1974), Exx. 2.8 and 2.10, pp. 12–13.

are carefully arranged to exhibit tonal coherence, a sense of motion, and a graceful contour. The overall range of a model seldom exceeds an octave, and its notes are of equal duration. Five of Etler's models are shown in Ex. 12–6. Readers who have studied species counterpoint will recognize the similarity between a model and a cantus firmus.

Example 12–5.   **Traditional and neotonal resolutions of diminished thirds and augmented sixths**

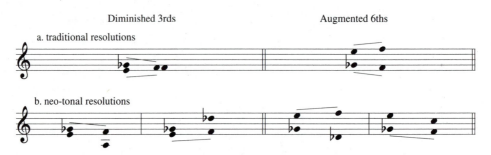

Example 12–6.   **Neotonal models***

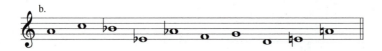

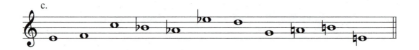

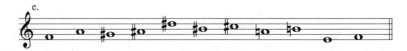

*Alvin Etler, *Making Music: An Introduction to Theory*, (New York: Harcourt Brace Jovanovich, 1974), Exx. 3.1, 3.16c, 3.38d, 3.40b, 3.42e.

Neotonal models begin and end on the same pitch, the tonic. The final tonic may be approached by step from above or below, or by a skip no larger than a perfect fifth. If a skip is elected, then the next-to-last pitch must be chosen with care so that it does not threaten the stability of the final tonic. That will not occur as long as the final tonic is the root of the final melodic interval (according to Hindemith's Series II).

The segment between the beginning and ending is termed the *departure*. Here the tonic should not be emphasized, but the other eleven pcs may be used freely as long as they form melodic intervals whose quality is perfect, major, or minor, and whose size is no larger than a perfect fifth. Augmented or diminished intervals are not allowed between adjacent pitches, but they may occur between nonadjacent pitches if resolved correctly. Successions of equal-sized intervals (e.g., major seconds) are permitted only if their first and last pitches form a very stable interval such as a major third. Etler noted that several factors can retard a sense of motion within the departure: repetition of a single pitch, outlining of conventional triads, scalar passages longer than three notes, and melodic sequences.

The most important aspect of models, for our purposes, is their tonal stability. Stability will be strengthened if a model is based entirely on a traditional scale type, such as major, natural minor, harmonic minor, or melodic minor. It is also affected by the strategic placement of the dominant, subdominant, and lower leading tone. Placing these scale degrees immediately before the final tonic (Ex. 12–6b, c, and e) will enhance stability; placing them nearer to the beginning of a model (see Ex. 12–6d) will weaken it.

Some models contain cross-relations, pairs of pitches that belong to the same name class but to different pitch classes. Example 12–6a has two instances of nc B (B natural and B flat) and two of nc A (A natural and A flat). Binomial representations (brs) for pitches and ordered intervals are listed below the staff.[4] A pair of cross-related pitches will form an augmented or diminished unison (or octave), and either pitch may form augmented or diminished intervals with other pitches. The tonal stability of a model is affected considerably by the placement of these "chromatic" pcs and by the treatment of the intervals formed between them.

EXERCISE 12–1

The following exercises pertain to the models shown in Ex. 12–6b–e.

1. List the br (binomial representation) for each pitch. In each case, use the tonic of the model as the reference pitch (pc 0 and nc 0). (Binomial representation was explained in Chapter Two, pp. 33–34.)
2. Locate and label the following scale degrees: tonic (T), dominant (D), subdominant (S), lower leading tone (LLT), and upper leading tone (ULT). Note their

---

[4]Recall that a pitch br consists of a pc number and an nc number; its prototype is, therefore, <pc,nc>. An interval br (ibr) gives the size of the interval in semitones and scale steps. For example, <3,2> indicates an interval of three semitones and two scale steps, or a minor third.

placement relative to the final tonic. Does it reinforce or weaken the tonal stability of the model?

3. Identify each melodic interval by its traditional name and its binomial representation. (Computation of br intervals was discussed in Chapter Two, pp. 41–42).

4. Locate any augmented or diminished intervals formed between nonadjacent pitches. Identify each of these intervals by its traditional name and its br name. Try to find another pitch (or pair of pitches) that resolves each interval as shown in Exx. 12–4 and 12–5.

5. Review the conditions that govern the approach to the final tonic of a model. Then select a tonic pitch and notate the eight possible endings for a model. Each ending will consist of two pitches; a nontonic pitch followed by the tonic.

6. Review the conditions that govern melodic intervals within a model. Then, using the same pitch as the initial tonic, write all the three-note beginnings that you can imagine.

7. Compose several models that continue your beginnings and conclude with a suitable ending. Analyze the tonal features of each according to Exercises 1–4 above.

Melodies

Neotonal melodies can often be parsed into segments that outline triads, seventh chords, or stable intervals such as P5, P4, M3, m3. We'll refer to these segments as *tonal cells*. The melody shown in Ex. 12–7 contains several tonal cells as indicated by brackets. Some of the brackets overlap because certain pitches are common to more than one cell. The roots of these cells form the *degree progression* of the melody.

Neotonal melodies often exhibit directed, stepwise motion between adjacent or nonadjacent notes. This feature, which Hindemith termed *step progression*, was especially prominent in music that he composed during the 1930s and 1940s. Example 12–8 shows Neumeyer's analysis of a melody that exhibits lengthy step progressions in both directions.

Example 12–7. **Analysis of a neotonal melody showing tonal cells and degree progression***

*Paul Hindemith, *The Craft of Musical Composition* (New York: Associated Music Publishers, 1942), Book I, Example 154, p. 184.

Example 12–8. Hindemith, *Nobilissima Visione Suite*, I. (Introduction or Meditation), mm. 1–13 (melody only) with analysis of step progressions*

*David Neumeyer, *The Music of Paul Hindemith* (New Haven: Yale University Press, 1986), Example 3.17, p. 70.

Meyer and Narmour have documented *linear* and *triadic* patterns in tonal melodies, but they insist that such patterns unfold at a relatively even pace. They have also documented *gap-fill* patterns. These begin with a skip that is usually filled by stepwise motion in the opposite direction. The fill may be complete or only partial, direct or indirect. A fourth category, *complementary* patterns, exhibit motion in one direction that is immediately followed by the same type of motion in the opposite direction.

Examples 12–9 and 12–10 contain two melodies that Etler derived from the model shown in Ex. 12–6a. Their distinctive character is determined by meter, rhythm, articulation, and note repetition, aspects not found in the model. Each

Example 12–9.   **Meyer-Narmour analysis of a neotonal melody***
(compare Ex. 12–6a)

**Alvin Etler, Making Music: An Introduction to Theory (New York: Harcourt Brace Jovanovich, 1974), Ex.
4–15, p. 66.*

melody has an intricate structure that is analyzed on the lower staff using symbols
devised by Meyer and Narmour.[5]

The melody in Ex. 12–9 contains three notes that are not found in its parent
model. The F_4 in m. 2 and the $C\sharp_5$ in m. 5 are passing tones. The B_4 in m. 7 is a
returning tone embellishing the climactic D_5. These simple figures should be familiar
from your study of tonal melody.

Now on to more complex patterns. The ascending third B_4–D_5 opens a gap in
m. 7 that is partially filled by the C_5 in m. 8. But before that fill can be completed,
another gap is opened by the descending fifth in m. 8. And before *that* interval is
filled, an ascending-fourth gap appears in m. 9. Because of these deferrals, the final
G_4 serves not only as a return to the initial tonic, but also as the goal of these three
gap-fill structures. Its triple function is indicated by the three tails on the stems of
the final note.

The melodic structure of Ex. 12–10 is even more complex. The descending G–E
third of its model (Ex. 12–6a) is elaborated by an ascending-fourth gap G_4–C_5, which
receives an immediate and direct fill that continues well beyond G_4 to E_4. Measure

[5]Leonard B. Meyer, *Explaining Music* (Chicago: University of Chicago Press, 1973), see Part II, Explorations in Tonal Melody; Eugene Narmour, *Beyond Schenkerism* (Chicago: University of Chicago Press, 1977). For a concise summary see J. Kent Williams, "Archetypal Schemata in Jazz Themes of the Bebop Era," *Annual Review of Jazz Studies* 4 (1988): 49–74.

Example 12–10.	**Meyer-Narmour analysis of a neotonal melody***
	(compare Ex. 12–6a)

*Alvin Etler, *Making Music: An Introduction to Theory* (New York: Harcourt Brace Jovanovich, 1974), Ex. 4–18, p. 68.

2 begins with another ascending fourth E_4–A_4, which is not filled. Instead, A_4 combines with the initial G_4 to imply a slow-paced linear ascent. This implication is strengthened when B_4 arrives on the first beat of m. 3, precisely where it was due. The linear pattern formed by these three notes (G_4–A_4–B_4) implies that C_5 will arrive on or slightly after the first beat of m. 4. C_5 arrives on schedule, but it is preceded by a complex of gap-fill patterns, the most important being the ascending-third gap formed by B_4 and D_5. The need to fill *that* gap motivates the lengthy and complex linear descent of the remainder of the melody. Notice that $D\sharp_5$ in m. 3 is transformed from a lower leading tone, that should resolve upward to E_5, to an upper leading tone that actually resolves downward to D_5. As noted above, enharmonic "puns" are a distinctive feature of neotonality.

EXERCISE 12–2

1. Create several neotonal melodies from the models shown in Ex. 12–6 or from other models that you compose. Try to make each melody sound distinctive by

paying careful attention to meter, tempo, register (models may be transposed), dynamics, and articulation. Compose each melody for a specific instrument, and have it played on that instrument.

2. Compose some more melodies in the same manner but add a few embellishing notes in the manner of Ex. 12–9.

3. Compose some more elaborate melodies by adding several notes in the manner of Ex. 12–10, but do not allow these notes to dominate the melody. They should merely reinforce and enhance the structural role of the model's pitches.

4. Analyze the melody given below in the same manner as Exx. 12–9 and 12–10. Explain and interpret your findings in a concise essay.

Hindemith, *Mathis der Maler*, I, mm. 39–47, principal melodic line

Neotonal Counterpoint

Example 12–11 shows a neotonal counterpoint exercise in first species. Each voice is a well-composed model, so it makes no difference which is the cantus firmus. When analyzed separately, the two voices have different tonics: G for the upper voice, E for the lower voice. When sounded together, they form harmonic intervals with roots of varying strength. A neotonal exercise must begin and end on an interval whose root is in the lower voice. Roots of the intervening intervals may appear in either voice.

Let's compare this exercise with a first species example by Fux (Ex. 12–12). Fux's example contains the diatonic degrees of the A minor scale plus G♯, but the neotonal Ex. 12–11 contains at least one instance of each chromatic pc. Fux's exercise begins and ends on a perfect consonance; the other intervals are perfect or imperfect

Example 12–11. Two-voice model*

*Alvin Etler, *Making Music: An Introduction to Theory* (New York: Harcourt Brace Jovanovich, 1974), Ex. 6.1. p. 89.

Example 12–12. Two-voice, first-species counterpoint*

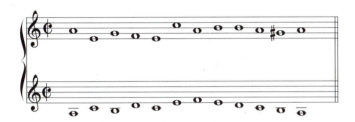

*Fux, *Gradus ad Parnassum*. Vienna, 1725. Translated and edited by Alfred Mann as *The Study of Counterpoint* (New York: W. W. Norton, 1965), Figure 22, p. 40.

consonances with a preference for the latter. Etler used seconds and sevenths but treated these "tense" intervals with care. Each is resolved by step motion in at least one voice to a less tense interval in accordance with Exx. 12–4 and 12–5. Furthermore, Etler's exercise contains only one minor second (ninth) that is placed right before the final tonic for maximum effect.

It is possible to create musical passages by elaborating first-species exercises.[6] As Ex. 12–13 shows, a neotonal duet can be derived from a first-species model (Ex. 12–11) by decorating either or both of the voices with neighboring tones, passing tones, suspensions, anticipations, escape tones, and chordal skips.

Identifying such tones is fairly easy in tonal counterpoint where there is usually a clear distinction between consonant and dissonant intervals. The task becomes more problematic, however, in the neotonal idiom where the distinction between consonance and dissonance is less clear.

---

[6]For examples see Felix Salzer and Carl Schachter, *Counterpoint in Composition* (New York: McGraw-Hill, 1969), Chapter 6, pp. 117–23.

Example 12–13. Two-voice model with both voices decorated*
(compare Ex. 14–11)

*Alvin Etler, *Making Music: An Introduction to Theory* (New York: Harcourt Brace Jovanovich, 1974), Ex. 6.2, p. 90.

In the present case it is helpful to have a duet's model available for comparison. Observe that the harmonic intervals of Ex. 12–11 occur one per measure in Ex. 12–13. Structural pitches of the model are emphasized by longer duration and/or stronger metric position. Neighbor and passing tones are usually shorter and metrically weaker, but they can receive emphasis (m. 5, upper voice). Skips generally occur on weaker beats and often form more consonant intervals with the other voice.

Example 12–14 shows how the upper voice of a first-species model may be decorated with suspensions. Two of these suspensions (m. 4 and m. 8) form an augmented or diminished octave with the lower voice, and those intervals resolve in accordance with Ex. 12–4. The other two suspensions (m. 6 and m. 10) are of the milder 6–5 type. Appoggiaturas would be resolved in a similar manner but approached by skip.

EXERCISE 12–3

1. Create two or three other duets by decorating only the upper voice of Ex. 12–11. Try to use at least two or three different types of figuration in each duet.
2. Add a few decorative pitches to the lower voice of the duets that you created above. Take care not to detract from the figuration that you added to the upper voice.

Example 12–14. Two-voice model with upper-voice decoration using suspensions*

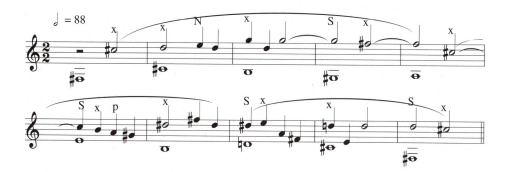

*Alvin Etler, *Making Music: An Introduction to Theory* (New York: Harcourt Brace Jovanovich, 1974), Ex. 6.32, p. 102.

Neotonal Harmony

Traditional harmonic analysis is inadequate for neotonality because it recognizes only tertian chords. Accordingly, Hindemith devised a new system of chord classification. In doing so, he proceeded from the assumption that chords are built of intervals, which vary in terms of harmonic stability as indicated in Series II (see Ex. 12–2). More stable intervals have prominent roots; less stable intervals have less prominent roots. Chords can, therefore, be classified according to the intervals that they contain, the relative stability of those intervals, and the relative prominence of their roots.

Hindemith's method involves four stages: (1) isolating the intervals within a chord; (2) evaluating the sonance, stability, and root of each interval; (3) determining the root of the entire chord (if possible); and (4) classifying the chord as shown in Fig. 12–1.

The task of isolating the intervals within a chord is similar to that of finding all of the unordered pairs of pcs within a set. As Ex. 12–15 shows, we could list the intervals between the lowest pitch and its higher pitches, then proceed to the next-to-lowest pitch, then to the next-to-next-to-lowest, etc. As each interval is isolated, its stability (according to Series II) and its root can be acknowledged.

Finding the root of an entire chord requires ranking its intervals in terms of harmonic strength. Hindemith thought that the root of a chord was the root of its "best" interval, as judged by Series II as well as by the registral placement of each interval's pitches. Because of the harmonic series (see Ex. 1–6, p. 9), stable intervals whose pitches are positioned lower within a chord will be more salient than those whose pitches are positioned higher. Classifying a chord involves answering a series of questions as shown in Fig. 12–1. Example 12–15 illustrates this procedure for several chords.

Figure 12–1.   **Hindemith's method of chord classification in flowchart representation**

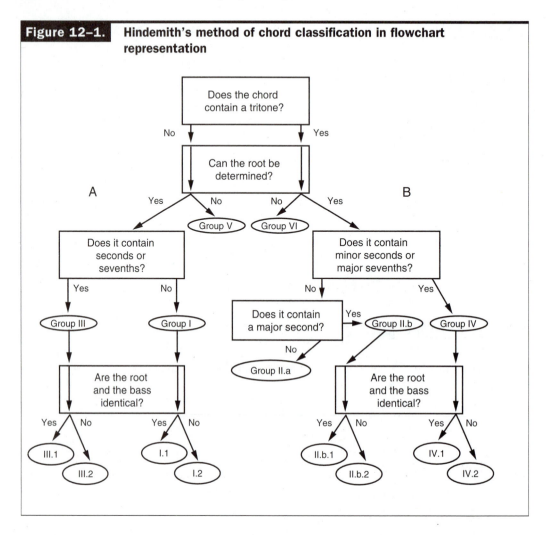

Hindemith avoided the terms *root position, first inversion, second inversion,* etc. because they imply that there is a preferred voicing for every chord, and that a chord may be revoiced without changing its root. He believed that revoicing a chord can have a marked effect upon its root. For example, the chord shown in Ex. 12–16a has D_4 as its root because that pitch is the root of its lowest best interval D_4–A_4. When the same four pitch classes are revoiced as shown in Ex. 12–16b, C_4 becomes the root of the lowest best interval and, by extension, of the entire chord.

Harmonic analysis also requires distinguishing chord tones from nonchord tones. In functional tonality, a pitch that does not belong to a standard chord type can usually be regarded as a nonchord tone. Since neotonality contains a wider range of chord types, how does one decide which pitches belong to a chord and which do not? There are no definite rules; such decisions can only be made with reference to specific contexts.

Example 12–15. Procedure for isolating intervals within a chord, determining their roots, and finding the root of the chord. Numbers beneath harmonic intervals indicate their relative stability as measured by Series II.

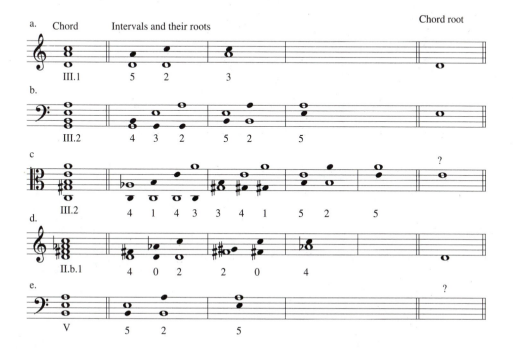

Example 12–16. Chords with the same pitch classes but different roots

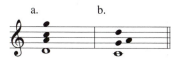

To illustrate, let's consider the opening bars of Hindemith's Piano Sonata No. 2 (Ex. 12–17a). The melody is accompanied by an Alberti bass pattern anchored to a tonic pedal. When the arpeggiations are verticalized, problems arise. The analysis on staff b shows the $B\flat_4$ in m. 2 as a passing tone that connects chord tones C_5 and A_4. The A_4 in m. 1 and the D_5 in m. 4 are also shown as nonchord tones, since they are short and metrically weak. But what type of nonchord tones are they? Staff c shows the $B\flat_4$ as a chord tone that is approached via passing motion from the G_4 in m. 1. This means that the chord tones (the stemmed notes in m. 2) form a diminished triad, an instance of Group V.

Each analysis has attractive and unattractive qualities. Analysis b shows consistent underlying harmony, but it treats melodic figuration inconsistently. Why, for

Example 12–17. Hindemith, Piano Sonata No. 2, I, mm. 1–6

example, should the A_4 in m. 1 be a nonchord tone when the same pitch in m. 2 is a chord tone? In analysis c, a triadic conception of harmony (in m. 2) produces richer melodic figuration (in mm. 1 and 2) but a less consistent harmonic background for the entire excerpt.

SUMMARY

To analyze and understand neotonal music, we need new theoretical concepts and criteria for evaluating crucial aspects of pitch organization. These include:

- relations of pitch classes to a tonic pc
- relative sonance and stability of intervals
- tonal coherence and structure of melodic lines
- control of dissonance in contrapuntal textures
- relative sonance and stability of chords

Neotonal analysis requires rethinking the concept of tonality. It assumes familiarity with the diatonic modes, synthetic scales, and the chromatic scale in addition to the familiar major and minor scales. Neotonal music may contain chords that cannot be explained by traditional harmonic analysis and intervals that are not resolved in the customary manner. Instead of projecting a consonant tonic sonority, such as a major or minor triad, it may project a more dissonant sonority, or simply a focal pitch class. In analyzing neotonal music, we must be more sensitive to the specific musical context and less bound by theoretical concepts associated with functional tonality.

QUESTIONS FOR REVIEW

1. Define the following terms: Series I, Series II, model, tonal cell, degree progression, step progression, interval root, chord root.
2. Write Hindemith's Series I from memory. Then notate two transpositions: one should begin on F, the other on A.
3. Write Hindemith's Series II from memory.
4. Explain the similarities and differences between Series I and interval cycle 5/7 (the circle of P4/P5).
5. Explain the similarities and differences between Series II and the harmonic series.
6. Explain how Etler's harmonic interval resolutions differ from those of functional tonality. Give some examples.
7. How does Hindemith's method of chord classification differ from traditional harmonic analysis? Give some examples.
8. How does Hindemith's method of chord classification differ form the method for determining the T_n/T_nI-type of an unordered pc set? Give some examples.

RECOMMENDED LISTENING AND ANALYSIS

Bartók, Forty-four Violin Duets
———, *Mikrokosmos*, II/59 and V/128 (Turek), VI/148 (Morgan)
Britten, Serenade, Op. 31, "Prologue" (Turek), "Sonnet" and "Epilogue" (Burkhart)
Diamond, Sonatina, I (DeLio-Smith)
Hindemith, Six Chansons, "Printemps" (Wen20), "A Swan" (Burkhart)
———, *Ludus Tonalis*, Interlude No. 2 (Morgan; WenAMSS), Interlude No. 3 (Wen20), Interlude No. 5 (Turek)
———, *Das Marienleben (The Life of Mary)*, "Vom Tode Mariä I," (Simms); "Pietà" (De-Lio-Smith)
———, *Kleine Kammermusik (Little Chamber Music)* for Five Winds, Op. 24, No. 2.
Milhaud, String Quartet No. 7, II (DeLio-Smith)
Prokofiev, *Visions Fugitives*, No. 1 (DeLiio-Smith)
Shostakovich, Twenty-Four Preludes, Op. 34, No. 1 (DeLio-Smith)
Tippett, *Songs for Ariel*, No. 2, "Full Fathom Five" (DeLio-Smith)

CHAPTER 13

Neotonality Analyzed

Hindemith, "A Swan"

Having laid a theoretical foundation in Chapter Twelve, we are now ready to analyze some representative neotonal pieces. Example 13–1b is a Schenkerian analysis of a polyphonic chanson by Hindemith (see Ex. 13–1a).[1] The graph reveals an elaborate tonal structure built around the tonic E and its dominant, B. This framework is projected most clearly during the opening and closing stanzas (mm. 1–5 and 18–22).

In the first stanza the soprano hovers around B_4 while the alto, tenor, and bass move between and around E and B. Notice that in m. 3 the bass reaches E_3 and forms a compound fifth with the soprano B_4. In m. 4 the soprano repeats B_4 while the lower three voices move, in parallel, to the dominant triad in m. 5.

The second stanza begins in m. 5 with a brief point of imitation among the upper three voices. When the bass enters, it reiterates E_3 for the better part of mm. 6 and 7 then descends to C_3, which forms a compound major third with the soprano's climactic E_5. Observe how Hindemith emphasized the word "aime" ("loves") by reiterating and pausing on a major triad (m. 9) rooted on $E^\flat$, the lower leading tone (as $D^\sharp$) to the tonic E. The same sonority serves as an upbeat to the final subphrase of this stanza (mm. 10–11). Here the music takes on a Phrygian inflection as F natural is introduced. The final chord, an $\frac{8}{5}$ sonority, is approached from a nontertian sonority rooted on D.

The third stanza begins with the bass and tenor restating the soprano's motive of m. 1. As the two lower voices project B_3 (m. 12), then E_3 and E_4 (m. 13), the soprano moves among B_4, E_5, and G_5, the tones of an E minor triad. The beginning of the phrase (m. 12) includes $G^\sharp$, $C^\sharp$, $F^\sharp$, and B, but as the phrase continues and each of these pcs is lowered a chromatic semitone, the mode changes from E Mixolydian, to Aeolian, to Phrygian, and finally to Locrian. Locrian inflections continue during the remainder of the stanza where there is a dramatic registral expansion from E_4 to the climactic D_3–F_5 tenth on the second beat of m. 16, then a contraction to the cadence on a $\frac{6}{4}$ chord in m. 17.

The final stanza (mm. 18–22) begins like the first but soon veers off to a surprising cadence in m. 21. Hindemith's approach to this $E^\flat$ major $\frac{6}{4}$ chord is smooth,

---

[1]Schenkerian analyses of other Hindemith works may be found in David Neumeyer, *The Music of Paul Hindemith* (New Haven: Yale University Press, 1986) and in Felix Salzer, *Structural Hearing,* 2 vols. (New York: Charles Boni, 1952; reprint New York: Dover Publications, 1962), see Vol. 2, Exx. 453, 489, and 505.

yet novel in keeping with the expanded possibilities for resolution shown in Ex. 12–4 (p. 219). The final E major triad is approached from a D-rooted chord as in mm. 10–11.

To summarize, the chanson is tonal, but its tonality is projected in less traditional ways. Notice, for example, that the work does not contain a single instance of a V–I root progression. Instead, the E-rooted cadential chords in mm. 11 and 22 are approached from more dissonant, nontertian sonorities rooted on D. The only allusion to dominant-tonic harmony is the half cadence in m. 5 where V is approached rather conventionally. The other interior cadences reach a chord whose root lies a half step above or below E (mm. 9 and 20, E♭ root; m. 17, F root), or a chord that includes E but is rooted on A (m. 14).

Most of the chords are mildly dissonant and the result of smooth voice leading. Parallel voice motion is common and often occurs at harmonic intervals that would be unacceptable in earlier styles (e.g., perfect fourths). $^6_4$ chords are used freely both within phrases and at interior cadences (mm. 14 and 17). In summary, the chanson's tonality derives from melodic and harmonic patterns that project E and B as the tonic and dominant of a tonal hierarchy.

EXERCISE 13–1

1. Classify each chord according to Hindemith's system, and plot chord roots on the bottom staff. Use roman numerals and Arabic subscripts to indicate chord classes as shown in Fig. 12–1 and Ex. 12–15 (pp. 230–31). Locate each progression in Ex. 13–1, and note its location in the space provided.

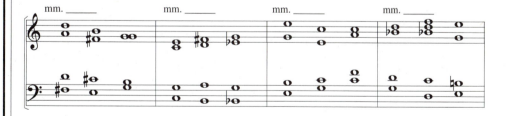

Roots

2. Locate at least one example of the following voice-leading patterns.
   a. bass and soprano in parallel 10ths
   b. bass and tenor in parallel 5ths, bass and alto in parallel 10ths
   c. tenor and alto in parallel 4ths while bass repeats a pitch
   d. bass and tenor in parallel 4ths, bass and alto in parallel 7ths
   e. bass and soprano in contrary motion

Example 13–1a. **Hindemith, "A Swan" from *Six Chansons* (1939)**

Example 13–1b. Schenkerian analysis of "A Swan"

3. Locate at least one example of the following sonorities.
   a. a major triad with root in bass and third doubled
   b. an $\frac{8}{5}$ (open fifth) sonority)
   c. a complete minor 7th chord
   d. an incomplete minor 7th chord (3rd or 5th missing)
   e. a chord whose figured bass is $\frac{7}{5}$
      $\frac{}{4}$

4. Compare and contrast the following passages in terms of harmony and voice leading.
   a. mm. 1, 12, and 18
   b. mm. 8–9 and 19/3–20/2
   c. mm. 10–11 and 16–17

Bartók, Dance in Bulgarian Rhythm No. 2

Some neotonal works establish their tonality more by assertion than by harmonic function or voice leading. Bartók's Dance in *Bulgarian Rhythm No. 2* (Ex. 13–2) begins on a reiterated C–G dyad. As its first melodic idea appears (mm. 4–7), so do three additional pcs to form a pentatonic collection. By emphasizing C as the upper and lower boundary of this melody, Bartók confirmed that it is also the tonic.

The abrupt shift in mm. 8–10 to a B♭–F dyad could be regarded as a change of key, or merely as a change of harmony within the prevailing key. For if the C–G dyad implies a C tonic, then the B♭–F dyad could imply a B♭ tonic. Notice, however, that Bartók did not introduce any new pitch classes; he merely emphasized B♭, a member of the prevailing collection. The issue of tonal focus becomes more interesting in mm. 11–12 as material from mm. 4–7 reappears. Again, the collection remains the same, but the focus changes to F. The ostinato pattern returns in mm. 13–15, where G is clearly the focus of the pentatonic collection [G-A-C-D-F]. When D and A are added the diatonic collection [C-D-E♭-F-G-A-B♭] is formed.

In retrospect, this passage can be conceived in the C Dorian mode but that fact is not obvious upon first hearing because Bartók never presented all seven pcs in close proximity. Instead, he used two pentatonic collections that have three pcs in common. The second [G-A-C-D-F], is oriented toward G, but the first emphasizes C in mm. 4–7, B♭ in mm. 8–10, and F in mm. 11–12. We may hear these shifts as changes of emphasis within the prevailing C Dorian scale, or as changes of tonic within the overall tonality of C. Example 13–2b shows that mm. 1–15 exhibit a conventional tonal plan. The passage begins by establishing C as the tonic pc and ends by emphasizing G as its dominant.

The tonality becomes less stable in m. 16, where Bartók introduced a scale built from two instances of [0, 1, 3, 5] realized as T_n type (0, 2, 4, 5), a tritone apart (see Ex. 13–2b). This synthetic scale is presented in ascending and descending form on G (mm. 16–20), and then in an ascending sequence that ends in m. 24. The focal A in mm. 24 through 30 sounds against E♭ with which it forms a tritone.

A_3 serves as axis for prime and inverted statements of the trichordal motive (mm. 24–25, RH). After a one-measure link, Bartók repeated this motive an octave lower (mm. 27–28, LH), then once more with C_3 as the axis. As Ex. 13–2 shows, each trichordal motive is an instance of set-type [0, 2, 5], a trichord that permeates the pentatonic collections on which mm. 4–12 and 13–15 are based.

The dynamic climax of the dance is reached in m. 31, where the bass accents and sustains F♯, the most distant relative of C, the overall tonic. In addition to this large-scale tritone, Bartók reiterated A–E♭, the tritone that dominated mm. 24–30.

The remaining pitch, D_3, combines with $F^\sharp_2$ and A_3 to form a D major triad, but that sonority is virtually masked by the dissonant minor second D–$E^\flat$.

The scalar motive recurs in m. 35 (RH), but its bounding pitches, C_4 and C_5, are rendered unstable by the sustained $F^\sharp_2$ in the bass. C also sounds in mm. 37–39, where C_3 and C_4 form a more stable major third above the bass $A^\flat_2$. (Note that $A^\flat$ appeared only briefly before, as $G^\sharp$ in m. 23.) The bass continues to ascend by step, reaching A_2 natural in mm. 40–41 and then $B^\flat_2$ in mm. 42–44. C is also prominent in these measures, but it forms unstable intervals with the other pcs.

The passage that begins in m. 45 features the scalar motive above reiterated triads. The F major triad in mm. 45 and 47, the only major triad in the entire dance, is embellished by lower-neighbor motion in the two lowest voices. A linear bass descent in mm. 47–51 leads to a chord built on $D^\flat_2$, which eventually resolves to the C–G tonic dyad. Bartók's spelling of the chord in mm. 51–54 obscures its triadic structure. He could have notated E_2 as $F^\flat_2$, but he chose to respell $F^\flat$ as E natural, apparently to avoid a cross-relation with F_5 in the treble.

In summary, Bartók used C extensively throughout the dance, but he never allowed it to be heard as the root of an interval or chord during mm. 16–54. Within this lengthy departure section, some passages are processive and others are relatively static. The processive passages serve as transitions, while the static ones are more developmental. Bartók undermined the tonal stability of each passage by including at least one unstable interval and/or one "new" pitch class.

EXERCISE 13–2

1. List all of the instances of [0, 2, 5] in the pentatonic collection [C-$E^\flat$-F-G-$B^\flat$]. Do the same for [G-A-C-D-F].
2. Compare the cadence in mm. 54–55 of Bartók's dance to the various cadences in Hindemith's chanson. Which of Hindemith's cadences does it most resemble and why?

Hindemith, Interlude in G

Example 13–3 shows the tonal plan of another neotonal dance piece, one modeled upon the Baroque *siciliano*. The harmonic reduction by David Neumeyer is in two stages. In Stage I (Ex. 13–3a), pitches that serve as local tonics are shown with open note heads in the bass staff. The function of these key areas relative to G, the overall tonic, is indicated beneath the staff with symbols devised by Hindemith (see Ex. 13–4). Neumeyer used solid note heads to indicate the root of the penultimate chord in each major cadence (see mm. 10 and 24). Stage II, a middle-level reduction (Ex. 13–3b), reveals that Hindemith wrote $\frac{8}{5}$ sonorities at these structural points, and that he approached each tonic sonority from a minor 7th chord rooted a chromatic half step above the tonic. Instead, however, of resolving the outer voices in the traditional manner, Hindemith expanded them to an octave as if they were augmented sixths (compare Exx. 12–4 and 12–5, pp. 219–20).

Example 13–2. Bartók, Dance in Bulgarian Rhythm No. 2 (*Mikrokosmos,* VI/149)

a. Score

Example 13–2. *Continued*

Example 13–2. *Continued*

[1 min. 10 sec.]

Example 13–2. *Continued*

b. Analysis of tonal plan. Ovals enclose pentatonic collections; rectangles enclose instances of
[0, 2, 5]

Example 13–3. Neumeyer's reductions of Hindemith's Interlude in G*

a. Stage I analysis

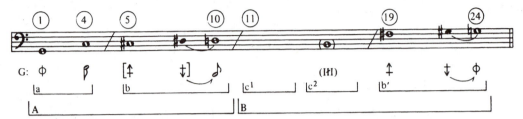

b. Stage II analysis

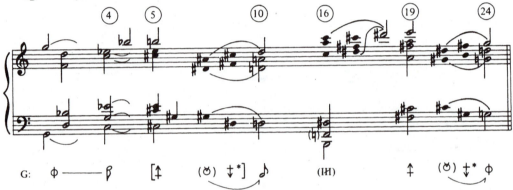

*David Neumeyer, *The Music of Paul Hindemith* (New Haven and London: Yale University Press, 1986), Ex. 3.2 and 3.3, pp. 52–53.

Example 13–4. Harmonic function symbols used by Hindemith*

*David Neumeyer, *The Music of Paul Hindemith*, Ex. 3.4, p. 55.

The underlying brackets in Ex. 13–3a show how the tonal plan of the Interlude is correlated with its melodic design and phrase structure. The piece is in continuous half-rounded binary form like many dance pieces of the Baroque and Classical eras.

Example 13–3b provides an orientation to the complete score (Ex. 13–5) of the Interlude. Both examples can serve as guides to Exercise 13–3 below.

Example 13–5. **Hindemith, Interlude in G from *Ludus Tonalis***

Example 13–6. **Rhythmic reduction of Interlude in G (to be completed)**

EXERCISE 13–3

1. Prepare a textural reduction of Hindemith's Interlude that displays less detail than the full score but more detail than Neumeyer's Stage II analysis (Ex. 13–3b).[2] Do this by continuing the worksheet provided in Ex. 13–6. Note that this exercise is *not* a Schenkerian reduction; you should use notes and rests in the traditional manner. The goal is to create a simplified score that can be performed in tempo. Before beginning your work, compare the completed portions of Ex. 13–6 with Ex. 13–5 noting the treatment of neighbor tones, passing tones, suspensions, and chordal arpeggiations.
2. Write a brief essay in which you compare the pitch organization of Bartók's Dance with that of Hindemith's Interlude. The term pitch organization can be taken to include scale, chord, and pc set-types, harmonic root progression, voice leading, and tonal plan.
3. Write an essay in which you compare David Neumeyer's analysis of Hindemith's Interlude in G with those by Felix Salzer and Robert Morgan.[3]

SUMMARY

Composers of neotonal music have devised varied tonal plans for their works. Many of these schemes emphasize the overall tonic and its dominant. However, neotonal works usually depart from tonal conventions in their middle sections where they modulate and shift to more remote key areas. These modulations often divide the scalar octave into equal-sized parts.

In the smaller dimensions, chord movement is regulated as much or more by voice leading than by functional root progressions. One often finds embellishing chords that result from simultaneous neighbor motion in several voices. The primary chords of a passage may be connected by passing motions in which two or more voices move in parallel.

Neotonal composers often modify the traditional V–I progression or replace it with alternatives. They typically avoid its leading-tone effect with indirect resolutions (e.g., 7–6–1), chromatic alteration of scale degree 7, or suspended fourths. Alternatives to V–I often involve substitute dominants with descending half-step motion to the tonic (e.g., ♭II–I).

Neotonal harmony consists of a wide variety of mildly dissonant chord types. These include extended tertian chords as well as subsets of the pentatonic set-type. The latter are often labeled in terms of their most prominent interval(s): e.g., quartal chords (perfect fourths), secundal chords (major seconds). Highly consonant sonorities, such as $\frac{8}{5}$, often appear at the ends of phrases.

---

[2]Upon completion, this reduction may be compared with Neumeyer's Stage IV and V analyses (*The Music of Paul Hindemith,* Ex. 3.22, pp. 76–79).

[3]Neumeyer, *The Music of Paul Hindemith,* pp. 75–81; Salzer, *Structural Hearing,* II: Fig 489; Robert Morgan, *Anthology of Twentieth-Century Music* (New York: Norton, 1992), pp. 251–53.

RECOMMENDED LISTENING AND ANALYSIS

Bartók, *Mikrokosmos,* IV/115 Bulgarian Rhythm (Burkhart), V/133 Syncopation (Burkhart), V/126 Change of Time (Wen20), VI/148 Dance No. 1 in Bulgarian Rhythm (Wen20; Morgan)

Britten, Serenade for Tenor Solo, Horn and Strings, Op. 31; "Sonnet" (Burkhart)

———, *Peter Grimes,* Op. 33: Act III, "To hell with all your mercy" (Palisca)

Debussy, from *Preludes,* Book II, "La puerta del Vino" (WenAMSS), "Canope" (WenAMSS); Book I, "Des pas sur la neige" (Wen20)

———, "La Soirée dans Grenade" (*Estampes* No. 2) (Morgan)

———, "Reflets dans l'eau" (*Images,* Book I) (Wen20)

Hindemith, Interlude from *Ludus Tonalis* (Wen20)

———, *Mathis der Maler:* Sechtes Bild (Palisca)

Ravel, *Le tombeau de Couperin,* Menuet (WenAMSS, Palisca), Rigaudon (WenAMSS)

———, Sonatine, first movement (Burkhart)

Schuman, *Three-Score Set,* second movement (Burkhart)

CHAPTER 14

Free Atonality

The music composed by Schoenberg, Berg, and Webern during the period 1908–1923 is often called *free atonality.* The designation "free" indicates that it was written before Schoenberg had devised the so-called "12-tone" or "serial" method of composition.

Transitional Works

Schoenberg, Second String Quartet

Schoenberg's Second String Quartet (1907–08) was one of his first ventures into atonality.[1] Its first three movements are in F$^\sharp$ minor, D minor, and E$^\flat$ minor, respectively, each with the appropriate key signature. The fourth movement has no key signature, although it retains vestiges of functional tonality and ends on an F$^\sharp$ major triad.

The quartet is also distinctive for its use of a soprano voice in the third and fourth movements. For texts, Schoenberg chose poems by Stefan George, a Symbolist poet and a member of the *Blaue Reiter* group. The third movement, a setting of the George poem *Litanei (Litany),* begins with the phrase "Deep is the sadness that overclouds me." The fourth movement is a setting of George's *Entrückung (Transport).* That poem's first line, "I feel the air of other planets," has often been cited as a prophetic metaphor for Schoenberg's venture into the atonal universe.

The fourth movement begins with the four stringed instruments presenting an 8-note motive at successively higher pitch levels (Ex. 14–1, m. 1). Schoenberg transposed the cello motive recursively by the same interval. (What is that interval? How would you demonstrate that these motives are T_n-related?)

The cello's pitches form discrete 4-note submotives with similar melodic contours (see Ex. 14–2). The last three notes of each submotive form an *appoggiatura* figure, a melodic pattern that permeates Post-Romantic music. Observe that the crucial second note of each figure is metrically strong, approached by an ascending skip, and left by a descending step. The only missing condition—that these notes be dissonant in their harmonic context—is met at the end of m. 1 and throughout

---

[1] For an extensive discussion of this issue see Allen Forte, "Schoenberg's Creative Evolution: The Path to Atonality," *Musical Quarterly* 64 (April 1978): 133–76.

Example 14–1. Schoenberg, Second String Quartet, Op. 10, fourth movement, mm. 1–10

m. 2 where the implied harmony consists of pcs {1 3 5 7 9 11}, the odd-numbered whole-tone collection (see Ex. 14–3). Since the circled notes are even-numbered pcs, they do *not* belong to that collection, and are, therefore, truly dissonant appoggiaturas. The tendency for melodic figures and chords to be based on whole-tone or "nearly whole-tone" hexachords is characteristic of many early atonal compositions.[2]

---

[2]See Bryan R. Simms, *Music of the Twentieth-Century* (New York: Schirmer Books, 1986), pp. 37–44.

Example 14–2. Cello motive parsed into submotives, each containing an appoggiatura figure

Example 14–3. Whole-tone collection in m. 2 of violin parts

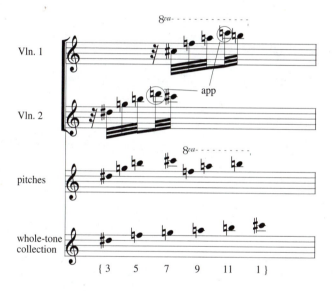

Berg, Four Songs, Op. 2

Berg's Op. 2, a collection of four songs on poems by Hebbel and Mombert, is another important transitional work. The second song (see Ex. 14–4) consists almost entirely of chords that are enharmonically equivalent to a dominant seventh with a lowered fifth (or raised fourth), or a French augmented sixth. The presence of two tritones in these chords weakens their stability, but their bass tones may still be regarded as roots because of the way the chords progress. As Ex. 14–5 reveals, root motion by descending perfect fifths or minor seconds implies a chain of secondary, or applied, dominants that belong alternately to the odd- or even-numbered whole-tone collection.

The song's key signature implies G♭ major or E♭ minor, but Berg provided an accidental for nearly every note. E♭ major is implied in mm. 11–12 and again in the last two measures. In fact, the V7–I progression in mm. 11–12 underscores the

Example 14–4. Berg, Four Songs, Op. 2, No. 2

song's dynamic and poetic climax, the phrases "über Gipfel, über Schlünde" ("over peaks, over abysses"). Furthermore, the B♭ chord in m. 11 is the only sonority in the entire song that contains a perfect fifth above its bass tone.

The melodic line resembles those of other Post-Romantic works where ascending-sixth leaps (see Ex. 14–4, mm. 2 and 14) are partially filled by descending half-step motion (compare also the motives of Ex. 14–2). But Berg's vocal melody has

Example 14–5. Berg, Op. 2, No. 2, mm. 1–4. Descending fifths progression implying alternate whole-tone collections

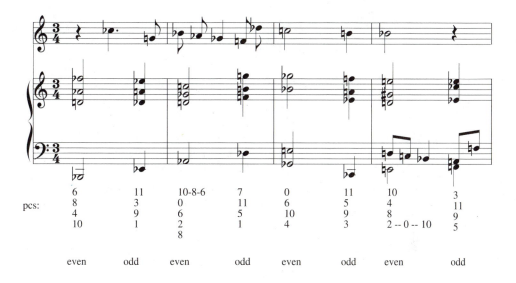

pcs:	6	11	10-8-6	7	0	11	10	3
	8	3	0	11	6	5	4	11
	4	9	6	5	10	9	8	9
	10	1	2	1	4	3	2 -- 0 -- 10	5
			8					

even	odd	even	odd	even	odd	even	odd

very few nonchord tones. Its pitches usually belong to their supporting harmony or to the implied whole-tone collection. The only notable exceptions occur in m. 1, where the vocal C♭$_5$ forms a minor second above the bass, and in m. 11 where E♭$_5$–D$_5$ form an appoggiatura figure above the bass B♭.

The third song of Berg's Op. 2 (see Ex. 8–3a, p. 134) has a key signature and an opening melodic phrase that imply A♭ minor. However, the music settles briefly onto a D minor triad in mm. 6–7 and ends on an E♭ major triad (V of A♭?). Here again Berg provided an accidental for nearly every note.

Schoenberg, Piano Piece, Op. 11, No. 1

Having examined two transitional works, we'll now turn to some examples of full-fledged, free atonality. The first eleven measures of Schoenberg's Piano Piece, Op. 11, No. 1 are given in Ex. 14–6. This passage contains a short phrase (mm. 1–3), a contrasting interpolation (mm. 4–8), and, finally, another short phrase that parallels the first. The interpolation, or B phrase, of this small A B A′ form consists of three statements of a two-note motive (E$_4$–G$_4$) with linear motion in the middle voices and a sustained G♯$_2$ in the bass.

In keeping with the practice acknowledged above (see Ex. 14–1), Schoenberg did not provide a key signature. Instead, he placed an accidental before nearly every pitch. He also avoided characteristic sonorities of functional tonality. In place of triads and seventh chords, he used an array of more dissonant and less familiar harmonic combinations.

Example 14–6.   Schoenberg, Piano Piece, Op. 11, No. 1, mm. 1–11

Our first task is to define the vocabulary of the passage. What types of sets does it contain? How many different set-types are represented? How many instances of each type? Is the distribution fairly even, or is it skewed in favor of one or a few types? Having answered these questions, we can correlate this knowledge with other aspects, notably form. Our analysis procedure will, therefore, comprise four stages as indicated below.

Stage 1: Parsing the Musical Score

The first stage is crucial, since it is here that we decide which notes form sets and which do not. Sets may be realized horizontally or vertically, as lines, chords, or combinations of lines and chords. The specific details of set realization will depend primarily upon texture. The texture of this passage is homophonic with the melody in the "soprano" voice and three supporting voices. Those voices form block chords in the two outer phrases (mm. 1–3, 9–11), but the "alto" and "tenor" become more linear during the interpolation (mm. 4–8).

Example 14–7 shows two ways to parse, or segment, the outer phrases. In Ex. 14–7a the notes have been grouped into a melodic line and its supporting chords. The melody, in turn, has been divided into two segments, each having a similar melodic contour and consisting of three notes Ex. 14–7b shows two chords per phrase and melodic-harmonic units that are congruent with the notated meter. These parsings have some attractive qualities. In addition to making musical sense, each

Example 14–7. Segmentation of phrases A and A′

a. melody vs. harmony

mm. 1-3

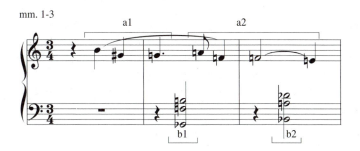

mm. 9-11

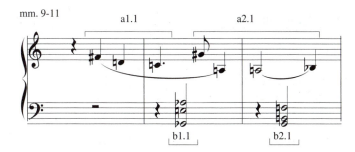

b. harmony with melody

mm. 1-3

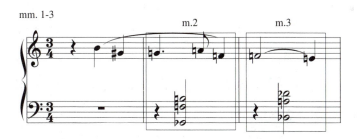

mm. 9-11

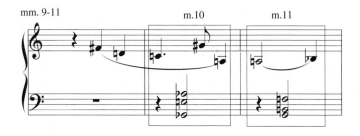

produces small sets of equal cardinality: trichords in Ex. 14–7a, pentachords in Ex. 14–7b.

The interpolation consists of three harmonized statements of a two-note motive. (How is this motive related to the first phrase?) Example 14–8 shows how Schoenberg avoided literal repetition by lengthening the second and third statements and realigning the voices.

Parsing the B phrase is not as easy because the alto and tenor parts are more melodic. A linear reading of the first statement (B.1) produces only two musically interesting sets: the "alto" trichord and "tenor" pentachord (see Table 14–1). A vertical reading (see Ex. 14–8) reveals a two-chord progression analogous to those in the A and A′ phrases (see Ex. 14–7b). Because of repetition, this reading produces only three sets, those labeled as x, x.1, and y in Table 14–1. It also seems appropriate

Example 14–8. **A vertical parsing of the interpolation**

mm. 4-5

mm. 5-6

mm. 7-8

TABLE 14-1. **Normalization and classification of unordered pc sets (to be completed by referring to Exx. 14–7 and 14–8)**

Identify each set's T_n/T_nI-type by underlining either its T_n- or T_nI-type as shown in the completed rows. Forte names and ic vectors can be referenced in Appendix A.

Set	Normal form	T_n-type	T_nI-type	Forte name	IC vector
a1					
a1.1					
a2					
a2.1					
b1					
b1.1					
b2					
b2.1					
m.2					
m.3					
m.10					
m.11					
alto	{10,11,0}	(0,1,2)	(0,1,2)	3-1	<2,1,0,0,0,0>
tenor	{6,9,10,11,2}	(0,3,4,5,8)	(0,3,4,5,8)	5-Z37	<2,1,2,3,2,0>
x	{10,0,4}	(0,2,6)	(0,4,6)	3-8	<0,1,0,1,0,1>
x.1	{10,0,1,4}	(0,2,3,6)	(0,3,4,6)	4-12	<1,1,2,1,0,1>
y	{6,7,8,9,10,11,2}	(0,1,2,3,4,5,8)	(0,3,4,5,6,7,8)	7-3	<5,4,4,4,3,1>
y.1	{7,8,11,2}	(0,1,4,7)	(0,3,4,7)	4-18	<1,0,2,1,1,1>
y.2	{7,8,11}	(0,1,4)	(0,3,4)	3-3	<1,0,1,1,0,0>

to isolate the first and last vertical sonorities of set y. These sets are labeled y.1 and y.2 in Ex. 14–8 and Table 14–1.

Stage 2: Normalizing the Sets

In Stage 2 we normalize the sets to facilitate comparison. You should complete this stage by filling in the blank cells of Table 14–1.[3]

---

[3]A number of computer programs are available to lighten the computational burden of set normalization. Your instructor may wish to recommend one for your use.

Stage 3: Tabulation and Additional Set Analysis

In Stage 3 you will tabulate the results by compiling a rank-order listing of the set-types in Table 14–1. In addition, you should indicate whether each type is an abstract subset of the diatonic set-type or the whole-tone set-type. (The concept of abstract subset is reviewed in the following paragraph.) The first and last rows of Table 14–2 have been completed. You may use these as models to complete the remaining rows.

It will also help to know whether the smaller sets are subsets of the larger sets. To review briefly, a smaller set is a *literal subset* of a larger set if all of its pcs are contained within the larger set. If that condition does not hold, then the smaller set could still be an *abstract subset* of the larger set. To determine this, we must find the T_n/T_nI-type of the smaller set and then show that the larger set contains one or more instances of that T_n/T_nI-type. The instances may, of course, be transpositions or transposed inversions.

Let's begin by testing whether the smaller sets of this passage are literal subsets of the larger sets. The cells of Table 14–3b contain a T or F to indicate whether or not the trichords (listed in the left column) are contained within the tetrachords and septachords (listed in the top row). Use this table as a model to complete Table 14–3a.

Tables 14–4a and b will aid in discovering abstract subsets. Here the T_n/T_nI-*types* of the various trichords are listed in the left column and the T_n/T_nI-*types* of the larger sets are listed in the top row. Again, Table 14–4b should be used as model for filling in Table 14-4a. Notice, however, that the cells of Table 14–4b contain

Table 14–2. **A rank-order listing of set-types in Table 14–1 by frequency of occurrence (to be completed by referring to Table 14–1)**

Forte name	T_n/T_nI-type	Occurs	Diatonic subset?	Whole-tone subset?
3-3	[0,1,4]	3	F	F
3-8	[0,2,6]	3	T	T
7-3	[0,1,2,3,4,5,8]	1	NA	NA

TABLE 14–3a. **Trichordal sets as literal subsets of pentachordal sets (to be completed using Table 14–3b as a model)**

	m.2 {5,6,7,9,11}	m.3 {1,4,5,9,10}	m.10 {0,4,6,8,9}	m.11 {5,7,9,10,11}	tenor {2,6,9,10,11}
a1 & y.2 {7,8,11}					
a1.1 {0,2,6}					
a2 {4,5,9}					
a2.1 {8,9,10}					
b1 {5,6,11}					
b1.1 {4,6,8}					
b2 {1,9,10}					
b2.1 {5,7,11}					
alto {0,10,11}					
x {0,4,10}					

integers instead of letters. Each integer indicates how many times the trichord in the left column occurs as an abstract subset of the larger set in the top row.

One way to discover abstract subsets is to compute the smaller set's superclass of 24 T_n- and T_nI-related sets (see Chapter Six, pp. 88–89), then check to see whether any of these sets are literal subsets of the larger set. For example, the superclass of [0,1,4] is comprised of the following sets:

{0,1,4}	{0,3,4}
{1,2,5}	{1,4,5}
{2,3,6}	{2,5,6}
{3,4,7}	{3,6,7}
{4,5,8}	{4,7,8}
{5,6,9}	{5,8,9}
{6,7,10}	{6,9,10}
{7,8,11}	{7,10,11}
{8,9,0}	{8,11,0}
{9,10,1}	{9,0,1}
{10,11,2}	{10,1,2}
{11,0,3}	{11,2,3}

TABLE 14–3b. Trichordal sets as literal subsets of larger sets

	x.1 {0,1,4,10}	y {2,6,7,8,9,10,11}
a1 & y.2 {7,8,11}	F	T
a1.1 {0,2,6}	F	F
a2 {4,5,9}	F	F
a2.1 {8,9,10}	F	T
b1 {5,6,11}	F	F
b1.1 {4,6,8}	F	F
b2 {1,9,10}	F	F
b2.1 {5,7,11}	F	F
alto {0,10,11}	F	F
x {0,4,10}	T	F

As shown below, [0,1,4] occurs once as an abstract subset of [0,2,3,6] and five times within [0,1,2,3,4,5,8].

Instances of [0,1,4] in [0,2,3,6]: {2,3,6}

Instances of [0,1,4] in [0,1,2,3,4,5,8]:
{0,1,4}   {0,3,4}   {1,2,5}   {1,4,5}   {4,5,8}

Stage 4: Interpreting the Findings

In the final stage, we reflect upon our findings and relate them to other observations.

Tables 14–2 and 14–3 reveal that this music is permeated with set-types [0,1,2], [0,2,6], and [0,1,4]. Let's look more closely to see how Schoenberg used these sets.

[0,1,2] is formed by set a2.1, the last three melodic pitches in mm. 10–11, by the "alto" set of the interpolation, and by the last three notes of the "tenor" set. It also occurs as an abstract trichordal subset of sets m.2 and m. 11, the first and last harmonic-melodic sets of the passage.

TABLE 14–4a. **Trichordal set-types as abstract subsets of pentachordal set-types (to be completed using Table 14–4b as a model)**

	5-9 [0,1,2,4,6]	5-22 [0,1,4,7,8]	5-26 [0,2,4,5,8]	5-Z37 [0,3,4,5,8]
3-1 [0,1,2]				
3-3 [0,1,4]				
3-4 [0,1,5]				
3-5 [0,1,6]				
3-6 [0,2,4]				
3-8 [0,2,6]				

TABLE 14–4b. **Trichordal set-types as abstract subsets of tetrachordal and septachordal set-types. A single integer within a cell indicates the multiplicity of the trichordal set-type within the larger set.**

	4-12 [0,2,3,6]	7-3 [0,1,2,3,4,5,8]	Total instances
3-1 [0,1,2]	0	8	
3-3 [0,1,4]	1	5	
3-4 [0,1,5]	0	4	
3-5 [0,1,6]	0	2	
3-6 [0,2,4]	0	4	
3-8 [0,2,6]	1	2	

Example 14–9.   Instances of [0,1,4] in mm. 1–11 of Schoenberg's Op. 11, No. 1

[0,2,6] and its close relative [0,2,4] typically occur wherever [0,1,2] is *not* found, although the first instance of each type occurs in m. 2.

[0,1,4] occurs as set a1, the first melodic trichord, and shortly thereafter as b2 [9,10,1], the second harmonic trichord. The pcs of set a1 recur literally as y2, the final vertical sonority of set y. In addition, [0,1,4] recurs as an abstract subset of each of the larger sets including set y. In fact, it is the only trichordal set-type that is evenly distributed throughout the passage.

To account for these occurrences, locate the pitches that form instances of [0,1,4] in each of the larger sets and notate them in Ex. 14–9. Table 14–4 will indicate how many instances occur in each set, but remember that these numbers include both T_n- and T_nI-related instances. For example, we noted above that [0,1,2,3,4,5,8] contains five instances of [0,1,4]. Three of these, {0,1,4}, {1,2,5}, and {4,5,8}, are T_n-related to [0,1,4], and the other two, {0,3,4} and {1,4,5}, are T_nI-related.

We can also compare the trichords to the larger sets. Table 14–2 shows that none of the larger sets is a subset of the diatonic or whole-tone set-type. Neither are the trichords [0,1,2] and [0,1,4]. On the other hand, [0,2,4] and [0,2,6] are subsets of *both* the diatonic and whole-tone collections. The remaining trichords, [0,1,5] and [0,1,6], *do* belong to any diatonic collection but *do not* belong to either whole-tone collection.

It is interesting to see how Schoenberg used [0,2,6] without realizing its tonal implications. The two most prominent instances are set x in mm. 4, 5, and 7 (see Ex. 14–8) and set a1.1 in mm. 9–10 (see Ex. 14–7a). In the former case, the trichord C_4–E_4–Bb_3 implies a dominant seventh chord in the key of F major or minor (see Ex. 14–10a). Schoenberg deliberately avoided that implication by moving to a chord that is more dissonant than a major or minor triad and foreign to those keys. The second case, D_4–$F\#_4$–C_4, implies V7 of G. Again, the chord of "resolution" is more dissonant than a triad, and the stable degrees of G major/minor are evaded. Example 14–10b shows how this phrase might have been composed in the tonal idiom of Post-Romanticism. From these examples we can see that Schoenberg *did* use certain sets that have tonal implications, but he avoided realizing those implications.

Finally, let's correlate our findings with the A B A′ phrase structure of this passage. We might expect that Schoenberg would have used the same types of sets for corresponding motives, but Table 14–1 reveals that he did not. Motives a1 and a1.1 belong to different set-types, as do motives a2 and a2.1. Nevertheless, we can still hear these phrases as parallel. (Can you explain why?)

Example 14–10. Hypothetical tonal resolutions of [0,2,6] (compare 14–7 and 14–8)

We have already seen how Schoenberg linked the A and B phrases by presenting the same three pcs melodically as set a1, and harmonically as set y2. In addition, he linked the beginning and ending by using instances of set-type [0,1,2,4,6] in m.2 and m.11. Although these sets are voiced somewhat differently, they contain exactly the same interval classes. Furthermore, they share four of their five pcs:

$$\text{m.2 } \{\underline{5},\underline{6},7,\underline{9},\underline{11}\}$$
$$\text{m.11 } \{\underline{5},\underline{6},9,10,\underline{11}\}$$

{5,6,9,11}, the set formed by those common pcs, is an instance of [0,1,4,6], one of only two tetrachordal set-types that contain all six interval classes.

Forte name	T_n/T_nI-type	IC vector
4-Z29	[0,1,3,7]	<1,1,1,1,1,1>
4-Z15	[0,1,4,6]	<1,1,1,1,1,1>

(The letter Z in the Forte names above indicates that sets of these types share the same ic vector, but they cannot be mapped onto each other by T_n or T_nI.)

The other all-interval tetrachord is [0,1,3,7]. Set y contains two instances of [0,1,3,7] as abstract subsets. (Can you find these in Ex. 14–8?) Because set y also contains literal or abstract instances of each of the trichordal types (see Tables 14–3b and 14–4b), it may rightfully be regarded as the "mother set" of this passage.

The above discussion has concerned only the first eleven measures of this famous piece. There are other aspects to be discovered about this passage, as well as about the rest of the piece. You are encouraged to study the entire piece more thoroughly and to read published analyses of it.

Webern, Five Pieces for String Quartet, Op. 5, No. 3

Having become gradually acquainted with this movement (see Ex. 14–11) in previous chapters (see the Analysis Projects for Chapters Three, Four, and Five), you should now be prepared to study it more thoroughly.

Example 14–11. Webern, Five Pieces for String Quartet, Op. 5, No. 3

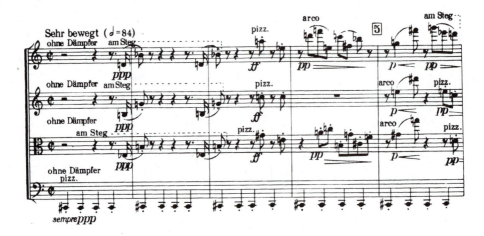

Example 14–11. *Continued*

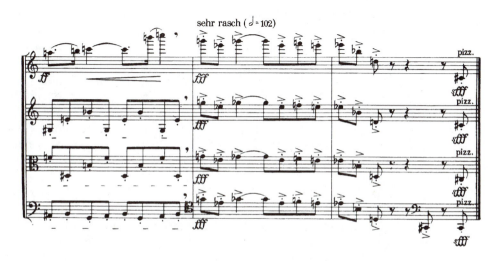

Our first task will be to discern its form. As with the Schoenberg excerpt, we cannot rely upon familiar events such as the cadential patterns of tonal harmony. But here the problem is more acute. Schoenberg's passage could be divided into two parallel phrases separated by a thrice-stated motive. For several reasons, the form of this piece is not as readily apparent. Nevertheless, there are clues that can be pursued.

The piece is divided approximately in half by an abrupt *ritard* in mm. 12–14 and an *a tempo* in m. 15. This articulation creates two sections: mm. 1–14 and mm. 15–23. The latter section has a gradual *accellerando* beginning in mm. 17–18, an abrupt *Luftpause* at the end of m. 20, and a frantic *sehr rasch* tempo in its final two measures. How do these affect its form?

Webern used several different textural combinations during this brief movement:

ostinato
> cello, mm. 1–6, 15–21
> joined by vln. 2 and vla. in mm. 18–21

stretto with entries related by T_n
> vln. 1 and vla, mm. 4–5
> all insts., mm. 10–12
> vln. 2, vla., vc., mm. 12–14
> vln. 2 and vla., mm. 18–21

stretto with entries related by T_nI
> vln. 1 and vc., m. 7

note-against-note/parallel motion
> vlns. 1 & 2, vla., mm. 1–3, 5, 6, 8

note-against-note/contrary motion (mirror writing)
> vln. 2 & vla. mm. 9–10, 15–17

octave unison
> all insts., mm. 22–23

solo instrument
> cello, m. 8; vln. 2, m. 14

Some of these combinations overlap. For example, in mm. 1–6 the cello repeats a $C^\sharp_2$ ostinato while the other instruments proceed in either rhythmic unison/parallel motion or stretto. Another arrangement (see mm. 9–10) has the first violin playing a two-measure phrase while the second violin and viola are coupled in rhythmic unison/contrary motion. Notice that the melodic phrase played tentatively by the first violin is restated more emphatically (*fff*) by all four instruments at the end of the movement. Finally, the first violin presents another phrase in mm. 12–14 while the lower three instruments engage in stretto. This phrase recurs in mm. 18–21, where the lower three instruments again repeat a three-note pattern in overlapping fashion.

Our analysis of texture leads to the discovery of the melodic relations summarized in Ex. 14–12. Here, as in Ex. 9–7 (p. 155), motives are vertically aligned to reveal their pitch contour. In Ex. 14–12, column a contains two- or three-note motives that move in one direction by large intervals; column b contains motives with a zig-zag contour, while column c includes motives with a unidirectional contour and smaller melodic intervals.

Example 14–12. Motivic relations in Webern's Op. 5, No. 3 (Motives are played *arco* unless otherwise indicated)

Before we begin to isolate sets in this piece, let's review what we know about its structure.

- The piece consists of a relatively few melodic ideas, most of which are quite brief (from 2 to 7 notes).
- It also has several distinctive textural combinations.
- The ostinato figures (in mm. 1–6 and 15–21) provide continuity, but there are few additional examples of repetition.
- Overlapping imitation (stretto) is used to develop melodic motives and integrate polyphonic textures. In most cases, the motives are related by pitch transposition, but inversion is used in m. 7. In a few cases, Webern displaced pitches to stay within the range of an instrument. These motives are related by pc transposition.
- Some textural combinations recur during the movement. For example, imitative passages provide an "accompaniment" to the first violin melody in mm. 12–14 and 18–21.

- Melodic ideas recur with varying degrees of exactness (see Exx. 14–11 and 14–12):
  —literal repetition—a1 & mm. 1–3
  —exact transposition—a2 & a3, b1 & b2, c2 & c3
  —transposed inversion—c4 & c5
  —transposed retrograde—b4 & b5
  —free transposition—a1 & a2, b3 & b4
  —free inversion—c1 & c2
  —lengthening or shortening—a3 & a4, b2 & b3
  —free paraphrase (first violin, mm. 12–14 & 18–21)
- Webern used a wide range of dynamic levels and styles of playing for such a brief piece. These lend further variety to the music and conceal similarities between motives.

As you can see, we already know a lot. With this knowledge at hand, we can probe more deeply using the tools of pc set analysis.

Stage 1: Parsing the Musical Score

As before, Stage 1 involves parsing, or segmenting, the score to isolate sets. In compiling Ex. 14–12 we isolated and labeled nearly all of the melodic ideas in the movement. We should also identify the harmonic trichords played by the two violins and viola in mm. 1–8. Example 14–13 has these trichords notated and labeled.

Example 14–13. Vertical trichords in mm. 1–8

Stage 2: Normalizing the Sets

Table 14–5 is provided for the purpose of normalizing the unordered pc sets. In completing it you will need to refer to Exx. 14–12 and 14–13.

Stage 3: Tabulation and Additional Set Analysis

Stage 3 involves tabulating the various set-types using Table 14–2 as your model. Here, however, you should tabulate how many times the various trichordal set-types occur in each of the larger sets. As you discovered in completing Table 14–5, the five larger sets represent only three T_n/T_nI-types. Since only a few trichord types are represented in this movement, the template provided as Table 14–6 should be sufficient.

Stage 4: Interpreting the Findings

As Tables 14–5 and 14–6 should reveal, [0,1,4] is the most abundant set-type in this piece. In fact, it permeates Webern's movement more extensively than Schoenberg's excerpt. All of the vertical trichords in mm. 1–8 are instances of [0,1,4], as are several of the melodic trichords. Measure 6 is especially interesting because Webern realized [0,1,4] both melodically and harmonically. Ex. 14–14 shows how three simultaneous statements of motive c.2 form three successive vertical trichords. All six of these sets are instances of [0,1,4]. Finally, [0,1,4] is an abstract subset of two of the three larger set-types in this piece (see Table 14–6).

[0,1,2] occurs as the first three notes of motive b6 (see Ex. 14–12). This motive recurs as part of the emphatic unison statement that ends the movement (see Ex. 14–11, m. 22, last three notes). Furthermore, [0,1,2] is abundant as an abstract subset of each of the three larger set-types.

[0,1,5] does not occur as frequently as [0,1,4], but it is still used as the final three notes of motive b.2 and its T_n-related counterpart in m. 23. Furthermore, it appears in the T_nI-related motives that interrupt the texture of mm. 1–6 (see Ex. 14–12, motives c4 and c5). (How many instances of [0,1,5] can you find there?)

Schoenberg's Op. 11, No. 1 and Webern's Op. 5, No. 3 are classic examples of free atonality, but each retains traces of functional tonality. In Ex. 14–10 we saw how Schoenberg used [0,2,6], a subset of the dominant-seventh chord type, but avoided resolutions that would imply a tonal center. He also ended phrases A and A′ with melodic figures that resemble suspensions (see Ex. 14–7). Suspension and appoggiatura figures are less apparent in Webern's piece, primarily because of its tempo and texture.

More relevant to the issue of tonality is the $C\sharp_2$ ostinato in the cello (mm. 1–6) and the emphatic ending on $C\sharp$. Webern also presented the two most expansive melodic phrases twice, once in each section (Ex. 14–11, first violin, mm. 9–10 and 22–23, mm. 12–14 and 18–21). The phrase played by the first violin in mm. 9–10 is restated at T_5 (a perfect fourth higher or perfect fifth lower) by all four instruments in mm. 22–23. The phrase played *arco* by the first violin in mm. 12–14 recurs in extended form in mm. 17–21; the second statement begins a perfect fifth lower than

TABLE 14–5.   Normalization and classification of unordered pc sets in Webern's Op. 5, No. 3

a. harmonic trichords (see Ex. 14–13)

Set	Normal form	T_n-type	T_nI-type	Forte name	IC vector
a					
b					
c					
d					
e					
f					
g					
h					
i					
j					
k					
l					
m					

b. melodic motives (see Ex. 14–12)

Set	Normal form	T_n-type	T_nI-type	Forte name	IC vector
a1	{10,2}	(0,4)	(0,4)	2-4	<0,0,0,1,0,0>
a2	{6,7}	(0,1)	(0,1)	2-1	<1,0,0,0,0,0>
a3	{11,0}	(0,1)	(0,1)	2-1	<1,0,0,0,0,0>
a4					
a5					
b1					
b2					
b3					
b4					
b5					
b6					
c1					
c2					
c3					
c4					
c5					

TABLE 14-6. **Trichordal set-types as abstract subsets of larger set-types in Webern's Op. 5, No. 3**

T_n/T_nI-types of the larger sets are listed at the top of columns 2–4. List the T_n/T_nI-types of the three most abundant trichordal sets at the left of rows 2–4. Then determine the multiplicity of each trichordal type in each larger set. Use Ex. 14–4b as your model.

	5-5 [0,1,2,3,7]	6-22 [0,1,2,4,6,8]	7-14 [0,1,2,3,5,7,8]

Example 14-14. Simultaneous melodic and harmonic realizations of [0, 1, 4]

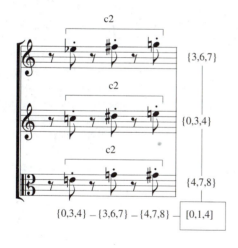

the first. If we correlate this evidence with aspects of tempo and texture cited above, we begin to realize that this movement could be regarded as a paraphrase of a continuous binary form. It divides into two main sections, begins and ends with the same focal pc (C♯), and presents the same two melodic phrases in each section. The second statement of each phrase is a perfect fifth lower than the first.

Finally, note that both Schoenberg and Webern used "nearly whole-tone" collections prominently (see Ex. 14–3). In Schoenberg's Op. 11 excerpt (see Table 14–1), sets m.2, m.3, m.10, m.11, x.1, and y contain either a 3-pc or 4-pc subset of

[0,2,4,6,8,10], the whole-tone set-type. In Webern's movement, the most prominent "nearly whole-tone" set is set b.1 in Ex. 14–12. (Which whole-tone collection does it imply? Which pc does not belong to that collection?)

SUMMARY

Properties of Free Atonality

Composers of free atonality preferred pitch combinations that do not occur within a diatonic collection. In the analyses above we discovered trichord types [0,1,2] and [0,1,4] and tetrachords (0,1,4,5), [0,1,4,6], and [0,1,6,7]. Each of these sets contains at least one instance of ic 1 and/or ic 6 (see Tables 14–1 and 14–5). Atonal composers also used whole-tone or "nearly whole-tone" hexachords, as well as other combinations. When using subsets of a diatonic collection, they preferred less stable combinations, such as [0,2,6] (also a whole-tone subset) and avoided tonal implications by "resolving" those sets in nontraditional ways (see Ex. 14–10).

To compensate for the absence of tonality, these composers resorted to other integrative devices, notably canonic imitation and motivic development. They used literal repetition, but only for ostinato patterns or within points of imitation. They also compensated by relying upon a text. The repertoire of free atonality includes several collections of songs, many based on the poetry of Stefan George, as well as other texted works. Instrumental works of the atonal repertoire are typically shorter and more introverted than the huge symphonies and orchestral tone poems of the Post-Romantic era. Robert Morgan has noted that Webern's entire compositional output, which comprises thirty-one opus numbers, requires less playing time than single compositions of some other composers (e.g., Richard Strauss or Gustav Mahler).[4] Some of the shortest atonal pieces can be found in Schoenberg's Op. 19 (Six Little Piano Pieces) and Webern's Op. 11 (Three Little Pieces for Cello and Piano).

Analysis of Free Atonality

Set theory is useful for discovering relations between sets of pitches or pitch classes and for correlating these discoveries with other aspects, notably form and texture. To make such discoveries, we must first parse a musical passage into sets, and to do this, we must become well acquainted with its sound and formal structure. Since the outcome of this stage influences that of later stages, we must exercise good musical judgment, making sure that each set can be heard as a distinct and perceptible element of the musical fabric.

Once sets have been isolated, they can be compared in numerous ways. The following is a concise summary.

---

[4]Robert P. Morgan, *Twentieth-Century Music* (New York: W. W. Norton, 1991), p. 80.

Relationships between sets of equal cardinality
  Ordered pitch sets
    Compare melodic motives and lines for
      T_n equivalence (identical pitch contour)
      T_nI equivalence (mirror-related pitch contour)
  Unordered pitch sets
    Compare harmonic intervals and chords for
      T_n equivalence (identical spacing)
      T_nI equivalence (mirror-related spacing)
  Ordered pc sets
    Compare melodic motives for
      T_n equivalence
      T_nI equivalence
  Unordered pc sets
    Compare all sets for
      T_n equivalence (same T_n-type)
      T_nI equivalence (different T_n-type, but same T_n/T_nI-type)
  Common subsets (sets share all but one or two elements)

Relationships between sets of differing cardinality
  Literal subsets
    pitches
    pcs
  Abstract subsets
    pcs

    Set theory is a useful analytical tool, but like all tools, it has limitations. Lerdahl has enumerated six:

1. It provides no criteria for segmenting a musical surface into sets.
2. It does not acknowledge varying degrees of structural prominence and analytical connections among the pitches in a set.
3. Its criteria for equivalence and similarity among sets *may not* be psychologically valid.
4. Theoretical descriptions of pitch-class and interval-class content do not seem to explain how we perceive atonal music in real-time listening experiences.
5. Set-theoretical relations are associational in nature. In contrast, tonal theory is mostly concerned with hierarchical relations among pitches, intervals, and chords. Psychologists have shown that hierarchical structuring is crucial for learning and memory in practically any domain, including music.
6. Set theory could be linked more closely with tonal theory in order to explicate the large body of 20th-century music that lies between the extremes of diatonic tonality and chromatic atonality (the repertoire that we have termed neotonality).[5]

---

[5]Fred Lerdahl, "Atonal Prologational Structure," *Contemporary Music Review* 4 (1989): 66–67. In this article Lerdahl suggests modifications to his Generative Theory of Tonal Music that make it useful for the atonal idiom. He demonstrates how the modified theory might be applied to three atonal excerpts including the opening measures of Schoenberg's Piano Piece, Op. 11, No. 1.

These limitations have prompted Lerdahl and other theorists to continue studying atonal music and the listening process with the goal of developing even more appropriate and powerful tools for analysis.

RECOMMENDED LISTENING AND ANALYSIS

Bartók, *Makrokosmos,* VI/144 "Minor Seconds, Major Sevenths" (Morgan)

Berg, Four Songs, Op. 2 (c. 1908–1910) (No. 2 in Burkhart, No. 3 in Wen20, No. 4 in Simms and Wen20; No. 4 is mislabeled as No. 3 in Turek)

———, Five Orchestral Songs, Op. 4 (1912) (Nos. 2 and 5 in Morgan)

———, Four Pieces for Clarinet and Piano, Op. 5 (1913) (No. 2 in DeLio-Smith)

———, *Wozzeck,* Op. 7 (1917–1921) (Act III, Scene 3. in Palisca; Act III, Scenes 4 & 5 in Kamien)

Ives, 114 Songs; "The Cage" (Burkhart); "From Paracelsus" (Simms)

Schoenberg, Three Piano Pieces, Op. 11 (1908) (No. 1 in Burkhart)

———, *The Book of the Hanging Gardens,* Op. 15 (1908); (No. 6 in Arlin)

———, Five Pieces for Orchestra, Op. 16 (1909); (Nos. 1 and 2 in Kamien; Nos. 1 & 5 in Morgan; No. 3 in Burkhart)

———, Six Little Piano Pieces, Op. 19 (1911) (Nos. 2, 4, & 6 in Wen20; No. 6 in DeLio-Smith and Turek)

———, *Pierrot Lunaire,* Op. 21 (1912) (Nos. 1 and 8 in WenAMSS; No. 7 in DeLio-Smith; No. 8 in Turek)

Webern, Five Pieces for String Quartet, Op. 5 (1909) (No. 1 in Wen20; No. 2 in Arlin; No. 3 in Turek & WenAMSS; No. 4 in Burkhart)

———, Six Pieces for Orchestra, Op. 6 (1909) (No. 1 in Wen20)

———, Six Bagatelles for String Quartet, Op. 9 (1913) (No. 1 in Godwin)

———, Five Pieces for Small Orchestra, Op. 10 (1913) (Nos. 3 & 4 in Kamien)

———, Three Little Pieces for Cello and Piano, Op. 11 (1914) (No. 3 in DeLio-Smith)

CHAPTER 15

Serialism

Fundamentals of Serial Composition

In the early 1920s, Arnold Schoenberg devised a "method for composition with twelve tones which are related only with one another." This technique has since come to be known as the *12-tone, dodecaphonic,* or *serial* method. The term *serial* indicates the presentation and manipulation of a predetermined *series, row,* or *set* of musical elements, usually twelve pitch classes. We'll begin by examining some of the more conventional modes of presentation.

Linear Presentation

Example 15–1 shows the beginning of Schoenberg's Fourth String Quartet. The texture of mm. 1–6 is homophonic with the first violin stating the melody and the other instruments providing chordal accompaniment. Schoenberg indicated that the first violin is the leading part by enclosing its notes within the symbols H⁻ and ¬. (The H⁻ stands for *Haupstimme,* the German term for principal voice.)

The first violin phrase can be reduced to an ordered pitch set by eliminating its repeated pitches. From these we can form an ordered set, or series, of pitch classes as shown in Ex. 15–2a. Notice that these pcs are numbered with reference to D, and that the entire set is labeled P_0 to indicate that it is the transposition of the *prime* form, which begins with pc zero. Ordered and unordered pc interval patterns are shown above and below the staff.

The next melodic statement occurs in mm. 6–9 of the second violin part. Example 15–2b shows a set derived from this line. Comparison of ordered interval patterns for sets *a* and *b* reveals that their corresponding intervals are complementary. These sets are, therefore, T_nI-related. Their interval of transposition can be found by adding any pair of corresponding pcs. Using the first pc of each set, we would get $0 + 5 = 5$. Since set *a* is the P_0 form, set *b* is the I_5 form, the inversion transposed by interval 5. The relationship between these two forms can be expressed as $T_5I(a) = b$.

The third melodic phrase (beginning in the first violin with the upbeat to m. 10) presents the P_0 form in reverse order. It can, therefore, be labeled RP_0 (the retrograde of P_0), as shown in Ex. 15–2c. Be sure to write in the numbers for the pitch classes and various types of intervals.

The retrograde operation can be applied to any I form to produce an RI (retrograde inversion) form. The staff in Ex. 15–2d has been left blank for you to notate

Example 15–1. Schoenberg, Fourth String Quartet, first movement, mm. 1–15.

Example 15–2. Basic set forms of Schoenberg's Fourth String Quartet

a. P₀ (compare Example 15–1, violin 1, mm. 1–6)

ip⟨a,b⟩:	-1	-4	+1	+7	-2	+1	+8	-4	-1	-1	+5
pcs:	0	11	7	8	3	1	2	10	6	5	4	9
ipc⟨a,b⟩:	11	8	1	7	10	1	8	8	11	11	5
ipc(a,b):	1	4	1	5	2	1	4	4	1	1	5

b. I₅ (compare Example 15–1, violin 2, mm. 6–9)

ip⟨a,b⟩:	+1	+4	-1	+5	-10	-1	+4	+4	-11	+25	-17
pcs:	5	6	10	9	2	4	3	7	11	0	1	8
ipc⟨a,b⟩:	1	4	11	5	2	11	4	4	1	1	7
ipc(a,b):	1	4	1	5	2	1	4	4	1	1	5

c. RP₀ (compare Example 15–1, violin 1, mm. 10–15) (to be completed)

ip⟨a,b⟩:

pcs:

ipc⟨a,b⟩:

ipc(a,b):

d. RI₅ (to be completed)

ip⟨a,b⟩:

pcs:

ipc⟨a,b⟩:

ipc(a,b):

the RI_5 form by writing the pitches of I_5 in reverse order. When you have finished, number the pitches and pcs and compute the various interval patterns.

To summarize, three basic operations (T_n, I, and R) can be applied to the prime form of an ordered set, or series, to produce four types of set forms. Each form is identified by a one- or two-letter label (P, I, RP, or RI) followed by a subscript that indicates the index of transposition. Thus,

$$P_n \quad = \quad T_n(P_0)$$
$$I_n \quad = \quad T_n I(P_0)$$
$$RP_n \quad = \quad T_n R(P_0)$$
$$RI_n \quad = \quad T_n RI(P_0)$$

Figure 15–1 illustrates the symmetrical relations between various set forms. Its dotted lines represent axes of symmetry. Pitches of Schoenberg's P_0 form (Ex. 15–2a) are plotted in the upper-left quadrant. The other quadrants contain its mirror images as reflected along the horizontal (inversional) and/or vertical (retrograde) axes. Actually, this figure oversimplifies because it represents serial operations at the *pitch* level. In 12-tone music those operations occur more typically at the *pitch class* level.

Vertical Presentation

Schoenberg contended that set forms could be presented in various ways: horizontally as motives and phrases, vertically as chords, homophonically as a melody with chordal accompaniment, or polyphonically as two or more lines. We have already seen an example of linear set presentation.

The vertical mode is illustrated in Ex. 15–3. Schoenberg segmented the basic set of this work into three tetrachords that he presented in m. 1. We cannot infer the exact order of the twelve pcs from this excerpt, but we can acknowledge the intervallic structure of each tetrachord (as shown by the numbers within the rectangles) and the order in which those chords are presented. That information can be used to identify the set form in m. 2. Underlying brackets (in Ex. 15–3) reveal *retrograde symmetry,* while the crossed diagonal lines show that R-related chords have I-related interval structures. From this we can deduce that if m. 1 contains the P_0 form, then m. 2 contains an RI form. In other words, m. 1 is presented upside down, backward, and transposed in m. 2.

In Ex. 15–4, from the Fourth Quartet, we can see that Schoenberg formed a chordal accompaniment from the four discrete trichords of the basic set. He presented the P_0 form both melodically and harmonically, but was careful to avoid duplicating pcs between these two textural elements. Notice, for example, that a given melodic trichord is never accompanied by the same harmonic trichord.

Polyphonic Presentation

Composers often present two or more sets, series, or row forms simultaneously. This technique is ideally suited for polyphonic textures. We have already seen

| **Figure 15–1.** | **Symmetrical relations between the forms of an ordered 12-pc set (compare Example 15–2)** |

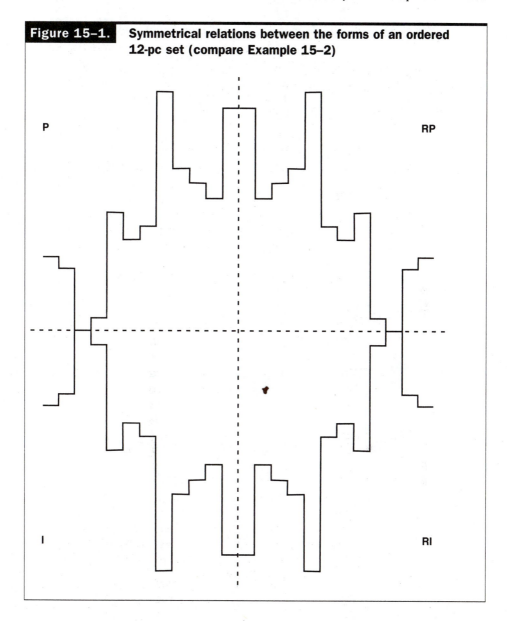

canonic imitation in pre-serial atonal works such as Webern's Op. 5, No. 3 (see Exx. 14–11 and 12, pp. 264–67). Webern continued to explore canonic writing even more rigorously in his 12-tone works. The second movement of his Variations for Piano, Op. 27 (see Ex. 15–8, p. 290) is canonic throughout. The succession of row forms is determined by *elision* as Webern begins a succeeding row form with the last pc of the preceding form.

Example 15–3.   Schoenberg, Piano Piece, Op. 33a, mm. 1–2*

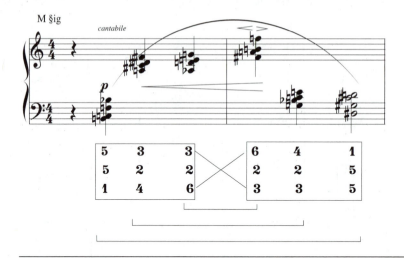

*Schoenberg's notation has been altered slightly to facilitate score reading.

Example 15–4.   Presentation of linear and vertical trichords in Schoenberg's Fourth Quartet (compare Example 15–1)†

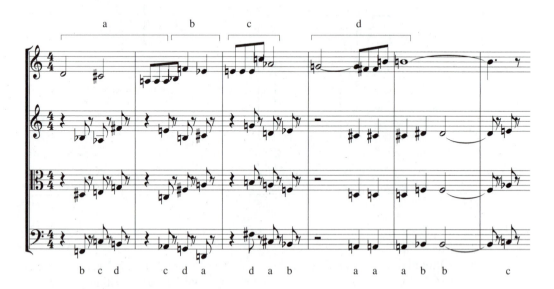

†Gary E. Wittlich, "Sets and Ordering Procedures in Twentieth-Century Music," in *Aspects of Twentieth-Century Music*, edited by Gary E. Wittlich (Englewood Cliffs, NJ: Prentice-Hall, 1975), Ex. 6–15, p. 410.

Matrix of Set Forms

Interpreting a Matrix

It is customary to list all 48 forms of the basic set in a matrix or "magic square." Figure 15–2 shows the matrix for Luigi Dallapiccola's *Quaderno musicale di Annalibera (Musical Notebook for* [his daughter] *Annalibera)*, a collection of eleven piano pieces, all based on the same 12-pc set. P and RP forms are listed in the rows of the matrix, while I and RI forms are listed in the columns. A given row form can be identified by its letter name followed by a subscript that indicates its index of transposition, for example, P_3, I_8, RP_2, RI_7. Note that P and I forms are indexed by their *first* pc, but RP and RI forms are indexed by their *last* pc, which is the first pc of the corresponding P or I form. Thus, the top row when read from right to left is called RP_0, and the left column when read from bottom to top is called RI_0. Specific pcs can be designated by their set form and *order number*, for example, P_3, order no. 5. Note that R-related forms share the same set of order numbers. Thus, P_0 has order number 0 as its *first* pc, but R_0 has order number 0 as its *last* pc. Likewise, I_0 *begins* with order number 0, while RI_0 *ends* with order number 0.

Computing a Matrix

To compute a matrix, we must first identify the P_0 form of the set. This form is often presented melodically at or near the beginning of the work (see Exx. 15–1 and 2). Some pieces, however, begin with a succession of chords (see Ex. 15–3) or with melody-accompaniment texture. In such cases, we must either look further for a linear presentation or infer the basic set from a combination of linear and/or vertical statements. For the present, we'll assume that the P_0 form is at hand and concentrate on computing its matrix.

As Figure 15–2 illustrates, the cells of a matrix may contain pc letter names or pc integers. Because serial operations are arithmetical, it is most efficient to use integers during the computation process. If letter names are preferred, they can be derived from the corresponding cells of the integer matrix.

A blank matrix form is provided for use in the following exercise (Fig. 15–3). Its rows and columns are labeled with order numbers. References to specific cells can be made in row/column format; for example, r3/c2 indicates the intersection of row 3 and column 2. Before beginning your work make several copies of this form for use in computing matrices for other sets.

To compute a **prime-by-inversion matrix:**

1. Write the pc numbers of the P_0 form from left to right in row 0. It is imperative that this form begin on pc zero. Indicate the letter name of pc zero in the blank provided.
2. Compute the I_0 form and write its numbers from top to bottom in column 0. I_0 begins with pc zero, which you will have already listed in cell r0/c0. Cell r1/c0 will contain

continued

Figure 15–2. **Matrix of set forms**

Composer: Dallapiccola
Work: *Quaderno musicale di Annalibera*
Reference pc: A$^{\sharp}$/B$^{\flat}$ = 0

		P 0	1	2	3	4	5	6	7	8	9	10	**R** 11		
I	0	0	1	5	8	10	4	3	7	9	2	11	6	0	**I**
	1	11	0	4	7	9	3	2	6	8	1	10	5	1	
	2	7	8	0	3	5	11	10	2	4	9	6	1	2	
	3	4	5	9	0	2	8	7	11	1	6	3	10	3	
	4	2	3	7	10	0	6	5	9	11	4	1	8	4	
	5	8	9	1	4	6	0	11	3	5	10	7	2	5	
	6	9	10	2	5	7	1	0	4	6	11	8	3	6	
	7	5	6	10	1	3	9	8	0	2	7	4	11	7	
	8	3	4	8	11	1	7	6	10	0	5	2	9	8	
	9	10	11	3	6	8	2	1	5	7	0	9	4	9	
	10	1	2	6	9	11	5	4	8	10	3	0	7	10	
RI	11	6	7	11	2	4	10	9	1	3	8	5	0	11	**RI**
		0 **P**	1	2	3	4	5	6	7	8	9	10	11 **R**		

---

the inverse mod 12 of the value in cell r0/c1; cell r2/c0 will contain the inverse of the value in cell r0/c2, etc.

3. Compute the remaining P forms by transposing P_0 by the appropriate interval. This interval will always equal the pc number in column 0 of a given row. Thus, to complete row 1, transpose P_0 by the value in cell r1/c0; to complete row 2, transpose P_0 by the value in cell r2/c0, etc.

4. Proofread your work by checking to see that there is only one instance of each pc number in each row and column. As a further test, make sure that the matrix has a diagonal of zeros running from cell r0/c0 through cell r11/c11.

The Compositional Process

Schoenberg noted that he began to compose a 12-tone work by inventing a melodic idea, usually one that contained all twelve pcs, such as the opening first violin phrase

Figure 15–2.	*Continued*

		P 0	1	2	3	4	5	6	7	8	9	10	**RP** 11		
I	0	A♯/B♭	B	D♯/E♭	F♯/G♭	G♯/A♭	D	C♯/D♭	F	G	C	A	E	0	**I**
	1	A	A♯/B♭	D	F	G	C♯/D♭	C	E	F♯/G♭	B	G♯/A♭	D♯/E♭	1	
	2	F	F♯/G♭	A♯/B♭	C♯/D♭	D♯/E♭	A	G♯/A♭	C	D	G	E	B	2	
	3	D	D♯/E♭	G	A♯/B♭	C	F♯/G♭	F	A	B	E	C♯/D♭	G♯/A♭	3	
	4	C	C♯/D♭	F	G♯/A♭	A♯/B♭	E	D♯/E♭	G	A	D	B	F♯/G♭	4	
	5	F♯/G♭	G	B	D	E	A♯/B♭	A	C♯/D♭	D♯/E♭	G♯/A♭	F	C	5	
	6	G	G♯/A♭	C	D♯/E♭	F	B	A♯/B♭	D	E	A	F♯/G♭	C♯/D♭	6	
	7	D♯/E♭	E	G♯/A♭	B	C♯/D♭	G	F♯/G♭	A♯/B♭	C	F	D	A	7	
	8	C♯/D♭	D	F♯/G♭	A	B	F	E	G♯/A♭	A♯/B♭	D♯/E♭	C	G	8	
	9	G♯/A♭	A	C♯/D♭	E	F♯/G♭	C	B	D♯/E♭	F	A♯/B♭	G	D	9	
	10	B	C	E	G	A	D♯/E♭	D	F♯/G♭	G♯/A♭	C♯/D♭	A♯/B♭	F	10	
RI	11	E	F	A	C	D	G♯/A♭	G	B	C♯/D♭	F♯/G♭	D♯/E♭	A♯/B♭	11	**RI**
		P 0	1	2	3	4	5	6	7	8	9	10	**RP** 11		

of Ex. 15–1. He then reduced this line to an ordered pc set (although he did not use that precise term), subjected the set to serial operations to produce additional forms, and, typically, divided those forms into smaller segments. To develop his idea, Schoenberg "realized" these set forms and segments to produce melodic motives and phrases, chords, accompaniment figures, and contrapuntal lines. In doing so, he made numerous choices about note duration, repetition, registration, articulation, melodic contour, chord spacing, and texture. From this summary it is evident that Schoenberg considered set *realization* to be the crux of the serial composition process. To underscore its importance, he predicted that

> *The time will come when the ability to draw thematic material from a basic set of twelve tones will be an unconditional prerequisite for obtaining admission into the composition class of a conservatory.*[1]

Experts may disagree as to whether Schoenberg's prediction has been fulfilled, but they would probably agree that the serial method is an important compositional technique.

---

[1] *Style and Idea,* p. 226.

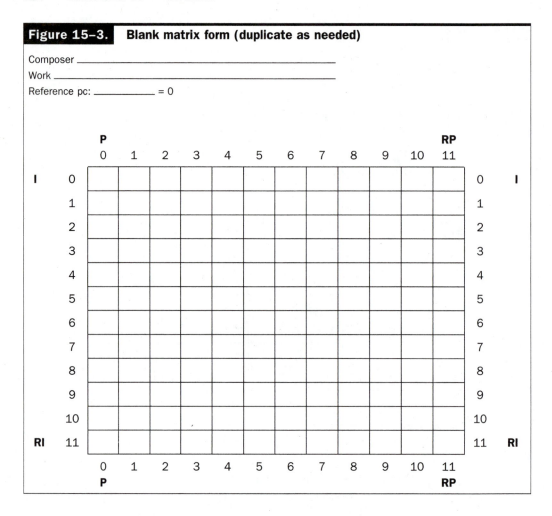

Figure 15–3. Blank matrix form (duplicate as needed)

Composer _____

Work _____

Reference pc: _____ = 0

Properties of 12-pc Sets

Interval Patterns

The distinctive quality of an ordered 12-pc set is determined by the interval pattern of its prime form and the patterns of its I, RP, and RI forms.

Ordered pc Intervals Since set forms are related by serial operations, their interval patterns are related, as well. The most obvious relationship occurs among sets related by transposition. These would include any pair of sets sharing the same label: P, I, RP, or RI. As you know from Chapter Three, T-related sets have the same ordered interval pattern. If related by pitch transposition (T^p_n), they have identical ordered pitch interval patterns *and* identical ordered pc interval patterns. If related only by pc transposition (T_n), their ordered pc interval patterns will match, but their pitch interval patterns will differ.

Deeper relationships exist between R-, I-, and RI-related forms, and these can be a bit puzzling at first glance. Table 15-1 lists the ordered pc interval patterns for the set forms of Schoenberg's Fourth Quartet. By comparing these patterns we can see that:

- I-related forms (P and I, RP and RI) have I-related interval patterns
- R-related forms (P and RP, I and RI) have RI-related interval patterns
- RI-related forms (P and RI, I and RP) have R-related interval patterns

The first observation makes sense, but the last two are a bit puzzling. It would seem that R-related forms should have R-related patterns, and RI-related forms should have RI-related patterns. Why is that not so? A bit of thought should reveal that the answer has something to do with the retrograde operation, since R is the factor that RP and RI have in common, and the one that distinguishes them from I. So let's consider the effect of an R operation upon a set's interval pattern.

When a set is retrograded, the order of its elements (pitches or pcs) is reversed, and so is the order of its intervals. Reversing the position of any two elements changes the direction of the interval that they form, and reversing the direction of an interval is the same as inverting it. To illustrate, consider the first interval in the P_0 form of Schoenberg's set (Ex. 15-2a). When pc 0 is followed by 11, ipc<0,11> = $11 - 0 = 11$, but if these pcs are reversed (as in Ex. 15-2c) ipc<11,0> = $0 - 11 = 1$. This explains why R-related forms have RI-related interval patterns. The R operation reverses the position of each interval within the pattern, but it also reverses the *direction* of each interval.

But what about the third observation: that RI-related forms have R-related interval patterns? In this case, applying RI to a P form is the same as applying I and then R. We already know that I inverts intervals, and that R both retrogrades and inverts them. Therein lies the explanation. R inverts intervals that have already been inverted by I, thus canceling out the effect of I and leaving the intervals "right side up" but in reverse order.

All 12-pc sets have the same pc content, but they differ considerably in terms of interval pattern. Some sets have been carefully arranged to contain one instance of each interval. These are designated as *all-interval sets*. Others exhibit less variety, with certain intervals occurring more than once and others missing altogether.

Unordered pc Intervals (Interval Classes)   Unordered pc interval patterns for Schoenberg's set forms are listed in Table 15–2. Notice that when a set's intervals are conceived at this more abstract level, there are only two distinct patterns: one

TABLE 15–1.   Ordered pc interval patterns for the set forms of Schoenberg's Fourth Quartet (compare Ex. 15–2)

P	11	8	1	7	10	1	8	8	11	11	5
I	1	4	11	5	2	11	4	4	1	1	7
RP	7	1	1	4	4	11	2	5	11	4	1
RI	5	11	11	8	8	1	10	7	1	8	11

for the P and I forms and another for the RP and RI forms. (How are these two patterns related?)

Table 15–3 shows how many times the various interval classes occur in the set for Schoenberg's Fourth Quartet. This table resembles an ic vector for an unordered set, except that it lists only those intervals formed by adjacent pcs. Here we can see that Schoenberg's set is abundant in ic 1 and void of ics 3 and 6. A glance back at Table 15–2 reveals, furthermore, that its most abundant ics are distributed unevenly; every set form has two consecutive instances of ics 1 and 4.

Subsets

Ordered 12-pc sets are often segmented into smaller sets that can be normalized as unordered sets. A large set may be parsed into *discrete subsets* or *overlapping subsets*. Example 15–4 shows discrete trichords in the basic set of Schoenberg's Fourth Quartet.

Example 15–5a shows the "all-interval" set on which Berg based his first 12-tone work, the 1925 setting of "Schliesse mir" (see Ex. 1–7, p. 12). Berg's song served as a preliminary study for a longer and more complex work, his six-movement *Lyric Suite* for string quartet. The opening phrase of that work is quoted in Ex. 15–5b. Its set can be segmented into two discrete hexachords, each of which is an instance of [0 2 4 5 7 9], the so-called *diatonic hexachord,* as shown in Ex. 15–5c. Those pitch classes can be rearranged to form a segment of interval cycle 5/7 (see Ex. 15–5d). In studying this example, be aware that the note heads in Ex. 15–5a and b represent pitches, whereas those in c and d represent pitch classes.

Webern also preferred rows that could be parsed into discrete subsets of the same type. The basic set of his Concerto for Nine Instruments, Op. 24 can be seen in Ex. 15–6. (The opening measures were shown in Ex. 5–1, p. 80) This series is

TABLE 15–2.   Unordered pc interval patterns (interval classes) for the set forms of Schoenberg's Fourth Quartet (compare Ex. 15–2)

P	1	4	1	5	2	1	4	4	1	1	5
I	1	4	1	5	2	1	4	4	1	1	5
RP	5	1	1	4	4	1	2	5	1	4	1
RI	5	1	1	4	4	1	2	5	1	4	1

TABLE 15–3.   Multiplicity of interval classes in the set forms of Schoenberg's Fourth Quartet

Interval class	1	2	3	4	5	6
Multiplicity	5	1	0	3	2	0

Example 15-5*

a. Basic set of Berg's "Schliesse mir die Augen beide" (1925) (compare Example 1–10, p. 16)

b. Opening violin phrase from Berg's *Lyric Suite,* first movement

c. Instances of the diatonic hexachord in Berg's set

d. Reordering of pcs within diatonic hexachords to form segments of interval cycle 5/7 (compare Figure 1–3, p. 9)

*Douglas Jarman, *The Music of Alban Berg* (Berkeley: University of California Press, 1979), Exx. 106 and 107, pp. 82–83.

especially interesting because its trichordal subsets are related as both ordered sets and unordered sets. The term *derived set* is often used to denote an ordered 12-pc set that can parsed into discrete subsets that are related to a "generator set," and to each other, by serial operations. In this case, trichords *b, c,* and *d* can be "generated" by applying serial operations to trichord *a.*

$$b = \mathrm{T_7RI}(a)$$
$$c = \mathrm{T_6R}(a)$$
$$d = \mathrm{T_1I}(a)$$

Example 15–6.   **Discrete trichordal subsets in the P_0 form of Webern's Concerto for Nine Instruments, Op. 24**

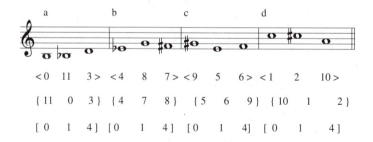

```
        a               b               c               d
```

< 0	11	3 >	< 4	8	7 >	< 9	5	6 >	< 1	2	10 >
{ 11	0	3 }	{ 4	7	8 }	{ 5	6	9 }	{ 10	1	2 }
[0	1	4]	[0	1	4]	[0	1	4]	[0	1	4]

As the bottom row of the example indicates, each trichord is an instance of T_n/T_nI-type [0 1 4], a particular favorite of Schoenberg and Webern (see Chapter Fourteen).

Invariance

The term *invariance* denotes a property that remains unchanged when a musical element is transformed by a certain operation. The most familiar types of invariance occur under transposition and inversion. A transposed set has the same *ordered* interval pattern as the original set (see Ex. 15–7a). An inverted set has the same *unordered* interval pattern (Ex. 15–7b). We could say, therefore, that a set's ordered interval pattern is invariant under T_n, and that its unordered interval pattern is invariant under T_nI.

Unordered sets also have invariant properties. Their interval-class and subset-type content remains invariant under T_n or T_nI. Finally, the pc content of symmetrical sets remains invariant under T_n or T_nI for certain values of n (Ex. 15–7c).

Composers may wish to know whether pcs that are adjacent in one set form will remain adjacent if the set undergoes various serial operations. This information may influence the choice of successive set forms. For example, Schoenberg may have chosen I_5 for the second violin phrase (see Ex. 15–1) because it is the only I form that presents D-C$\sharp$-A, the first trichord of P_0, in retrograde order. This enabled him to link the three phrases of this expository passage. The D-C$\sharp$-A trichord occurs in its P form at the beginning of the first phrase (m. 1), in its R form within the second phrase (m. 8), and again in its R form at the end of the third phrase (mm. 13–14).

Composers also rely upon invariant properties when selecting set forms to be presented simultaneously. The second movement of Webern's Variations for Piano, Op. 27 is famous for its pairing of T_nI-related set forms whose corresponding pcs lie equidistant from an axis. From Ex. 15–8 we can see that Webern consistently selected a pair whose index numbers sum to zero mod 12: P_{11} and I_1, P_6 and I_6, I_0 and P_0, and I_8 and P_4.[2] As a result, the corresponding pcs are inversionally symmetrical

---

[2]The pcs have been numbered with reference to A so that the inversionally symmetrical aspects will be most apparent.

Example 15–7. **Examples of invariance**

a. ordered pc interval pattern invariant under T₄

pcs: < 5 8 4 11 3 >   < 9 0 8 3 7 >

ipc<a,b>: 3 8 7 4   3 8 7 4

b. unordered pc interval pattern invariant under T₀I

pcs: < 5 8 4 11 3 >   < 7 4 8 1 9 >

ipc(a,b): 3 4 5 4   3 4 5 4

c. pc content invariant under T₆

pcs: (4 5 10 11)   (10 11 4 5)

around A₄, and these same pcs remain paired throughout the movement. The pairing is shown below for P₁₁ and I₁.

	Hexachord A					||	**Hexachord B**				
P₁₁	G♯	A	F	G	E	F♯	C	C♯	D	B♭	B	D♯
I₁:	B♭	A	C♯	B	D	C	F♯	F	E	G♯	G	E♭
P₁₁:	11	0	8	10	7	9	3	4	5	1	2	6
I₁:	1	0	4	2	5	3	9	8	7	11	10	6
	0	0	0	0	0	0	0	0	0	0	0	0

Combinatoriality

Comparison of the corresponding hexachords (see above) reveals that they have only one pc in common. These common pcs occupy the same position within each hexachord and form unison vertical dyads (pc 0 in hexachord A, pc 6 in hexachord B) that recur throughout the movement. The remaining five pcs occur in the opposite hexachord of the I-related form. Thus, the opposite hexachords of P₁₁ and I₁ are nearly identical, while the corresponding hexachords are nearly exclusive.

Example 15–8. Webern, Variations for Piano, Op. 27, second movement

In his later 12-tone works, Schoenberg carried this principle one step further by combining set forms that have mutually exclusive hexachords. This technique, termed *combinatoriality,* enabled him to present two forms simultaneously without duplicating, and thus inadvertently emphasizing, a given pc. Example 15–9 shows a typical passage when combinatorial forms are stated in the first violin and cello from m. 73 to 78. The excerpt begins with the pairing of P_7 and I_0, then continues with RP_7 and RI_0. Schoenberg could have used other pairings, as well, since the same relationship exists between any two set forms that are related by T_5I, for example, P_1 and I_6, or RP_4 and RI_9. The same concern for avoiding octave duplication was seen earlier in Ex. 15–3, even though only one form was presented there. Theorists often use the term *aggregate* to denote an unordered collection of all twelve pcs.

Aural Perception of Serial Music

The fact that laymen and some musicians find serial music difficult to comprehend has been acknowledged by a number of writers. Meyer and Lerdahl, for example, contend in separate essays[3] that for music to be meaningful a listener must be able to deduce its hierarchical structure solely through listening. Lerdahl does not claim that listeners are unable to infer any structure whatsoever from serial music, but he does wonder why competent listeners do not hear tone rows.[4] He attributes this to the fact that serialism is a *permutational* rather than *elaborational* system of pitch organization. Pitch relations in elaborational systems are relatively easy to hear and remember; those generated through permutations are more difficult.

Lerdahl also notes that Schoenberg tried to "emancipate" dissonant intervals by freeing them from a need to resolve to consonant intervals. Though well-intentioned, this practice led Schoenberg and his followers to deny that intervals are intrinsically consonant or dissonant and, hence, to create "musical contexts that are not apprehended hierarchically."[5]

Finally, Lerdahl asserts that the system of pitch space induced by serial music does not correlate well with the mind's preferred methods of measuring distances between pitches. The distinction between steps and skips, our most fundamental criterion of intervallic size, is not reinforced in the structure of a 12-pc series. It is unclear, for example, whether a step in serial music should be regarded as the distance from one pc to the pc that lies a semitone above or below in the chromatic scale, or to the pc that lies before or after in the series. Because of this ambiguity, "The Listener . . . has difficulty locating a pitch as close to or far from another pitch."[6]

---

[3]See Meyer, *Music, The Arts, and Ideas,* Part III—Formalism in Music: Queries and Reservations; Fred Lerdahl, "Cognitive Constraints on Compositional Systems," in John A. Sloboda, ed., *Generative Processes in Music* (New York: Oxford University Press, 1988), pp. 231–259; Fred Lerdahl and Ray Jackendoff, *A Generative Theory of Tonal Music* (Cambridge: MIT Press, 1983), Section 11.6 "Remarks on Contemporary Music," pp. 296–301.

[4]Lerdahl based this contention on the results of an experiment described in Robert Francès, *The Perception of Music,* trans. W. Jay Dowling, Hillsdale, NJ: Lawrence Erlbaum, 1988, pp. 122–27.

[5]Lerdahl, "Cognitive Constraints," p. 254. See also William Thomson, *Schoenberg's Error* (Philadelphia: University of Pennsylvania Press, 1991), Chapter 6.

[6]"Cognitive Constraints," p. 254.

Example 15–9. Combinatoriality in Schoenberg's Fourth Quartet, first movement

a. mm. 71–79

Example 15–9. *Continued*

b. Combinatorial set forms I₀ (violin 1) and P₇ (cello)

Several researchers have devised experiments to test whether listeners can perceive serial operations. While a thorough review of their findings is not possible here, some general principles can be summarized.

1. Serial relations are more perceptible when musical units are smaller. Thus, relations between 3-, 4-, 5-, or 6-element sets are perceived more easily than those between larger sets.
2. Serial relations are more perceptible when pitches are presented slowly, and less perceptible at faster tempos.
3. Serial relations are more perceptible when other aspects, especially duration, are held constant.
4. Pitch relations are more perceptible than pitch-class relations, since the former preserve melodic contour.
5. T relations are more perceptible than I relations, which are more perceptible than RP relations, which are more perceptible than RI relations. RP and RI relations make especially high demands on short-term memory because they require the comparison of sounds heard most recently to those heard least recently.
6. When hearing a prime form and two variants, listeners are often unable to distinguish between the variant that preserves exact interval size and the one that preserves overall melodic contour but varies interval size.
7. With sufficient knowledge and exposure, listeners can develop strategies for hearing serial music on its own terms rather than those of functional tonality.

It is important to consider these findings when developing approaches for listening and score analysis. In particular, we should guard against the tendency to dwell on aspects of serial technique that can be seen but not heard. Knowledge of serial operations and set structure is useful, but other features may be more apparent and crucial to the basic premise of the work. As you become acquainted with a number of serial masterworks, you will discover that each has unique properties.

The analysis project below is designed to acquaint you with four movements of a particularly accessible serial work. For each movement be sure to do the listening *before* the score study. It is important that you encounter each piece as musical sound, not merely as symbols on a printed page.

Analysis Project

Luigi Dallapiccola, Quaderno musicale di Annalibera

This work exists in two versions: as the *Quaderno (Notebook),* a collection of piano pieces that Dallapiccola dedicated to his daughter, Annalibera, and as his *Variations for Orchestra.* The keyboard version is modeled after the *Notebook for Anna Magdalena Bach,* a collection of pieces assembled by J. S. Bach and his sons.[7] The Bach and Dallapiccola collections are separated by a time span of more than two centuries, and they differ in several respects, but they do have certain attributes in common.

The matrix of set forms for the entire *Quaderno* (see Fig. 15–2) may be used for some of the analytical tasks below. In many cases, however, you will be better served by ignoring the matrix and trying to identify set forms from evidence in the score.

Piece No. 4, "Linee" (WenAMSS)

A. Listening

1. Describe the texture both in general terms (homophonic, polyphonic, etc.) and in more specific terms (number of voices, pulse-level ratios, relative melodic motion). How many textural components are there? Do any of the components imply more than one voice?
2. Describe the form. Into how many parts does the piece divide? What is the basis for this division?
3. Can you discern a metric structure? If so, describe it. How many pulse levels are there? How are they related? Which is the beat-level pulse? What is a possible meter signature?
4. How are the 12 pitch classes realized in this work? Do you hear any instances of repetition, either of a single pitch or of small groups of pitches? In light of your observations, predict how many row statements occur during this piece. Do you think row forms are stated simultaneously? Why or why not?
5. Notate the "melody" on staff paper. Don't be too concerned about the rhythmic accuracy of your notation; concentrate instead on the pitches. (The first pitch is A^b_4.) Is the melody a complete row statement? Why or why not? Does it contain tonal cells?

B. Score study

1. Use your findings to orient yourself to the score. Do you find any aspects of Dallapiccola's notation surprising? How might the score be reduced for analysis?

---

[7]Four pieces from that collection are given in Charles Burkhart, *Anthology for Musical Analysis,* 5th ed.

2. Do the pitches of mm. 1–5 form an aggregate (an unordered set of the 12 pcs)? What about mm. 6–10? Are any pcs duplicated between the two staves within each of these sections?

3. Using your answers to question 2 above and the matrix of row forms (Fig. 15–2), identify and label the various row statements. Describe how they relate to the texture of the movement.

4. Consider mm. 4–5 and m. 6 to be unordered pc sets. Which pcs do these two sets have in common? Are they instances of the same T_n/T_nI-type? Can you think of any parallels between this practice and the tonal plan of a movement of a Baroque dance suite?

Piece No. 5, *"Contrapunctus secundus"* (WenAMSS)

A. Listening

1. The texture of this movement is similar in many respects to that of Webern's Op. 27, II. Listen to both movements several times and describe the similarities and differences between them.

2. Does the form of this movement resemble that of the Webern, or that of the Dallapiccola's "Linee"? Be sure to consider all aspects including pitch, rhythm, dynamics, articulation, and texture.

B. Score study

1. How is the music of the two staves related? Does the same relationship hold throughout the movement? Be sure to consider both pitch contour and temporal delay in your answer.

2. Considering the implications of your answer to question 1 above, identify and label the various row forms.

3. What pitch is the axis of symmetry for mm. 1–2? Does this axis prevail throughout the piece? If not, where does it change, and what is the new axis?

4. The *Luftpause* sign (//) that appears above the staff at the end of m. 4 implies a two-part division for the movement. Compare the two sections carefully and comment on their similarities and differences.

5. Both this movement and Webern's Op. 27, II are based upon a limited number of "figures." How do Dallapiccola's figures compare with Webern's? Are any of Dallapiccola's figures associated with a certain pc set-type? Can any be regarded as tonal cells?

Piece No. 6, *"Fregi"* (WenAMSS)

A. Listening

1. Listen for aspects of texture and form. Does this movement divide into two equal-sized parts? If so, how are these parts related?

2. Can you discern a metric framework from listening? If so, describe it in as much detail as possible.

3. How much pitch repetition do you hear in each component of the texture?

B. Score study

1. Use your knowledge of the texture and form of the movement to help in identifying the various row forms. You should find it easy to identify row forms that are presented in the melody; those of the dyadic accompaniment may present more of a challenge.
2. How many different row forms are presented melodically during the course of the piece? How many within each section? How are the row forms within each section related? What is the relationship between row forms that have analogous positions within their respective sections?
3. Look carefully at the notation in mm. 4 and 9. Why did Dallapiccola place two different notes on the same staff line?
4. How did the composer cover the "seam" between the two major sections of this piece?

Piece No. 11, "Quartina" (Burkhart)

A. Listening

1. The title of this piece is the Italian word for quatrain. How does the structure of the music correspond to a four-line stanza of poetry?
2. How would you describe the texture? Which of the above pieces does it most closely resemble?
3. How many instances of pitch repetition can you hear?

B. Score Study

As you may have discovered through listening, the piece divides into four four-measure phrases. Its texture implies the use of one set form for the melody and another for the chordal accompaniment of each phrase.

1. Compare the four melodic phrases in terms of melodic interval pattern. Be careful to observe the changes of clef in mm. 5, 7, 8–9, and 13. Which phrases have I-related patterns? R-related patterns? RI-related patterns? Use these findings to identify the various set forms on the score. Record your findings in the table below. Be sure to review the earlier discussion concerning the relationship between interval patterns and set forms (see p. 285).
2. Compare the interval structure of the chords between the phrases. Can you find chords that have similar interval content? How do these findings aid the identification of set forms? Label the set forms used for the accompaniment of each phrase and record these labels in the table below.
3. Study the completed table. Does it reveal any pattern in the choice of set forms?

	Phrase 1	Phrase 2	Phrase 3	Phrase 4
Melody	_____	_____	_____	_____
Accompaniment	_____	_____	_____	_____

4. Within a given measure, how do the melody and chordal accompaniment compare in terms of pc content? Can their pcs be combined to form any familiar collections or set-types?

SUMMARY ASPECTS

1. Analyze Dallapiccola's basic set using the methods outlined above in the section entitled "Properties of 12-pc Sets." Of the other sets discussed in this chapter, which does it most closely resemble?
2. Listen carefully to the Variations version of this work and comment upon the composer's choice of orchestral timbres. Do these reveal or obscure the structure of the work?

ANALYSIS EXERCISES

1. Using the matrix for Dallapiccola's *Quaderno* (Fig. 15–1) locate the following row forms or row elements and list their pcs in the space provided.

P_9 _____

RI_2 _____

I_4 _____

R_6 _____

P_5, order no. 3 ___ P_6, order no. 10 ___

I_9, order no. 2 ___ I_3, order no. 9 ___

R_7, order no. 4 ___ R_8, order no. 1 ___

RI_1, order no. 6 ___ RI_0, order no. 8 ___

2. What is the serial operation that maps the discrete hexachords of Berg's *Lyric Suite* set (see Ex. 15–5a) onto each other?
3. Construct a table showing the multiplicity of adjacent interval classes for each of the following ordered sets: Webern, Op. 24 (see Ex. 15–6), Webern, Op. 27 (see Ex. 15-8), Berg, *Lyric Suite* (see Ex. 15–5a), Dallapiccola, *Quaderno* (see Fig. 15–2). Use Table 15–3 as your model. When you have finished, compare these tables noting how evenly the various interval classes are distributed. Are any of these examples all-interval sets?

COMPOSITION EXERCISES

1. Write a melody (about 16 measures) that is based on one of the ordered 12-pc sets discussed in this chapter. Use at least two set forms in your melody. To make your melody sound as much as possible like real music do the following:
   a. Review the procedure for realizing a pc set (See Exercise 1–2 (pp. 17–18) and the section entitled "The Compositional Process" in this chapter.
   b. Compose your melody for a specific instrument or voice.
   c. Try to evoke a definite mood or topic. This should help you decide about other features such as tempo, rhythmic patterns, register, and dynamics.
   d. Invent one or two short motives (2–6 notes) and try to develop them extensively throughout your melody.

2. Write a homophonic passage that illustrates hexachordal combinatoriality. Use one set form in the melody and another for the accompaniment. You may use one of the homophonic examples studied above as your model.

RECOMMENDED LISTENING AND ANALYSIS

Babbitt, "Play on Notes" (Burkhart)
———, Semi-Simple Variations (Burkhart, DeLio-Smith, Morgan)
Berg, Lyric Suite, first movement (Morgan)
———, Violin Concerto (excerpts of Andante and Adagio movements in Wen20)
———, "Lied der Lulu" from *Lulu* (Simms)
Dallapiccola, *Goethe-Lieder* (Nos. 1, 2, and 3 in Wen20)
Krenek, Suite for Violoncello Solo, Op. 84, first movement (Burkhart)
Schoenberg, Five Piano Pieces, Op. 23 (No. 4 in Simms)
———, Suite for Piano, Op. 25 (Prelude in DeLio-Smith, Menuett and Trio in Wen20)
———, Variations for Orchestra, Op. 31 (Introduction, Theme, and Variation 1 in Wen20)
———, Piano Piece, Op. 33a (Burkhart, Morgan, WenAMSS)
———, Fourth String Quartet, Op. 37, first movement (Simms)
Stravinsky, Dirge-Canons from *In Memoriam Dylan Thomas* (Burkhart, Wen20)
Webern, Quartet for Violin, Clarinet, Tenor Saxophone, and Piano, Op. 22, first movement (Burkhart)
———, Concerto, Op. 24, third movement (WenAMSS)
———, "Wie bin ich froh!" No. 1 of *Drei Lieder,* Op. 25 (Burkhart)
———, String Quartet, Op. 28, second movement (Morgan)
Wuorinen, Twelve Short Pieces (Nos. 3 and 11 in DeLio-Smith)

Part V

RECENT DEVELOPMENTS

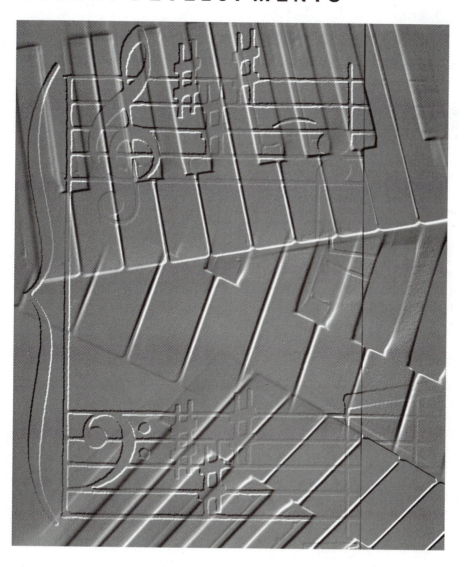

CHAPTER 16

Chance and Indeterminacy

Introduction

The ideas of intentionality, control, and authority are crucial to Western art music. From experience, we assume that a musical masterwork is the product of a great deal of thought and planning, that its composer intended for it to sound a certain way. To convey those intentions to listeners, a composer usually creates a score, an elaborate set of instructions for performing a work. To realize the composer's intentions a performer studies the score carefully and practices in order to execute its instructions faithfully. But a performer must also be capable of reading "between the lines" in order to supply missing information and make decisions about details that are assumed.

Chance is the very opposite of intention. When we attribute an event to chance, we indicate that it was not necessarily meant to happen; rather, it was merely one of several possible outcomes. The terms *aleatory* and *aleatorical* are often used as synonyms for chance. They come from *aleae*, the Latin word for dice, and refer to any type of chance procedure, such as playing cards, rolling dice, or entering a lottery. *Indeterminacy* has a rather different meaning. It means that an issue cannot be decided, or an outcome cannot be predicted, because certain essential information required for making a decision or prediction is unavailable.

John Cage and His Disciples

These terms are most closely associated with the music and ideas of a small but influential group of composers who came to prominence during the 1950s. The leader and philosopher of this movement was John Cage (1912–1992). To more fully understand the meaning of the terms defined above, let's look at an excerpt from Cage's *Aria* (Ex. 16–1).

Our first hint that this is an unconventional work comes from the composer's preface to the score. Cage states that "The Aria may be sung in whole or in part to provide a program of a determined time length, alone or with the *Fontana Mix* [an electronic work] or with any parts of the *Concert* [for piano and orchestra]."[1] In other words, there is no such thing as an authoritative version. A performer may

---

[1] Cage, score to *Aria* (New York: Henmar Press, 1960).

Example 16–1.   John Cage, Aria, beginning

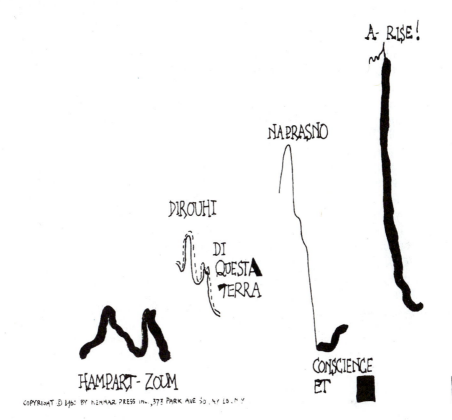

start practically anywhere and end somewhere later. The Aria's precise content and length are *indeterminate*; they can not be discerned from the composer's score. Texture is indeterminate, as well, but Cage did specify a limited range of options: solo performance or an "accompaniment" consisting of *Fontana Mix* or part of the *Concert*.

Cage also used a type of notation that left the pitch and duration of notes undetermined. In fact, he didn't even use notes for the vocal melody, just straight or wavy lines. He directed the performer to select ten different styles of singing and associate each style with a specific colored line (not reproduced here). The composer also called for an indefinite number of "unmusical" vocal sounds, but he let the vocalist decide which sounds to use and where to use them. Finally, Cage wrote that "All aspects of a performance (dynamics, etc.) which are not notated may be freely determined by the singer."[2]

---

[2]Cage, *Aria*, preface to score.

As you can see, the vocalist has a great deal of freedom in performing this work. In fact, she is more than an interpreter; she is very much a co-creator. The final result will depend as much or more upon her decisions as upon Cage's. It would appear that the text is the only fixed aspect, but if the singer may perform the work in whole or in part, then the extent of the text is indeterminate. Only the ordering of words, syllables, and vocal sounds has been fixed by the composer.

Cage began to build indeterminacy into his music during the 1940s. At first he left only timbre undetermined. For example, his *Living Room Music* (1940) has percussion parts that may be played on any household element, such as table, desks, or walls. In later works, such as *Aria*, other aspects were left indeterminate, as well.

Cage also began to disassociate form and content by placing musical ideas arbitrarily into formal "containers" without concern for their sequential ordering or structural function. These ideas were often severely limited. Instead of expansive themes, he often used short melodic figures that bore little or no relationship to their immediate surroundings. Cage considered silence to be as valuable as sound; neither was superior to the other. Finally, he began to rely upon chance operations for making musical decisions. For example, in composing his *Music for Changes* (1951), an extended piece for piano, he chose pitches, durations, timbres, dynamics, and tempos by tossing coins and then consulting *I Ching*, the Oriental *Book of Changes*.

The ultimate realization of Cage's philosophy was his *4'33"* (Ex. 16–2). The work's title refers to the sum of the durations of its three "movements." But its score contains nothing more than the word "tacet," indicating each movement consists solely of silence. To add to the irony, Cage noted that the piece can be "played" by any instrument or combination of instruments.

Cage's ideas about music were radical, but they influenced other composers. Among Americans, Morton Feldman (1926–87) and Earle Brown (1926–) are considered Cage's closest disciples. All three were close to the Abstract Expressionists, a group of avant-garde painters active in New York during the 1950s and 60s. The influence can be seen in certain scores created by Cage, Feldman, and Brown. For example, Watkins has noted the similarity between Earle Brown's score for *December 1952* (Ex. 16–3a) and Piet Mondrian's *Pier and Ocean* (1915).[3] Mondrian's close friend, Fritz Glarner (1899–1972), also explored numerous ways that a small number of simple colors and shapes can be combined. One of his several Relational Paintings is shown in Ex. 16–3b.

Composers who use idiosyncratic notation have often provided instructions that a performer may need to decode the various symbols. In his preface to *December 1952* Brown indicated that the work may be played by "one or more instruments and/or sound producing media." He also noted that "The composition may be performed in any direction from any point in the defined space for any length of time and may be performed from any of the four rotational positions in any sequence." Thus, Brown's score is highly indeterminate. To perform this work one must make numerous decisions about matters that are normally taken for granted.

---

[3]Glenn Watkins, *Soundings* (New York: Schirmer Books, 1988), pp. 565–66.

Example 16–2. John Cage, *4′33″* (1952); complete score

I

TACET

II

TACET

III

TACET

NOTE: The title of this work is the total length in minutes and seconds of its performance. At Woodstock, N.Y., August 29, 1952, the title was 4' 33" and the three parts were 33", 2' 40", and 1' 20". It was performed by David Tudor, pianist, who indicated the beginnings of parts by closing, the endings by opening, the keyboard lid. However, the work may be performed by an instrumentalist or combination of instrumentalists and last any length of time.

FOR IRWIN KREMEN   JOHN CAGE

Brown's scores to his *Available Forms* I and II are typical of his more recent work. A page from *Available Forms I* (1961), a work for eighteen players with conductor, is shown in Ex. 16–4. Each member of the ensemble reads from a copy of the score and performs a designed part. The score consists of various musical events that are indicated by large numerals. During a performance a conductor controls the sequence and pacing of these events.

Example 16–5 is another example of graphic notation. Feldman's notation may be somewhat indeterminate, but his instructions are rather precise. The following is a paraphrase and summary.

- Instrumental timbres and playing techniques are indicated, for the most part, by capital letters.
  B indicates bell-like sounds
  C indicates cymbal
  G indicates gong
  Δ indicates triangle
  S indicates skin instruments (membranophones)
  R indicates roll
  TR indicates timpani roll
  GR indicates gong roll

Example 16–3a. Earle Brown, *December 1952*

Example 16–3b. Fritz Glarner, Relational Painting No. 74 (1954)*

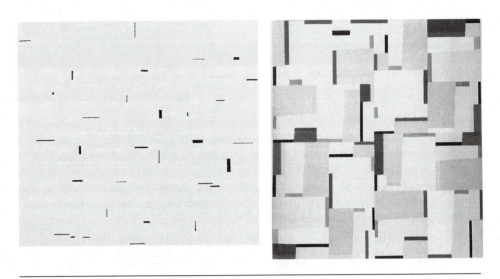

*Margit Staber, *Fritz Glarner* (Zurich: ABC Verlag, 1976), p. 89.

- Duration is indicated by equally spaced vertical lines. The performance tempo should be about MM. 66–92 per measure.
- Approximate pitches are indicated by the vertical placement of symbols on the four-line staff.
- Tone clusters are indicated by thick horizontal lines.
- Sustained sounds are indicated by broken lines.
- Simultaneous sounds are indicated by Roman numerals.
- Specific numbers of single sounds in all registers are indicated by large Arabic numerals.
- Specific numbers of single sounds in a specific register are indicated by small Arabic numerals.

Feldman wrote specific pitches for the vibraphone and directed that it should be played without the fan motor (which produces an amplitude vibrato). He also indicated that all of the percussion instruments should be played without sticks or mallets at dynamic levels that "are extremely low, and as equal as possible." The result, an extremely calm piece of music that lacks even a hint of drama, passion, or lyricism, is an excellent example of *nonlinear time* (see Chapter Nine, pp. 162–64).

Among European composers, Boulez and Stockhausen were most influenced by Cage's philosophy. During the early 1950s, both were staunch advocates of *integral serialism*, the application of serial procedures to other aspects, such as duration, dynamics, and timbre. But in 1954, after hearing Cage's music played by the American pianist David Tudor, they began to realize that it was not much different

Example 16–4. Earle Brown, Available Forms I (1961), excerpt

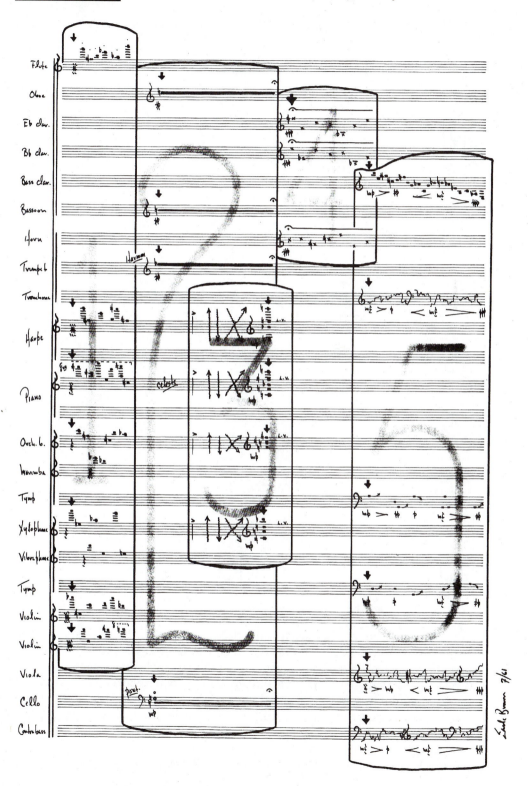

Example 16–5. Morton Feldman, *The King of Denmark* (1964) for solo percussionist, p. 1 of score

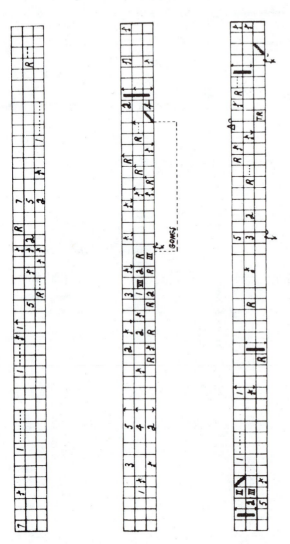

from their own. Integral serialism and indeterminacy were diametrically opposite approaches to composition, but they produced virtually the same musical result. As Morgan has noted, "Stockhausen, Boulez, and their serialist colleagues had come to realize that the more precisely musical events were determined, the more random and haphazard they tended to sound."[4] As a result, Boulez and Stockhausen began to build indeterminacy into their music although in a more limited way.

[4]Robert P. Morgan, *Twentieth-Century Music* (New York: W. W. Norton, 1991), pp. 370–71.

Stockhausen designed the score of his *Zyklus* so that it can be read right side up or upside down (see Ex. 16–6). Furthermore, he indicated that the performer could begin at any point on any page, but once a starting point was chosen, the score should be read in the normal direction (left to right) from that point to that point. Thus, the work's title (*Zyklus* is German for cycle) refers to its form. To augment the possibilities for realization, Stockhausen provided alternative passages at several points in the score. The percussionist is supposed to choose from among the various alternatives during a performance.

Example 16–6. **Karlheinz Stockhausen, *Zyklus* (1959) for solo percussion, excerpt**

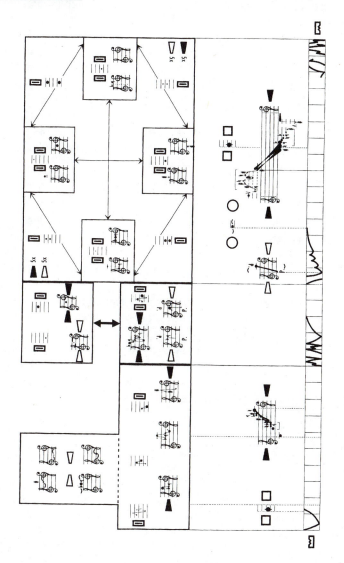

Analysis of Indeterminate and Chance Music

Analysis is a systematic and rigorous procedure for making sense out of something. When we analyze we make a significant leap of faith; we assume that there is sense to be made. In doing so, we unwittingly adopt a Western mindset that emphasizes rational and logical thought processes, assumes intentionality, and seeks to discover cause-effect relationships.

Cage and his disciples created their music under a different set of rules. By using chance procedures and indeterminate notation, they undermined the belief that music embodies rational thought processes and that it can be explained through analysis. From his studies of Oriental philosophy Cage developed the conviction that art should not be created by imposing one's will upon a set of materials. Rather an artist should subordinate his or her ego, reject the "masterpiece mentality," and create works that calm, rather than stimulate, the mind.

It is practically impossible to analyze music that was designed to thwart the mind's propensity to remember, compare, and understand. About all that one can do is try to explain how the composer achieved a type of music that defies explanation, a difficult and unrewarding task. We can also read the composer's account of the creation process (if there is one) and study the score and performance directions. From these we should learn which aspects of the work are determinate and which are partially or wholly indeterminate. Finally, we can study live or recorded performances. By comparing the performance to the score we can better understand the roles of composer and performer in the creation process.

PROJECTS AND EXERCISES

1. Read Leonard Ratner's description of *Ars combinatoria* in his *Classic Music* (pp. 99–103). How does this method compare with the procedures that Cage used for his *Music of Changes?*
2. Perform Cage's *4'33"* then write an account of the performance in which you describe *everything* that you heard.
3. Experiment with an interactive computer program designed to automate musical composition and/or improvisation.[5] Over the course of several work sessions keep a journal in which you describe the processes and results of each session as well as the musical decisions that you made and those that the program made for you.

RECOMMENDED LISTENING AND ANALYSIS

Robert Ashley, *In Memoriam . . . Esteban Gomez* (quartet) (DeLio-Smith)
Boulez, Piano Sonata No. 3
Brown, *Available Forms I* and *II*

---

[5]For example, *GenTrax* (IBM). Denton, TX: MusTech Software Developers, 1993; *Sound Globs* (IBM). Winston-Salem, NC: Cool Shoes Software, 1990; *Jam Factory* (Macintosh). Needham, MA: Dr. T's Music Software, 1992; *M* (Macintosh/Atari ST/Amiga). Needham, MA: Dr. T's Music Software, 1992.

Herbert Brun, *Mutatis mutandis* (DeLio-Smith)
Cage, *Aria with Fontana Mix*
———, *Concert for Piano and Orchestra*
———, *Music of Changes*
———, *For Paul Taylor and Anita Dencks* (Burkhart)
Feldman, *The King of Denmark*
Stockhausen, *Zyklus*
———, *Piano Piece XI*
Christian Wolff, *Burdocks*, Section V (DeLio-Smith)

CHAPTER 17

Minimalism

Influences

The terms *minimalism, pattern music, process music, pulse music,* and *trance music* denote a musical style that emerged during the 1960s. Minimalism has certain features in common with indeterminacy: meager melodic resources and the avoidance of hierarchical structures and goal-directed processes. But while Cage, Brown, and Feldman achieved these qualities by avoiding repetition, the minimalists have embraced it wholeheartedly.

Repetition has been an integral feature of Western music throughout most of its history; the simplest way to continue a musical passage is merely to repeat it. Excessive repetition induces boredom, but on the other hand, excessive novelty produces incoherence. Composers and improvisers have usually struck an acceptable balance between these two extremes by limiting repetitions and varying the content of repeated passages.

Literal and persistent repetition are more characteristic of non-Western musics. Their use in the West reflects a widespread and growing interest in the musics of other cultures. Steve Reich, one of the leading minimalist composers, predicted in 1970 that

> *Non-Western music in general and African, Indonesian and Indian music in particular will serve as new structural models for Western musicians.*
> *Music schools will be resurrected through offering instruction in the practice and theory of all the world's musics. Young composer/performers will form all sorts of new ensembles growing out of one or several of the world's musical traditions.*[1]

Reich's predictions have come true in many ways. During the past quarter century numerous American music schools have added the study of non-Western musics to their curricula.

Minimalism also evolved from techniques used in the early days of electronic tape music. Terry Riley (b. 1935) and Steve Reich (b. 1936) both experimented with tape loops for repeating musical segments and with phase shifting for bringing them into and out of synchronization. Reich composed the tape pieces *It's Gonna Rain* (1965), *Come Out* (1966), and *Melodica* (1966) using these techniques. Later, he

---

[1]Steve Reich, "Some Optimistic Predictions (1970) about the Future of Music" in *Writings About Music* (Universal Edition, 1974), p. 28.

used phase shifting in a series of live performance, acoustical works including *Piano Phase* (1967), *Violin Phase* (1967), *Phase Patterns* (1970), and *Clapping Music* (1972).

Steve Reich's *Piano Phase*

To see how phase shifting works, let's take a look at Reich's *Piano Phase* for two pianos or two marimbas. Example 17–1 shows several measures of the work's two-page score. We'll refer to the performers as Top (plays music on the top staff) and Bottom (plays music on the bottom staff).

Example 17–1.   Steve Reich, *Piano Phase* excerpts

1. Top begins by playing and repeating the pattern in m. 1. Notice that this 12-note pattern contains only five different pitches. (Do they form a pentatonic collection?)
2. After a short period, Bottom fades in playing the same pattern in perfect unison (pitch and rhythm). They "lock in" with each other and continue to play for about 12 to 18 repetitions.
3. Top holds a steady tempo while Bottom accelerates slightly until (s)he locks into another rhythmic unison with Top. The pitches of the two parts will, however, be out of phase as shown in m. 3. Observe that the first note of Bottom's pattern from m. 2 appears at the end of m. 3.
4. Top and Bottom play m. 3 together for about 16–24 repetitions.
5. Top holds a steady tempo while Bottom accelerates slightly until (s)he locks into another rhythmic unison with Top. The pitches of the two parts will, however, be out of phase as shown in m. 4. Notice that the first note of Bottom's pattern from m. 3 appears at the end of m. 4.

Then a shorter phase-shifting process begins:

1. Top changes to the 8-note pattern shown in m. 16 of Ex. 17–1. Since this pattern contains the same five pitches played as evenly as possible, the change is barely perceptible.
2. Bottom enters with another 8-note pattern as shown in m. 17. (How many pitches does it contain? How do they relate to Top's pattern?)
3. Bottom accelerates gradually until (s)he moves one rotation ahead of Top (m. 18).

This process continues through eight cycles until the parts are back together in perfect unison.

The work ends with one more phase-shifting process whose first two cycles are shown at mm. 28 and 29. Since the basic pattern contains only four notes, the two parts achieve pitch unison after only four shifts.

Since the above description summarizes what happens in this piece, the score is superfluous. Reich recognized this when he wrote:

> As a musician, you know what this [phase-shifting] means, but you don't have to read music to do it; as a matter of fact, what is there to read but a lot of dotted lines? So one learns the musical material of the piece and puts the score aside because it is no longer necessary, it would only be a distraction. What you have to do to play the piece is to listen carefully in order to hear if you've moved one beat ahead or if you've moved two by mistake, or if you've tried to move ahead but have instead drifted back to where you started. Both players listen closely and try to perform the musical process over and over again until they can do it well. Everything is worked out, there is no improvisation whatsoever, but the psychology of performance, what really happens when you play, is total involvement with the sound; total sensuous-intellectual involvement.[2]

---

[2]Reich, *Writings About Music*, p. 52.

Terry Riley's *In C*

Terry Riley is another Minimalist who grew up in California and came of age during the turbulent 1960s. The score for his composition *In C* (1964) is shown in Ex. 17–2. This piece may be played by any number of instruments with piano. The pianist reiterates the top two Cs to keep a steady eighth-note pulse throughout the entire process. The other instrumentalists begin independently and move slowly through the 53 notated patterns, repeating each as many times as desired. If the process

Example 17–2. Terry Riley, *In C*, complete

unfolds as intended, one hears gradual tonal-harmonic motion beneath the reiterated C pedal tones.

Frederic Rzewski's *Les Moutons de Panurge*

This well-known work, also for an indeterminate ensemble of melody instruments, is based on another type of process, one that involves the gradual lengthening and/or shortening of melodic material. Rzewski's score presents the basic melody (see Ex. 17–3) along with the following performance instructions:

> *Read from left to right, playing the notes as follows: 1, 1–2, 1–2–3, 1–2–3–4, etc. When you have reached note 65, play the whole melody once again and then begin subtracting notes from the beginning: 2–3–4– . . . –65, 3–4–5– . . . –65, . . . , 62–63–64–65, 63–64–65, 64–65, 65. Hold the last note until everybody has reached it. Then begin an improvisation using any instruments. In the melody above, never stop or falter, always play loud[ly]. Stay together as long as you can, but if you get lost, stay lost. Do not try to find your way back into the fold. Continue to follow the rules strictly.*[3]

As these directions imply, the instrumentalists will inevitably drift out of phase with each other. It is impossible to predict when such drifts will occur or the extent of the drifting. One can only say that given the complexity of the task and the

Example 17–3. Frederic Rzewski, *Les Moutons de Panurge* (1972), basic melody*

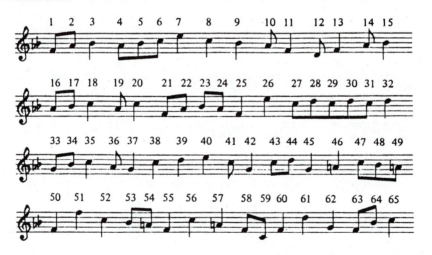

*As shown in Jonathan Kramer, *The Time of Music* (New York: Schirmer Books, 1988), Example 12.1, p. 390.

---

[3]As quoted in Jonathan D. Kramer, *The Time of Music* (New York: Schirmer Books, 1988), p. 389.

frailties of human concentration, some or all of the performers will "get lost." Nevertheless, they will all be headed in the same general direction and should complete the subtractive process at about the same time, give or take a few seconds. (Do you now understand the significance of the title? Hint: what is the English equivalent of *les moutons?*) And this is apparently what the composer intended, a loosely controlled stampede to the last note.

Analyzing Musical Processes

Minimalism has been called "process music" for good reason. It is more concerned with what happens to materials than with the structure of the materials themselves. Indeed, this is why composers use a minimal amount of musical material. They want listeners to focus upon transformations rather than objects.

If processes are the substance of minimalism, then they should be the primary concern of our analyses. But describing processes can be frustrating, especially if a score is sketchy or nonexistent. As noted earlier (see Chapter Nine, pp. 159–62), we try to describe processes by isolating stages, moments when the music achieves and maintains a steady state. If this can be done, then we can try to explain how one stage is transformed into the next.

The stages of Steve Reich's *Piano Phase* are shown as numbered measures in the score (see Ex. 17–1). In fact, Reich notated only those stages. He did not try to show in musical notation *how* Bottom accelerates until (s)he has gotten a beat ahead of Top. He just told the performers to do it.

In a simple process, like phase shifting, each successive stage is derived by applying the same operation to the preceding stage. In *Piano Phase*, that operation is Bottom's acceleration. The term *recursion* is often used to describe such processes. We could say that mm. 2–24 of *Piano Phase* involve the recursive application of acceleration to Bottom's part. In other words, m. 2 is accelerated to produce m. 3, m. 3 to produce m. 4, etc.[4]

People who analyze processes often represent them with flowcharts.[5] Figure 17–1 is a chart of the first process that Bottom performs in mm. 2–14 of Reich's *Piano Phase*. Notice that the diagram has containers with different shapes. These represent various components of the process:

- ovals represent start and stop points
- rectangles represent operations or tasks to be performed
- diamonds represent questions to be asked
- the labels "Yes" or "No" represent answers to those questions
- arrows represent the direction of flow

Earlier we noted that player Bottom executes three phase-shifting processes during a performance of *Piano Phase*. The diagram in Fig. 17–1 represents the first

---

[4]For other examples of recursion see Chapters Nine and Ten.
[5]For another example of a flowchart see Fig. 12–1 (p. 230).

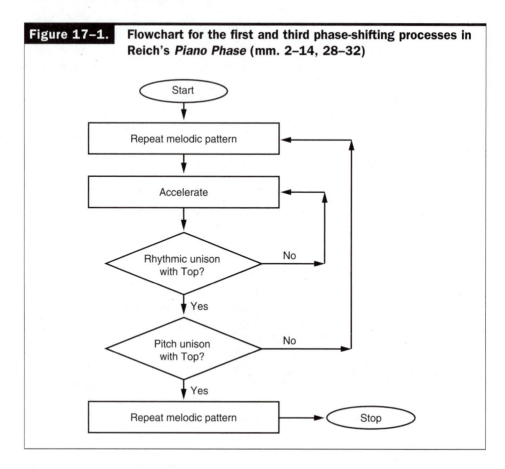

Figure 17–1. Flowchart for the first and third phase-shifting processes in Reich's *Piano Phase* (mm. 2–14, 28–32)

such process, the one that begins when Bottom enters in m. 2 and ends when Bottom exits in m. 15. It also represents the third phase-shifting process (in mm. 28–32), even though the melodic pattern used there has fewer notes and contains different pitches. In fact, this diagram represents *any* phase-shifting process that begins and ends with the two parts in perfect unison. Because it represents numerous instances of the same type of process, we can say that the diagram has a certain degree of *generality*. People who study processes (computer programmers, economists, business planners, etc.) like to achieve generality. By doing so they attain a deeper understanding of a process, an explanation that fits several cases.

The flowchart in Fig. 17–1 does not represent the second phase-shifting process (mm. 17–25) because the two parts do not begin and end in perfect unison (pitch and rhythm). for that process we would need the diagram shown in Fig. 17–2. The crucial difference between these two charts is the *stop rule*, the condition that halts the entire process. The process in Fig. 17–1 stops when Bottom achieves a perfect unison with Top. In Fig. 17–2 it stops when Bottom's pattern has been rotated eight times.

Fig. 17–2 begins by setting values for two variables: N is set to 8, the number of notes in the pattern; I is set to 0 so that it can be used to count the rotations. Every time Bottom accelerates to a position another beat ahead of Top, the value of I is incremented by 1, and then I is compared to N. When I equals N, after the eighth rotation, the process stops.

Now let's consider generality once more. Our new diagram represents Reich's process adequately, and it would represent any similar process that rotated an 8-note pattern. But it wouldn't work for shorter or longer patterns. We have not yet defined this process in terms that are sufficiently general to accommodate a pattern of any length. That could be done, however, by changing just one assignment statement. Instead of saying let N = 8, we could say let N = the number of notes in the melodic pattern. (Would this revision make the chart general enough to describe the first and third processes?)

The discussion above has shown how flowcharting might be used in musical analysis. Admittedly, the processes in *Piano Phase* are not very complex, but neither are the charts that represent them. The point is that flowcharts can be expanded to accommodate processes of much greater complexity. Do not assume, however, that every minimalist composition can be reduced to a flowchart. Some can, but

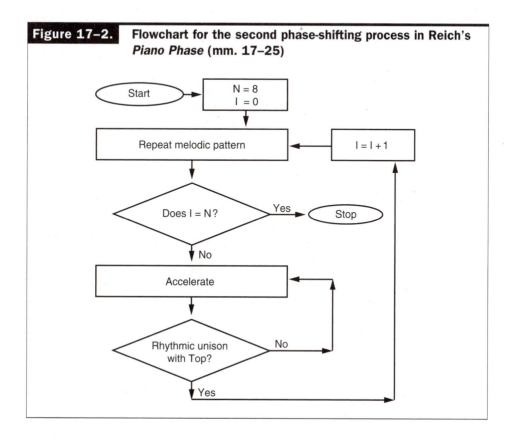

Figure 17–2.   **Flowchart for the second phase-shifting process in Reich's *Piano Phase* (mm. 17–25)**

others cannot. Nevertheless, if a process is the topic of a minimalist work, then we should try to understand it. Flowcharts may be helpful in this regard.

SUMMARY

The above examples provide an introduction to Minimalism through some of its most accessible works. We have seen that minimalist pieces are often based on brief nondescript melodic ideas, additive and subtractive melodic processes, homogeneous texture, and often homogeneous timbres, as well. These factors enable the various parts to blend into an undifferentiated mass of pulsing sounds.

The pitch materials used in minimalism typically comprise a complete diatonic collection, or one of its subsets. Consonant intervals are often abundant; dissonant and/or unstable intervals are relatively rare.

Minimalistic works often have tonal focus, but they lack the sense of progression and goal orientation that is characteristic of functional tonality. Process pieces evolve very slowly, and one is often uncertain when or where they will stop. Kramer notes that

> *Because in such pieces the motion is unceasing and its rate gradual and constant, and because there is no hierarchy of phrase structure, the temporality is more vertical than linear. The motion is so consistent that we lose any point of reference, any contact with faster or slower motion that might keep us aware of the music's directionality. The experience is static despite the constant motion in the music.*[6]

Kramer also observes that "Nonlinear music can induce in a dedicated and sympathetic listener a truly extended present, a real disassociation from the past and future, a now that is eternal even though it is destined to stop."[7] But for that to happen

> *the listener must become a creative participant in making the music. He or she must chunk [group] it according to individual criteria (since the music usually lacks unequivocal cues). He or she must create hierarchies. He or she must provide contrast, by focusing attention on different aspects. The listener can become more important to the music than the composer. In this way he or she becomes a part of the music, and thus the distinction between the self and the other, the listener and the music, is minimized.*[8]

Rather than conceiving their works in the abstract, minimalists have composed for specific ensembles and have often led those groups in public and recorded performances. They have also helped to break down the barrier between classical and popular music. Steve Reich, Terry Riley, Philip Glass, and John Adams have reached a much wider audience than many other contemporary composers. In fact,

---

[6]Kramer, *The Time of Music*, p. 57. "Vertical" time was discussed in Chapter Nine (see pp. 163–64).
[7]Ibid., p. 382.
[8]Ibid., p. 384.

Glass and Adams have expanded the scope and variety of their music to the point of composing full-length operas (e.g., Glass, *Einstein on the Beach*; Adams, *Nixon in China*). The minimalist influence is also evident in a number of recent Broadway musicals (e.g., Stephen Sondheim's *Sunday in the Park with George*).

PROJECTS AND EXERCISES

1. Study and perform Steve Reich's *Clapping Music* (DeLio-Smith, Burkhart, Wen20, Morgan). Then represent its phase-shifting process with a flowchart. Use Figs. 17–1 and 17–2 as your model.

2. Review the discussion of diatonic and pentatonic modes in Chapter Ten (pp. 168–84). Then study Exx. 17–1 and 17–2 and identify the various modes and scale types. Can you find any examples of a complete modal scale? If not, which scale degrees are missing? Why do you think Reich omitted them?

3. Perform Terry Riley's *In C* (Ex. 17–2). Then study the score to discern its tonal plan. What is that plan? How does it compare to a typical sonata-form movement in C major by Haydn or Mozart?

4. Explain how phase shifting is related to set rotation. You may need to review the discussion of normal form in Chapter Five (pp. 76–78).

5. Is it possible to draw a flowchart that describes the process(es) of Terry Riley's *In C*? Why or why not?

6. The beginning of Rzewski's *Les moutons* is notated below through the addition of note 5.[9] Using Ex. 17–3 and the performance directions as your guide, continue this example through the addition of note 11. Use beams instead of flags whenever two or more eighth notes occur in succession.

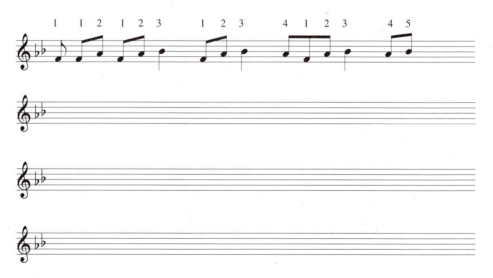

---

[9]Ibid., Ex. 12.2, p. 390.

7. The ending of Rzewski's *Les moutons* is notated below through the deletion of note 52. Notice that bar lines and meter signatures are used here. Study this example carefully to discern the criteria for placing bar lines and choosing meter signatures. When you feel certain that you understand these criteria, continue in the same manner through the final sustained note (see Ex. 17–3 and the performance directions). Then compare your barring with Jonathan Kramer's.[10]

8. Construct a flowchart that represents the additive and subtractive melodic processes of Rzewski's *Les moutons*.

9. Analyze the pitch collection used in each process of Reich's *Piano Phase* as follows:

   a. Consider each collection as an unordered pc set, compute its T_n/T_nI-type and its interval-class vector. Which interval classes are most abundant; which are least abundant? Are any of the sets symmetrical?

[10]Ibid., Ex. 12.3, p. 392.

    b. Consider each collection as a sonority with each pitch having a specific register. Classify each sonority using Hindemith's system of chord classification (see Fig. 12–1, p. 230).

10. Study the notated beginning of Rzewski's *Les moutons* (see item 6 above). What is the scale basis of this passage? Why is the addition of note 11 a significant event?

11. Study the notated ending of Rzewski's *Les moutons* (see item 7 above). On what pc collection is this entire ending based? What is the T_n/T_nI-type of this collection? As notes are deleted, which scale degrees are discarded first? Which are retained the longest? How does this priority compare with Krumhansl's tonal hierarchy and Hindemith's Series I? (See Fig. 1–2, p. 8, and Ex. 12–1, p. 216.)

RECOMMENDED LISTENING AND ANALYSIS

John Adams, *Short Ride in a Fast Machine*
———, *Phrygian Gates*
———, *Common Tones in Simple Time*
———, *Grand Pianola*
———, *Harmonielehre*
———, *Nixon in China*
Philip Glass, *Music in Fifths*
———, *Music in Similar Motion*
———, *Music in Changing Parts*
———, *Music in Twelve Parts*
———, *Another Look at Harmony*
———, *Two Pages*
———, *Einstein on the Beach*
Steve Reich, *It's Gonna Rain; Come Out; Melodica*
———, *Piano Phase* for two pianos
———, *Violin Phase*
———, *Four Organs*
———, *Clapping Music (Music for Pieces of Wood)* (DeLio-Smith, Burkhart, Wen20, Morgan)
———, *Drumming*
———, *Music for 18 Musicians*
Riley, *In C* (Schirmer Scores; Turek)
———, *A Rainbow in Curved Air*

CHAPTER 18

Eclecticism and the Revival of Tonality

Introduction

Tonality did not die during the 20th century, but it did go out of fashion in certain musical circles due to the influence of *modernism*. Modernist composers believed that their art should not stand still or look backward. Science and technology were making incredible strides and music should keep pace, as well.

The argument against modernism has been made by George Rochberg, who contends that:

> *To be a victim of the idea of change for its own sake . . . is nothing short of a curse on the artist. For it deprives him on every side of the reality and value of the past experience of human beings whose earlier contributions must be considered as valid as his own . . . if his own are to be considered valid by others who will come later.[1]*

Rochberg cites several examples where 19th- and 20th-century composers have renewed their music by using and reinterpreting earlier works.[2] He contends that

> *All such acts . . . renew both that past drawn upon and that present in which the act occurs. Far from being acts of weakness or signs of the depletion of creative energy, they reveal a profound wisdom about the paradox of time, which does not consume itself and its products as if it were fire, but gathers up into itself everything which has occurred in it, preserving everything as the individual mind preserves its individual memories. The myth is more important than the fact.[3]*

Modernism has waned considerably during the past two decades as composers have found ways to make peace with their musical past. In doing so, many have revived tonality as a binding force in their music.

George Rochberg's "Sfumato"

To document this revival we'll analyze the "Sfumato" movement of Rochberg's *Carnival Music* (1971), a suite for piano solo. Rochberg has defined "sfumato" as

---

[1]George Rochberg, "Reflections on the Renewal of Music," In *The Aesthetics of Survival*, ed. William Bolcom (Ann Arbor: University of Michigan Press, 1984), p. 233.

[2]In this regard see also Joseph N. Straus, *Remaking the Past* (Cambridge, MA: Harvard University Press, 1990).

[3]Rochberg, "Reflections on the Renewal of Music," pp. 233–34.

"A style of painting during the Renaissance in which figures, shapes, objects emerged out of misty, veiled, dreamy backgrounds."[4] The figures, shapes, and objects of this work come from two keyboard works of earlier eras: Bach's Three-Part Sinfonia No. 9 in F minor (S. 795), and Brahms's Capriccio in C, Op. 76, No. 8. The misty, veiled, dreamy background results from Rochberg's skillful handling of pitch, register, time, and sonority.

Example 18–1 shows the opening of this movement. Notice that Rochberg did not provide a meter signature, but he did indicate that the quarter note should be regarded as the basic pulse. He also directed that the eighth notes should not be played in strict time (*sempre senza misura*), but the groups of four and six eighth notes should be observed carefully. Additional performance directions include the extremely soft dynamic level (*ppp*) and the extensive use of the sostenuto pedal. All of these features contribute to the impression of a veiled and dreamy background.

Pitch organization contributes, as well. Example 18–2 contains two reductions that reveal the presence of set-types [0,1,2,3] and [0,1,2,3,4]. Notice how Rochberg softened the dissonance of these semitonal clusters by spreading the pitch classes over three octaves. During most of the movement he presented [0,1,2,3] as shown at the left of Ex. 18–2a, but periodically he revoiced it as shown at the right. These revoicings articulate the flow of time with brief and barely perceptible changes. In addition, [0,1,2,3] is occasionally transposed up four semitones as shown in Ex. 18–2b.

The figures and shapes that emerge gradually from the background are formed by notes marked tenuto in the upper staff of each system (see Ex. 18–1). The first figure begins with the last note in the first system. This three-note motive comes from Bach's Sinfonia, specifically the passage shown in Ex. 18–3a. Notice how the soprano and bass present the eighth-note motive in stretto while the alto sounds an augmentation in quarter notes. At the end of m. 16, the voices exchange roles. The soprano takes the quarter-note pattern, the alto assumes the eighth-note motive, and the bass sounds a variant of that motive. (How was the variant derived from the original motive?) As Ex. 18–3b shows, Rochberg's figure has the same pitch contour as Bach's variant, but the corresponding intervals are not equal in size.

Rochberg presented Bach's motive twice then followed with an extended variant. The motive and its variant combine to form an antecedent-consequent group, but they actually come from different sources. The *y* motive in Ex. 18–4a was derived from the Brahms passage shown in Ex. 18–4b. It is interesting that both the Bach and Brahms motives come from passages that occur well after the beginning of their respective source pieces. By using variants instead of originals Rochberg was able to evoke vague associations without risking positive identifications.

Eventually, however, the original images come into clearer focus. Brahms's *Capriccio* is the first to emerge. Example 18–5 shows how Rochberg quoted its

---

[4]Rochberg, *Carnival Music* (Bryn Mawr, PA: Theodore Presser Co., 1975), p. 24.

Example 18–1.   Rochberg, *Carnival Music*, IV. "Sfumato," opening

Example 18–2. Instances of [0,1,2,3] and [0.1,2,3,4] in the background of "Sfumato"

a. from first page of score

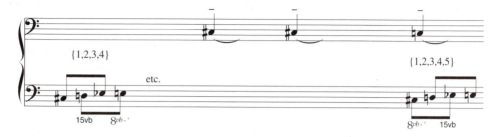

b. from second page of score

opening measures by starting slightly after the beginning and blurring the tonality by evading the F major triads in mm. 3 and 7. To be more precise, the blurring is accomplished by replacing Brahms's F major arpeggios (left hand) with the pc set shown in Ex. 18–2b. Rochberg voiced this set exactly as before, but here the context is ostensibly tonal.

After the brief fermata (not shown) at the end of Ex. 18–5a, the music lapses back into its dreamy state. Rochberg presented essentially the same motives as before (see Ex. 18–4a), first over set {5,6,7,8} (see Ex. 18–2b), then over {1,2,3,4} (see Ex. 18–2a). Eventually, he introduced the primary motive of the Bach Sinfonia, first against the atonal background, then in a foreground stretto passage (see Ex. 18–6a, p. 330). Example 18–6b (p. 331) shows how Rochberg varied Bach's variant by displacing its final note.

The crescendo of Rochberg's stretto passage ends abruptly with a *subito pp* and another lapse into the musical dream world. As before, motives and variants are presented against the background of two transpositions of [0,1,2,3]. After a while, the pianist is directed to slow down as though ending, and to bring the music to a lengthy fermata on the sonority shown in Ex. 18–7a (p. 332) (see second system).

Example 18–3.

a. J. S. Bach, Three-Part Sinfonia No. 9 in F minor (S. 795), mm. 15–20

b. Comparison of ordered pitch interval patterns

Example 18-4.

a. Rochberg, "Sfumato," motivic statements from opening (compare Exx. 18–1 and 18–3)

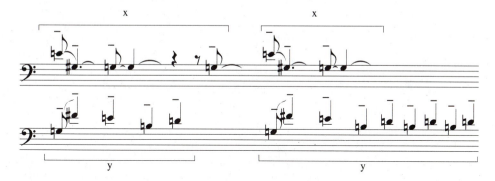

b. Brahms, *Capriccio* in C, Op. 76, No. 8, mm. 36–43

Then Rochberg quoted another Brahms excerpt, the passage that leads to the Capriccio's first V7–I cadence in C major (see Ex. 18–7b mm. 56–57). The significance of that cadence can only be appreciated by listening to the entire piece. In a functionally tonal work that is ostensibly in C major, Brahms wrote fifty-five measures of music before providing an authentic cadence in the overall tonic key. If mm. 1–15 are repeated as indicated, then the cadence in m. 57 occurs 88 percent of the way through the piece. Another, more decisive V7–I cadence occurs in mm. 61–63. This technique of implying a key yet avoiding confirmation of that key is typical of functional tonality in its more advanced form.

Example 18–5.

a. Rochberg, "Sfumato," excerpt from third page of score

Example 18–5. *Continued*

b. Brahms, *Capriccio* in C, mm. 1–9

Comparison of Exx. 18–7a and b reveals that Rochberg quoted Brahms rather closely but, as before, blurred important harmonies. In this case, the blurring occurs on the last beats of mm. 53 and 54 where Rochberg replaced Brahms's bass notes with the D_1–E_2 of his {1,2,3,4} tetrachord. But the most dramatic effect is Rochberg's avoidance of Brahms's tonic triad. Instead of continuing to the C major triad at the beginning of m. 57, Rochberg lapsed one last time into the dreamy state and ended the movement by repeating the ascending minor third B_3–D_4 over the dissonant sonority that has prevailed throughout. Notice, however, that Rochberg ended on a slightly different sonority, the same one that he used for the fermata chord near the beginning of this excerpt.

In discussing this movement, Rochberg observed that tonality and atonality are not really distant opposites (as implied by Fig. 1–1, p. 2) but close relatives.[5] In the analysis above, we have seen how Rochberg exploited a link between the tonal idiom of Bach and Brahms and the atonal idiom of Schoenberg, Berg, Webern. That

---

[5]Informal lecture, University of North Carolina–Greensboro, February 2, 1992.

Example 18–6.

a. Rochberg, "Sfumato," paraphrase of Bach Sinfonia (compare Example 18–3a)

Example 18–6. *Continued*

b.

Bach's primary motive   Bach's variant   Rochberg's variant

link is most apparent in the stretto passage of the F minor Sinfonia (see Ex. 18–3a). In treating the basic motive to an ascending sequence Bach spelled his own name.[6] As Ex. 18–8a (p. 334) shows, this succession produces the unordered pc set {9,10,11,0}, an instance of [0,1,2,3].

Rochberg's dreamy background was built, for the most part, from two other instances of that set-type (see Ex. 18–2). Notice that he used the two transpositions that complement the B-A-C-H transposition. As Ex. 18–8 illustrates, these three sets are mutually exclusive; they have no pcs in common. Collectively, they form the entire chromatic collection or aggregate.

In an essay on his Third String Quartet, Rochberg noted that

> *By embracing the earlier traditions of tonality and combining them with the more recently developed atonality, I found it possible to release my music from the overintense, expressionistic manner inherent in a purely serially organized, constant chromaticism, and from the inhibition of physical pulse and rhythm which has enervated so much recent music. With the enlargement of this spectrum came an enlargement of perspective which potentially placed the entire past at my disposal. I was freed of the conventional perceptions which ascribe some goal-directed, teleological function to that past, insisting that each definable historical development supersedes the one that has just taken place either by incorporating it or nullifying it.[7]*

Rochberg is one of several composers who have acknowledged the expressive and dynamic qualities of music from earlier eras. By rejecting modernism and adopting an eclectic attitude, these composers have breathed new life into an art that, in the opinions of some critics, had grown arcane and esoteric. Rather than trying to turn back to the "good old days" of functional tonality, these composers have realized that tonality is one of several possible musical idioms. Each has strengths and weaknesses that a composer can exploit as needed to express the full range and complexity of the human experience.

---

[6]The German names for B flat and B natural are B and H, respectively.
[7]George Rochberg, "On the Third String Quartet" In *The Aesthetics of Survival*, p. 239.

Example 18-7.

a. Rochberg, "Sfumato," last page of score

Example 18–7.   *Continued*

b. Brahms, *Capriccio* in C, mm. 50–end

Example 18–8.

SUMMARY

Eclecticism is a musical movement that draws freely upon musical idioms of the past and present. Eclectic composers have incorporated tonality, neotonality, and atonality into their music as they deem appropriate. In some cases, references to tonality are made by literally quoting musical masterworks of earlier eras. In other cases, composers have created original tonal music of their own.

The adjective *eclectic* has occasionally been used to deprecate the work of a composer or artist who has borrowed from others. That connotation is not intended here. Borrowing and imitating were widespread practices during most of the history of Western art music. Some of our most revered composers based many of their compositions on ideas, forms, or processes that they gleaned from the music of their contemporaries or predecessors.

EXERCISES AND PROJECTS

1. Find several additional instances of set-type [0,1,2,3] in Ex. 18–3a.
2. Determine the T_n/T_nI-type of the sonority used at the fermata and at the end of Ex. 18–7a. Compute or look up its ic vector. How does it compare to the vector of [0,1,2,3]?
3. Classify Rochberg's final sonority using Hindemith's method of chord classification (see Fig. 12–1, p. 230).
4. Determine the set-types of the trichordal subsets of Rochberg's final sonority and of [0,1,2,3]. Locate instances of these in the Bach and Brahms excerpts (Exx. 18–3a, 18–4b, 18–5b, 18–7b).
5. What is the T_n/T_nI-type of the motive shown on the upper staff of Ex. 18–3b? In what other works have you encountered that set-type? Can you find instances of it in the Bach or Brahms excerpts?
6. Look carefully at the sonority that Rochberg used for the chord marked *più f* in the third system of Ex. 18–7a. Compare this sonority to set b.1 in Ex. 14–12 (p. 267). Consider both as unordered pc sets.

7. The motives shown in Ex. 18–6b are related by which of the following operations: T^p_n, T_n, T^p_nI, T_nI? What is the interval of transposition?

8. Could Rochberg have notated "Sfumato" using meter signatures? If so, what might they be? Would they make the score easier or more difficult to read?

9. Compare Rochberg's "Sfumato" to other works that evoke a dream-like state (see Ex. 14–4, p. 252).

RECOMMENDED LISTENING AND ANALYSIS

Dominick Argento, Franz Schubert (To a Friend) and Johann Sebastian Bach (To the Town Council)

Warren Benson, *Songs for the End of the World*

Britten, *Six Metamorphoses after Ovid*, "Niobe" (DeLio-Smith)

Crumb, Ancient Voices of Children, V. "Se ha llenado" (WenAMSS)

———, *Makrokosmos*, Vol. I, "Dream Images [Love-Death Music]" and "Spiral Galaxy" (Godwin)

———, Madrigals, Book IV, No. 1 "¿Por qué nací entre espejos?" (Burkhart)

———, *Black Angels*, VI and VII (Simms)

David Del Tredici, *Final Alice*

Lukas Foss, *Baroque Variations*

Henryk Górecki, Symphony No. 3

John Harbison, Piano Concerto

———, *Miribai Songs*

Mauricio Kagel. *Ludwig Van*

Tobias Picker. *Old and Lost Rivers* (Kamien)

Rochberg, *Carnival Music*

———, Third String Quartet

———, Sixth String Quartet, III (Variations on Pachelbel) (Simms)

———, *Music for the Magic Theater*

———, *Nach Bach*

———, *Caprice Variations*

Schuller, *Seven Studies on Themes of Paul Klee*, "Little Blue Devil" (Wen20)

Joseph Schwantner, *Wild Angels of the Open Hills*

Yehudi Wyner. Three Short Fantasies for Piano

Ellen Taaffe Zwilich, *Passages*, I. Eyesight (Wen20)

———, Symphony No. 1

Appendix A

Table of T_n/T_nI-types[1]

Trichords / Nonachords

Tn/TnI-type	D.S.	IC Vector	Forte Names	IC Vector	D.S.	Tn/TnI-type
[0, 1, 2]	2	<2, 1, 0, 0, 0, 0>	3-1/9-1	<8, 7, 6, 6, 6, 3>	2	[0, 1, 2, 3, 4, 5, 6, 7, 8]
[0, 1, 3]	1	<1, 1, 1, 0, 0, 0>	3-2/9-2	<7, 7, 7, 6, 6, 3>	1	[0, 1, 2, 3, 4, 5, 6, 7, 9]
[0, 1, 4]	1	<1, 0, 1, 1, 0, 0>	3-3/9-1	<7, 6, 7, 7, 6, 3>	1	[0, 1, 2, 3, 4, 5, 6, 8, 9]
[0, 1, 5]	1	<1, 0, 0, 1, 1, 0>	3-4/9-4	<7, 6, 6, 7, 7, 3>	1	[0, 1, 2, 3, 4, 5, 7, 8, 9]
[0, 1, 6]	1	<1, 0, 0, 0, 1, 1>	3-5/9-5	<7, 6, 6, 6, 7, 4>	1	[0, 1, 2, 3, 4, 6, 7, 8, 9]
[0, 2, 4]	2	<0, 2, 0, 1, 0, 0>	3-6/9-6	<6, 8, 6, 7, 6, 3>	2	[0, 1, 2, 3, 4, 5, 6, 8, 10]
[0, 2, 5]	1	<0, 1, 1, 0, 1, 0>	3-7/9-7	<6, 7, 7, 6, 7, 3>	1	[0, 1, 2, 3, 4, 5, 7, 8, 10]
[0, 2, 6]	1	<0, 1, 0, 1, 0, 1>	3-8/9-8	<6, 7, 6, 7, 6, 4>	1	[0, 1, 2, 3, 4, 6, 7, 8, 10]
[0, 2, 7]	2	<0, 1, 0, 0, 2, 0>	3-9/9-9	<6, 7, 6, 6, 8, 3>	2	[0, 1, 2, 3, 5, 6, 7, 8, 10]
[0, 3, 6]	2	<0, 0, 2, 0, 0, 1>	3-10/9-10	<6, 6, 8, 6, 6, 4>	2	[0, 1, 2, 3, 4, 6, 7, 9, 10]
[0, 3, 7]	1	<0, 0, 1, 1, 1, 0>	3-11/9-11	<6, 6, 7, 7, 7, 3>	1	[0, 1, 2, 3, 5, 6, 7, 9, 10]
[0, 4, 8]	6	<0, 0, 0, 3, 0, 0>	3-12/9-12	<6, 6, 6, 9, 6, 3>	6	[0, 1, 2, 4, 5, 6, 8, 9, 10]

Tetrachords / Octachords

Tn/TnI-type	D.S.	IC Vector	Forte Names	IC Vector	D.S.	Tn/TnI-type
[0, 1, 2, 3]	2	<3, 2, 1, 0, 0, 0>	4-1/8-1	<7, 6, 5, 4, 4, 2>	2	[0, 1, 2, 3, 4, 5, 6, 7]
[0, 1, 2, 4]	1	<2, 2, 1, 1, 0, 0>	4-2/8-2	<6, 6, 5, 5, 4, 2>	1	[0, 1, 2, 3, 4, 5, 6, 8]
[0, 1, 2, 5]	1	<2, 1, 1, 1, 1, 0>	4-4/8-4	<6, 5, 5, 5, 5, 2>	1	[0, 1, 2, 3, 4, 5, 7, 8]
[0, 1, 2, 6]	1	<2, 1, 0, 1, 1, 1>	4-5/8-5	<6, 5, 4, 5, 5, 3>	1	[0, 1, 2, 3, 4, 6, 7, 8]
[0, 1, 2, 7]	2	<2, 1, 0, 0, 2, 1>	4-6/8-6	<6, 5, 4, 4, 6, 3>	2	[0, 1, 2, 3, 5, 6, 7, 8]
[0, 1, 3, 4]	2	<2, 1, 2, 1, 0, 0>	4-3/8-3	<6, 5, 6, 5, 4, 2>	2	[0, 1, 2, 3, 4, 5, 6, 9]
[0, 1, 3, 5]	1	<1, 2, 1, 1, 1, 0>	4-11/8-11	<5, 6, 5, 5, 5, 2>	1	[0, 1, 2, 3, 4, 5, 7, 9]
[0, 1, 3, 6]	1	<1, 1, 2, 0, 1, 1>	4-13/8-13	<5, 5, 6, 4, 5, 3>	1	[0, 1, 2, 3, 4, 6, 7, 9]
[0, 1, 3, 7]	1	<1, 1, 1, 1, 1, 1>	4-Z29/8-Z29	<5, 5, 5, 5, 5, 3>	1	[0, 1, 2, 3, 5, 6, 7, 9]
[0, 1, 4, 5]	2	<2, 0, 1, 2, 1, 0>	4-7/8-7	<6, 4, 5, 6, 5, 2>	2	[0, 1, 2, 3, 4, 5, 8, 9]
[0, 1, 4, 6]	1	<1, 1, 1, 1, 1, 1>	4-Z15/8-Z15	<5, 5, 5, 5, 5, 3>	1	[0, 1, 2, 3, 4, 6, 8, 9]
[0, 1, 4, 7]	1	<1, 0, 2, 1, 1, 1>	4-18/8-18	<5, 4, 6, 5, 5, 3>	1	[0, 1, 2, 3, 5, 6, 8, 9]
[0, 1, 4, 8]	1	<1, 0, 1, 3, 1, 0>	4-19/8-19	<5, 4, 5, 7, 5, 2>	1	[0, 1, 2, 4, 5, 6, 8, 9]
[0, 1, 5, 6]	2	<2, 0, 0, 1, 2, 1>	4-8/8-8	<6, 4, 4, 5, 6, 3>	2	[0, 1, 2, 3, 4, 7, 8, 9]
[0, 1, 5, 7]	1	<1, 1, 0, 1, 2, 1>	4-16/8-16	<5, 5, 4, 5, 6, 3>	1	[0, 1, 2, 3, 5, 7, 8, 9]
[0, 1, 5, 8]	2	<1, 0, 1, 2, 2, 0>	4-20/8-20	<5, 4, 5, 6, 6, 2>	2	[0, 1, 2, 4, 5, 7, 8, 9]
[0, 1, 6, 7]	4	<2, 0, 0, 0, 2, 2>	4-9/8-9	<6, 4, 4, 4, 6, 4>	4	[0, 1, 2, 3, 6, 7, 8, 9]
[0, 2, 3, 5]	2	<1, 2, 2, 0, 1, 0>	4-10/8-10	<5, 6, 6, 4, 5, 2>	2	[0, 2, 3, 4, 5, 6, 7, 9]
[0, 2, 3, 6]	1	<1, 1, 2, 1, 0, 1>	4-12/8-12	<5, 5, 6, 5, 4, 3>	1	[0, 1, 3, 4, 5, 6, 7, 9]
[0, 2, 3, 7]	1	<1, 1, 1, 1, 2, 0>	4-14/8-14	<5, 5, 5, 5, 6, 2>	1	[0, 1, 2, 4, 5, 6, 7, 9]
[0, 2, 4, 6]	2	<0, 3, 0, 2, 0, 1>	4-21/8-21	<4, 7, 4, 6, 4, 3>	2	[0, 1, 2, 3, 4, 6, 8, 10]
[0, 2, 4, 7]	1	<0, 2, 1, 1, 2, 0>	4-22/8-22	<4, 6, 5, 5, 6, 2>	1	[0, 1, 2, 3, 5, 6, 8, 10]

---

[1]John Rahn, *Basic Atonal Theory* (New York: Longman, 1980), Table II, pp. 140–143; as corrected in Paul W. Metz, "The Clock Diagram: An Effective Visual Tool in Set Theory Pedagogy," *Theory and Practice* 14/15 (1989/90), p. 115, fn. 8.

Tetrachords   Octachords

Tn/TnI-type	D.S.	IC Vector	Forte Names	IC Vector	D.S.	Tn/TnI-type
[0, 2, 4, 8]	2	<0, 2, 0, 3, 0, 1>	4-24/8-24	<4, 6, 4, 7, 4, 3>	2	[0, 1, 2, 4, 5, 6, 8, 10]
[0, 2, 5, 7]	2	<0, 2, 1, 0, 3, 0>	4-23/8-23	<4, 6, 5, 4, 7, 2>	2	[0, 1, 2, 3, 5, 7, 8, 10]
[0, 2, 5, 8]	1	<0, 1, 2, 1, 1, 1>	4-27/8-27	<4, 5, 6, 5, 5, 3>	1	[0, 1, 2, 4, 5, 7, 8, 10]
[0, 2, 6, 8]	4	<0, 2, 0, 2, 0, 2>	4-25/8-25	<4, 6, 4, 6, 4, 4>	4	[0, 1, 2, 4, 6, 7, 8, 10]
[0, 3, 4, 7]	2	<1, 0, 2, 2, 1, 0>	4-17/8-17	<5, 4, 6, 6, 5, 2>	2	[0, 1, 3, 4, 5, 6, 8, 9]
[0, 3, 5, 8]	2	<0, 1, 2, 1, 2, 0>	4-26/8-26	<4, 5, 6, 5, 6, 2>	2	[0, 1, 3, 4, 5, 7, 8, 10]
[0, 3, 6, 9]	8	<0, 0, 4, 0, 0, 2>	4-28/8-28	<4, 4, 8, 4, 4, 4>	8	[0, 1, 3, 4, 6, 7, 9, 10]

Pentachords   Septachords

Tn/TnI-type	D.S.	IC Vector	Forte Names	IC Vector	D.S.	Tn/TnI-type
[0, 1, 2, 3, 4]	2	<4, 3, 2, 1, 0, 0>	5-1/7-1	<6, 5, 4, 3, 2, 1>	2	[0, 1, 2, 3, 4, 5, 6]
[0, 1, 2, 3, 5]	1	<3, 3, 2, 1, 1, 0>	5-2/7-2	<5, 5, 4, 3, 3, 1>	1	[0, 1, 2, 3, 4, 5, 7]
[0, 1, 2, 3, 6]	1	<3, 2, 2, 1, 1, 1>	5-4/7-4	<5, 4, 4, 3, 3, 2>	1	[0, 1, 2, 3, 4, 6, 7]
[0, 1, 2, 3, 7]	1	<3, 2, 1, 1, 2, 1>	5-5/7-5	<5, 4, 3, 3, 4, 2>	1	[0, 1, 2, 3, 5, 6, 7]
[0, 1, 2, 4, 5]	1	<3, 2, 2, 2, 1, 0>	5-3/7-3	<5, 4, 4, 4, 3, 1>	1	[0, 1, 2, 3, 4, 5, 8]
[0, 1, 2, 4, 6]	1	<2, 3, 1, 2, 1, 1>	5-9/7-9	<4, 5, 3, 4, 3, 2>	1	[0, 1, 2, 3, 4, 6, 8]
[0, 1, 2, 4, 7]	1	<2, 2, 2, 1, 2, 1>	5-Z36/7-Z36	<4, 4, 4, 3, 4, 2>	1	[0, 1, 2, 3, 5, 6, 8]
[0, 1, 2, 4, 8]	1	<2, 2, 1, 3, 1, 1>	5-13/7-13	<4, 4, 3, 5, 3, 2>	1	[0, 1, 2, 4, 5, 6, 8]
[0, 1, 2, 5, 6]	1	<3, 1, 1, 2, 2, 1>	5-6/7-6	<5, 3, 3, 4, 4, 2>	1	[0, 1, 2, 3, 4, 7, 8]
[0, 1, 2, 5, 7]	1	<2, 2, 1, 1, 3, 1>	5-14/7-14	<4, 4, 3, 3, 5, 2>	1	[0, 1, 2, 3, 5, 7, 8]
[0, 1, 2, 5, 8]	1	<2, 1, 2, 2, 2, 1>	5-Z38/7-Z38	<4, 3, 4, 4, 4, 2>	1	[0, 1, 2, 4, 5, 7, 8]
[0, 1, 2, 6, 7]	1	<3, 1, 0, 1, 3, 2>	5-7/7-7	<5, 3, 2, 3, 5, 3>	1	[0, 1, 2, 3, 6, 7, 8]
[0, 1, 2, 6, 8]	2	<2, 2, 0, 2, 2, 2>	5-15/7-15	<4, 4, 2, 4, 4, 3>	2	[0, 1, 2, 4, 6, 7, 8]
[0, 1, 3, 4, 6]	1	<2, 2, 3, 1, 1, 1>	5-10/7-10	<4, 4, 5, 3, 3, 2>	1	[0, 1, 2, 3, 4, 6, 9]
[0, 1, 3, 4, 7]	1	<2, 1, 3, 2, 1, 1>	5-16/7-16	<4, 3, 5, 4, 3, 2>	1	[0, 1, 2, 3, 5, 6, 9]
[0, 1, 3, 4, 8]	2	<2, 1, 2, 3, 2, 0>	5-Z17/7-Z17	<4, 3, 4, 5, 4, 1>	2	[0, 1, 2, 4, 5, 6, 9]
[0, 1, 3, 5, 6]	2	<2, 2, 2, 1, 2, 1>	5-Z12/7-Z12	<4, 4, 4, 3, 4, 2>	2	[0, 1, 2, 3, 4, 7, 9]
[0, 1, 3, 5, 7]	1	<1, 3, 1, 2, 2, 1>	5-24/7-24	<3, 5, 3, 4, 4, 2>	1	[0, 1, 2, 3, 5, 7, 9]
[0, 1, 3, 5, 8]	1	<1, 2, 2, 2, 3, 0>	5-27/7-27	<3, 4, 4, 4, 5, 1>	1	[0, 1, 2, 4, 5, 7, 9]
[0, 1, 3, 6, 7]	1	<2, 1, 2, 1, 2, 2>	5-19/7-19	<4, 3, 4, 3, 4, 3>	1	[0, 1, 2, 3, 6, 7, 9]
[0, 1, 3, 6, 8]	1	<1, 2, 2, 1, 3, 1>	5-29/7-29	<3, 4, 4, 3, 5, 2>	1	[0, 1, 2, 4, 6, 7, 9]
[0, 1, 3, 6, 9]	1	<1, 1, 4, 1, 1, 2>	5-31/7-31	<3, 3, 6, 3, 3, 3>	1	[0, 1, 3, 4, 6, 7, 9]
[0, 1, 4, 5, 7]	1	<2, 1, 2, 2, 2, 1>	5-Z18/7-Z18	<4, 3, 4, 4, 4, 2>	1	[0, 1, 4, 5, 6, 7, 9]
[0, 1, 4, 5, 8]	1	<2, 0, 2, 4, 2, 0>	5-21/7-21	<4, 2, 4, 6, 4, 1>	1	[0, 1, 2, 4, 5, 8, 9]
[0, 1, 4, 6, 8]	1	<1, 2, 1, 3, 2, 1>	5-30/7-30	<3, 4, 3, 5, 4, 2>	1	[0, 1, 2, 4, 6, 8, 9]
[0, 1, 4, 6, 9]	1	<1, 1, 3, 2, 2, 1>	5-32/7-32	<3, 3, 5, 4, 4, 2>	1	[0, 1, 3, 4, 6, 8, 9]
[0, 1, 4, 7, 8]	2	<2, 0, 2, 3, 2, 1>	5-22/7-22	<4, 2, 4, 5, 4, 2>	2	[0, 1, 2, 5, 6, 8, 9]
[0, 1, 5, 6, 8]	1	<2, 1, 1, 2, 3, 1>	5-20/7-20	<4, 3, 3, 4, 5, 2>	1	[0, 1, 2, 5, 6, 7, 9]
[0, 2, 3, 4, 6]	2	<2, 3, 2, 2, 0, 1>	5-8/7-8	<4, 5, 4, 4, 2, 2>	2	[0, 2, 3, 4, 5, 6, 8]
[0, 2, 3, 4, 7]	1	<2, 2, 2, 2, 2, 0>	5-11/7-11	<4, 4, 4, 4, 4, 1>	1	[0, 1, 3, 4, 5, 6, 8]
[0, 2, 3, 5, 7]	1	<1, 3, 2, 1, 3, 0>	5-23/7-23	<3, 5, 4, 3, 5, 1>	1	[0, 2, 3, 4, 5, 7, 9]
[0, 2, 3, 5, 8]	1	<1, 2, 3, 1, 2, 1>	5-25/7-25	<3, 4, 5, 3, 4, 2>	1	[0, 2, 3, 4, 6, 7, 9]
[0, 2, 3, 6, 8]	1	<1, 2, 2, 2, 1, 2>	5-28/7-28	<3, 4, 4, 4, 3, 3>	1	[0, 1, 3, 5, 6, 7, 9]
[0, 2, 4, 5, 8]	1	<1, 2, 2, 3, 1, 1>	5-26/7-26	<3, 4, 4, 5, 3, 2>	1	[0, 1, 3, 4, 5, 7, 9]
[0, 2, 4, 6, 8]	2	<0, 4, 0, 4, 0, 2>	5-33/7-33	<2, 6, 2, 6, 2, 3>	2	[0, 1, 2, 4, 6, 8, 10]
[0, 2, 4, 6, 9]	2	<0, 3, 2, 2, 2, 1>	5-34/7-34	<2, 5, 4, 4, 4, 2>	2	[0, 1, 3, 4, 6, 8, 10]
[0, 2, 4, 7, 9]	2	<0, 3, 2, 1, 4, 0>	5-35/7-35	<2, 5, 4, 3, 6, 1>	2	[0, 1, 3, 5, 6, 8, 10]
[0, 3, 4, 5, 8]	2	<2, 1, 2, 3, 2, 0>	5-Z37/7-Z37	<4, 3, 4, 5, 4, 1>	2	[0, 1, 3, 4, 5, 7, 8]

Hexachords[2]

Tn/TnI-type	D.S.	IC Vector	Forte Names	Tn/TnI-type
[0, 1, 2, 3, 4, 5]	2	<5, 4, 3, 2, 1, 0>	6-1	
[0, 1, 2, 3, 4, 6]	1	<4, 4, 3, 2, 1, 1>	6-2	
[0, 1, 2, 3, 4, 7]	1	<4, 3, 3, 2, 2, 1>	6-Z36/6-Z3	[0, 1, 2, 3, 5, 6]
[0, 1, 2, 3, 4, 8]	2	<4, 3, 2, 3, 2, 1>	6-Z37/6-Z4	[0, 1, 2, 4, 5, 6]
[0, 1, 2, 3, 5, 7]	1	<3, 4, 2, 2, 3, 1>	6-9	
[0, 1, 2, 3, 5, 8]	1	<3, 3, 3, 2, 3, 1>	6-Z40/6-Z11	[0, 1, 2, 4, 5, 7]
[0, 1, 2, 3, 6, 7]	1	<4, 2, 2, 2, 3, 2>	6-5	
[0, 1, 2, 3, 6, 8]	1	<3, 3, 2, 2, 3, 2>	6-Z41/6-Z12	[0, 1, 2, 4, 6, 7]
[0, 1, 2, 3, 6, 9]	2	<3, 2, 4, 2, 2, 2>	6-Z42/6-Z13	[0, 1, 3, 4, 6, 7]
[0, 1, 2, 3, 7, 8]	2	<4, 2, 1, 2, 4, 2>	6-Z38/6-Z6	[0, 1, 2, 5, 6, 7]
[0, 1, 2, 4, 5, 8]	1	<3, 2, 3, 4, 2, 1>	6-15	
[0, 1, 2, 4, 6, 8]	1	<2, 4, 1, 4, 2, 2>	6-22	
[0, 1, 2, 4, 6, 9]	1	<2, 3, 3, 3, 3, 1>	6-Z46/6-Z24	[0, 1, 3, 4, 6, 8]
[0, 1, 2, 4, 7, 8]	1	<3, 2, 2, 3, 3, 2>	6-Z17/6-Z43	[0, 1, 2, 5, 6, 8]
[0, 1, 2, 4, 7, 9]	1	<2, 3, 3, 2, 4, 1>	6-Z47/6-Z25	[0, 1, 3, 5, 6, 8]
[0, 1, 2, 5, 6, 9]	1	<3, 1, 3, 4, 3, 1>	6-Z44/6-Z19	[0, 1, 3, 4, 7, 8]
[0, 1, 2, 5, 7, 8]	1	<3, 2, 2, 2, 4, 2>	6-18	
[0, 1, 2, 5, 7, 9]	1	<2, 3, 2, 3, 4, 1>	6-Z48/6-Z26	[0, 1, 3, 5, 7, 8]
[0, 1, 2, 6, 7, 8]	4	<4, 2, 0, 2, 4, 3>	6-7	
[0, 1, 3, 4, 5, 7]	1	<3, 3, 3, 3, 2, 1>	6-Z10/6-Z39	[0, 2, 3, 4, 5, 8]
[0, 1, 3, 4, 5, 8]	1	<3, 2, 3, 4, 3, 0>	6-14	
[0, 1, 3, 4, 6, 9]	1	<2, 2, 5, 2, 2, 2>	6-27	
[0, 1, 3, 4, 7, 9]	2	<2, 2, 4, 3, 2, 2>	6-Z49/6-Z28	[0, 1, 3, 5, 6, 9]
[0, 1, 3, 5, 7, 9]	1	<1, 4, 2, 4, 2, 2>	6-34	
[0, 1, 4, 5, 7, 9]	1	<2, 2, 3, 4, 3, 1>	6-31	
[0, 1, 3, 6, 7, 9]	2	<2, 2, 4, 2, 2, 3>	6-30	
[0, 2, 3, 6, 7, 9]	2	<2, 2, 4, 2, 3, 2>	6-Z29/6-Z50	[0, 1, 4, 6, 7, 9]
[0, 1, 4, 5, 6, 8]	1	<3, 2, 2, 4, 3, 1>	6-16	
[0, 1, 4, 5, 8, 9]	6	<3, 0, 3, 6, 3, 0>	6-20	
[0, 2, 3, 4, 5, 7]	2	<3, 4, 3, 2, 3, 0>	6-8	
[0, 2, 3, 4, 6, 8]	1	<2, 4, 2, 4, 1, 2>	6-21	
[0, 2, 3, 4, 6, 9]	2	<2, 3, 4, 2, 2, 2>	6-Z45/6-Z23	[0, 2, 3, 5, 6, 8]
[0, 2, 3, 5, 7, 9]	1	<1, 4, 3, 2, 4, 1>	6-33	
[0, 2, 4, 5, 7, 9]	2	<1, 4, 3, 2, 5, 0>	6-32	
[0, 2, 4, 6, 8, 10]	12	<0, 6, 0, 6, 0, 3>	6-35	

---

[2]In the 20 cases where no entry appears in the rightmost column, the complementary hexachords are of the same type. In the remaining cases, only the type of the complement is given, since mutually complementary hexachords have the same ic vector and degrees of symmetry.

Appendix B

Glossary of Jazz Chord Symbols

Listed below are common extended tertian chords in root- and close-position voicing. The chord symbols are based on those in Dan Haerle, *Jazz Piano Voicing Skills* (New Albany, IN: Jamey Aebersold Jazz, 1994). Note the generic use of sharp and flat signs to indicate raising or lowering a pitch by a chromatic semitone.

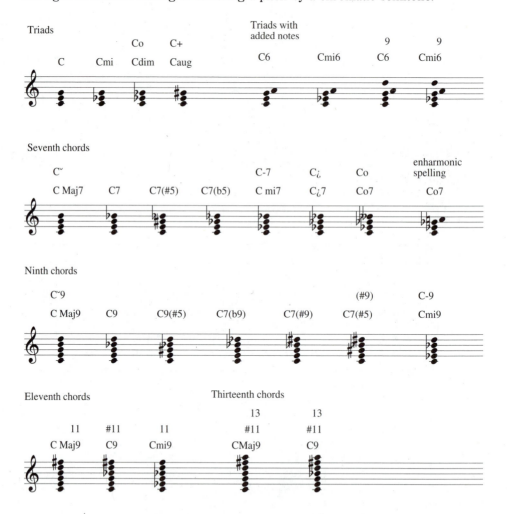

Bibliography

Aldwell, Edward and Carl Schachter. *Harmony and Voice Leading*. 2nd ed. Fort Worth, TX: Harcourt Brace Jovanovich, 1989.

Antokoletz, Elliott. *The Music of Béla Bartók*. Englewood Cliffs, NJ: Prentice-Hall, 1992.

———. *Twentieth-Century Music*. Englewood Cliffs, NJ: Prentice-Hall, 1992.

Baker, James. "Schenkerian Analysis and Post-Tonal Music," In *Aspects of Schenkerian Theory*, ed. David Beach. New Haven and London: Yale University Press, 1983.

Beach, David W. "Pitch Structure and the Analytic Process in Atonal Music: An Interpretation of the Theory of Sets." *Music Theory Spectrum* 1 (1979): 7–22.

Bent, Ian with William Drabkin. "Set-Theory Analysis," In *Analysis*. New York: W. W. Norton, 1987, pp. 100–08.

Berry, Wallace. *Structural Functions of Music*. Englewood Cliffs, NJ: Prentice-Hall, 1976.

Boulez, Pierre. "Aléa" In *Notes of an Apprenticeship*. New York: Knopf, 1968, pp. 35–51.

Brinkman, Alexander R. *Pascal Programming for Music Research*. Chicago: University of Chicago Press, 1990.

Browne, Richmond. "Tonal Implications of the Diatonic Set." *In Theory Only* 5/6–7 (July-August 1981): 3–21.

Bruner, Cheryl L. "The Perception of Contemporary Pitch Structures." *Music Perception* 2/1 (1985): 25–40.

Butler, David. "A Study of Event Hierarchies in Tonal and Post-Tonal Music." *Psychology of Music* 18 (1990): 4–17.

Butler, David and Helen Brown. "Describing the Representation of Tonality in Music." In *Musical Perceptions*, ed. Rita Aiello, New York: Oxford University Press, 1994.

Cage, John. *Silence*. Middletown, CT: Wesleyan University Press, 1961.

——— *A Year from Monday*. Middletown, CT: Wesleyan University Press, 1967.

——— *Notations*. New York: Something Else Press, 1969

Cogan, Robert and Pozzi Escot. *Sonic Design*. Englewood Cliffs, NJ: Prentice-Hall, 1976; reprint Cambridge, MA: Publication Contact International, 1985.

Cooper, Grosvenor and Leonard B. Meyer. *The Rhythmic Structure of Music*. Chicago: University of Chicago Press, 1960.

Cope, David H. *New Directions in Music*. 5th ed., Dubuque, IA: Wm. C. Brown, 1989.

Creston, Paul, *Principles of Rhythm*. New York: Franco Columbo, 1964.

DeLone, Peter. "Timbre and Texture in Twentieth-Century Music," In *Aspects of Twentieth-Century Music*. ed. Gary E. Wittlich. Englewood Cliffs, NJ: Prentice-Hall, 1975.

Dowling, W. Jay. "Recognition of Melodic Transformations: Inversion, Retrograde, and Retrograde Inversion." *Perception and Psychophysics* 12/5 (1972): 417–421.

Dunsby, Jonathan and Arnold Whitall. *Music Analysis in Theory and Practice*. New Haven: Yale University Press, 1988.

Epstein, David. *Beyond Orpheus*. New York: Oxford University Press, 1987.

Escot, Pozzi. "Non-Linearity as a Conceptualization in Music," In *Contiguous Lines: Issues and Ideas in the Music of the '60s and '70s*. ed. Thomas DeLio. Lanham, MD: University Press of America, 1985.

Etler, Alvin. *Making Music: An Introduction to Theory*. New York: Harcourt Brace Jovanovich, 1974.

Forte, Allen. *The Structure of Atonal Music*. New Haven: Yale University Press, 1973.

———. "Schoenberg's Creative Evolution: The Path to Atonality." *Musical Quarterly* 64/2 (April 1978): 133–176.

Francès, Robert. "The Perception of Serial Music," In *The Perception of Music*, translated by W. Jay Dowling. Hillsdale, NJ: Lawrence Erlbaum, 1988.

Gauldin, Robert. "A Pedagogical Introduction to Set Theory." *Theory and Practice* 3/2 (September 1978): 3–14.

Gena, Peter and Jonathan Brent, eds. *A John Cage Reader*. New York: Peters, 1982.

Goldman, Richard Franko. *Harmony in Western Music*. New York: W. W. Norton, 1965.

Hasty, Christopher. "Segmentation and Process in Post-Tonal Music." *Music Theory Spectrum* 3 (1981): 54–73.

———. "Phrase Formation in Post-Tonal Music." *Journal of Music Theory*, 28 (1984): 167–90.

Hindemith, Paul. *The Craft of Musical Composition*. Vol. I: Theoretical Part, trans. Arthur Mendel. New York: Associated Music, 1942. Vol II: Exercises in Two-Part Writing, trans. Otto Ortmann, New York: Associated Music, 1941.

Huron, David. "Interval Class Content in Equally Tempered Pitch-Class Sets: Common Scales Exhibit Optimum Tonal Consonance." *Music Perception* 11/3 (Spring 1994): 289–305.

Imberty, Michel. "How Do We Perceive Atonal Music? Suggestions for a Theoretical Approach." *Contemporary Music Review* 9 (1993): 191–205.

Jarman, Douglas. *The Music of Alban Berg*. Berkeley and Los Angeles: University of California Press, 1979.

Kostelanetz, Richard, ed. *John Cage: An Anthology*. New York: Praeger, 1970.

Kostka, Stefan. *Materials and Techniques of Twentieth-Century Music*. Englewood Cliffs, NJ: Prentice-Hall, 1989.

Kramer, Jonathan. *The Time of Music*. New York: Schirmer Books, 1988.

Krumhansl, Carol L. *Cognitive Foundations of Musical Pitch*. New York: Oxford University Press, 1990. See Chapter 10.

Lansky, Paul and George Perle. "Atonality," In *The New Grove Dictionary of Music and Musicians*. ed. Stanley Sadie. London: Macmillan, 1980.

Lansky, Paul and Malcolm Goldstein. "Texture," In *The Dictionary of Contemporary Music*. ed. John Vinton. New York: E. P. Dutton, 1974.

Larson, Steve. "A Tonal Model of an 'Atonal' Piece." *Perspectives of New Music* 25/1 & 2 (1987): 418–433.

LaRue, Jan. *Guidelines for Style Analysis*. New York: W. W. Norton, 1970.

Lerdahl, Fred. "Cognitive Constraints on Compositional Systems." In *Generative Processes in Music*, ed. John Sloboda, Oxford: Clarendon Press, 1988, pp. 231–259.

Lerdahl, Fred. "Atonal Prolongational Structure." *Contemporary Music Review* 4 (1989): 65–87.

Lerdahl, Fred and Ray Jackendoff. "Remarks on Contemporary Music," In *A Generative Theory of Tonal Music*. Cambridge: MIT Press, 1983. pp. 296–301.

Lester, Joel. *The Rhythms of Tonal Music*. Carbondale: Southern Illinois University Press, 1986.

———. *Analytical Approaches to Twentieth-Century Music*. New York: W. W. Norton, 1989.

Machlis, Joseph. *Introduction to Contemporary Music*. 2nd ed. New York: W. W. Norton, 1979.

Marvin, Elizabeth West. "The Perception of Rhythm in Non-Tonal Music: Rhythmic Contours in the Music of Edgard Varèse." *Music Theory Spectrum* 13 (Spring 1991): 61–78.

Mertens, Wim. *American Minimal Music*, trans. J. Hautekeit. New York: Alexander Broude, 1983.

Messiaen, Oliver. *Technique de mon langage musical*. Paris: Alphonse Leduc et Cie, Editions Musicales, 1944; trans. by John Satterfield as *The Technique of My Musical Language*. Paris: Alphonse Leduc, 1956.

Metz, Paul W. "The Clock Diagram: An Effective Visual Tool in Set Theory Pedagogy." *Theory and Practice* 14/15 (1989/90): 105–121.

———. "Set Theory, Clock Diagrams, and Berg's Op. 2, No. 2." *In Theory Only* 12/1 & 2 (1991): 1–17.

Meyer, Leonard B. *Music, The Arts, and Ideas*. Chicago: University of Chicago Press, 1967.

———. *Explaining Music*. Chicago: University of Chicago Press, 1973.

Morgan, Robert P. "Dissonant Prolongations: Theoretical and Compositional Precedents." *Journal of Music Theory* 20 (1976): 49–91.

———. *Twentieth-Century Music*. New York: W. W. Norton, 1991.

Morris, Robert. *Composition with Pitch Classes*. New Haven and London: Yale University Press, 1987.

———. "Recommendations for Atonal Music Pedagogy in General; Recognizing and Hearing Set-Classes in Particular." *Journal of Music Theory Pedagogy* 8 (1994): 75–134.

Neumeyer, David. *The Music of Paul Hindemith*. New Haven and London: Yale University Press, 1986.

Neumeyer, David and Susan Tepping. *A Guide to Schenkerian Analysis*. Englewood Cliffs, NJ: Prentice-Hall, 1992.

Owen, Harold. *Modal and Tonal Counterpoint: From Josquin to Stravinsky*. New York: Schirmer Books, 1992.

Perle, George. *Serial Composition and Atonality*, 6th ed., revised., Berkeley and Los Angeles: University of California Press, 1991.

Persichetti, Vincent. *Twentieth-Century Harmony*. New York: W. W. Norton, 1961.

Rahn, John. *Basic Atonal Theory*. New York: Longman, 1980.

Reich, Steve. *Writings about Music*. Halifax: University of Nova Scotia Press, 1974.

Reti, Rudolph. *Tonality, Atonality, Pantonality*. New York: Macmillan, 1958; reprinted as *Tonality in Modern Music*. New York: Collier Books, 1962.

Rochberg, George. *The Aesthetics of Survival*. Ann Arbor: University of Michigan Press, 1984.

Salzer, Felix. *Structural Hearing: Tonal Coherence in Music*. New York: Dover, 1962.

Salzer, Felix and Carl Schachter. *Counterpoint in Composition*. New York: McGraw-Hill, 1969.

Salzman, Eric. "Milton Babbitt and John Cage, Parallels and Paradoxes." *Stereo Review* 22/4 (1969): 60.

Schachter, Carl. Rhythm and Linear Analysis: Durational Reduction." *The Music Forum* 5 (1980): 197–232.

Schoenberg, Arnold. *Style and Idea*. New York: Philosophical Library, 1950.

Schwartz, Elliott and Daniel Godfrey, *Music Since 1945*. New York: Schirmer Books, 1993.

Sessions, Roger. "Problems and Issues Facing the Composer Today," In *Problems of Modern Music*, ed. Paul Henry Lang, New York: W. W. Norton, 1962. pp. 21–33.

Simms, Brian R. *Music of the Twentieth Century: Style and Structure*. New York: Schirmer Books, 1986.

Smith, J. David and Jordon N. Witt. "Spun Steel and Stardust: The Rejection of Contemporary Compositions." *Music Perception* 7/2 (1989): 169–86.

Straus, Joseph N. "The Problem of Prolongation in Post-Tonal Music." *Journal of Music Theory* 31 (1987): 1–21.

———. *Remaking the Past: Musical Modernism and the Influence of the Tonal Tradition*. Cambridge, MA: Harvard University Press, 1990.

———. *Introduction to Post-Tonal Theory*. Englewood Cliffs, NJ: Prentice-Hall, 1990.

———. "A Primer for Atonal Set Theory." *College Music Symposium* 31 (1991): 1–26.

Thomson, William. "Hindemith's Contributions to Music Theory." *Journal of Music Theory* 9 (1965): 52–71.

———. *Schoenberg's Error*. Philadelphia: University of Pennsylvania Press, 1991.

Tischler, Hans. "Hindemith's *Ludus Tonalis* and Bach's *Well-Tempered-Clavier*—A Comparison." *Music Review* 21 (1960): 217–227.

van den Toorn, Pieter C. *The Music of Igor Stravinsky*. New Haven and London: Yale University Press, 1983.

Watkins, Glenn. *Soundings: Music in the Twentieth Century*. New York: Schirmer Books, 1988.

Wennerstrom, Mary H. "Form in Twentieth-Century Music," In *Aspects of Twentieth-Century Music*, ed. Gary E. Wittlich, Englewood Cliffs, NJ: Prentice-Hall, 1975.

Westergaard, Peter. "Webern and 'Tonal Organization'." *Perspectives of New Music* 1/2 (1963): 107–120.

Williams, J. Kent. "Logo as a Medium for Exploring Atonal Theory." *Journal of Music Theory Pedadogy* 5/1 (1991): 47–78.

Wilson, Paul. *The Music of Béla Bartók*. New Haven and London: Yale University Press, 1992.

Winold, Allen. "Rhythm in Twentieth-Century Music ," In *Aspects of Twentieth Century Music*. ed. Gary E. Wittlich, Englewood Cliffs, NJ: Prentice-Hall, 1975.

Wittlich, Gary E. "Sets and Ordering Procedures in Twentieth-Century Music" In *Aspects of Twentieth-Century Music*, ed. Gary E. Wittlich, Englewood Cliffs, NJ: Prentice-Hall, 1975.

Wuorinen, Charles. *Simple Composition*. New York: Longman, 1979.

York, Wesley. "Form and Process." In Thomas DeLio, ed., *Contiguous Lines*, Lanham, MD: University Press of America, 1985.

Credits

Example 7-10: Paul Hindemith STRING QUARTET OP. 22, © 1923 B. Schott's Soehne, Mainz, © renewed. All rights reserved. Used by permission of European American Music Distributors Corporation, sole U.S. and Canadian agent for B. Schott's Soehne, Mainz.

Example 7-11: EIGHT PIECES FOR FOUR TIMPANI by Elliott Carter. Copyright © 1968 by Associated Music Publishers, Inc. (BMI) International Copyright Secured. All rights reserved. Reprinted by permission. ("Canaries," mm. 1-24.)

Example 7-12: Prelude to "The Afternoon of a Faun" piano arrangement by Leonard Borwick, mm. 79-85, by Claude Debussy. Public domain.

Example 7-13: "Dirge" by Benjamin Britten, SERENADE Op. 31. © Copyright 1944 by Hawkes & Son (London) Ltd.; Copyright Renewed. Reprinted by permission of Boosey & Hawkes, Inc.

Example 7-16: "The Unanswered Question" by Charles Ives. © Copyright 1984 by Peer International Corporation. International Copyright Secured. All Rights Reserved. Used by permission. Copyright 1923 by Southern Music Publishing Co. Inc.

Example 7-18: "Density 21.5" (mm. 1-23) by Edgar Varèse, published by Colfranc, New York.

Example 7-21: CONCERTO FOR ORCHESTRA, (mm. 1-9, snare drum part) by Bela Bartók. © Copyright 1946 by Hawkes & Son (London) Ltd.; Copyright Renewed. Reprinted by permission of Boosey & Hawkes, Inc.

Example 7-22: "Summertime" from *Porgy & Bess*, by George Gershwin, mm. 1-8 (voice part only). Published by Warner/Chappell Music.

Example 7-23: Gunther Schuller SEVEN STUDIES ON THEMES OF PAUL KLEE © 1962 by Universal Edition (London) Ltd., London © renewed. All Rights Reserved. Used by permission of European American Music Distributors Corporation, sole U.S. and Canadian agent for Universal Edition (London) Ltd., London.

Example 7-24: "Psalm 13" mm. 1-16 by Bruce Saylor, originally published in *Anthology for Musical Analysis* by Burkhart, 5th ed., by Harcourt Brace & Company, © by the author.

Example 7-25: Berg, WOZZECK, (Act III, Scene 2, Murder Movement, bass drum) copyright 1926 by Universal 1926 by Universal Edition A.G., Wien, copyright renewed. All Rights Reserved. Used by permission of European American Music Distributors Corporation, sole U.S. and Canadian agent for Universal Edition A.G., Wien.

Example 8-1: Hovhaness, "Visionary Landscape" No. 1 (systems 1-4) © 1967 by C. F. Peters Corp. Used by permission.

Example 8-2: LE TOMBEAU DE COUPERIN, RIGAUDON by Maurice Ravel. © 1918 S.A. Editions Musicales Joint Publication, Editions A.R.I.M.A. & Durand S.A. Editions Musicales. Used by permission of the publisher. Sole representative U.S.A. & Canada, Theodore Presser Company.

Example 8-3a: "Four Songs, Opus 2, No. 3" by Alban Berg. Reprinted by permission of Robert Lienau Muskiverlag, Germany.

Example 8-4: "Game of the Couples" from CONCERTO FOR ORCHESTRA by Béla Bartók. © Copyright 1946 by Hawkes & Son (London) Ltd.; Copyright Renewed. Reprinted by permission of Boosey & Hawkes, Inc.

Example 8-5: IN MEMORIAM, DYLAN THOMAS by Igor Stravinsky. © Copyright 1954 by Boosey & Hawkes, Inc.; Copyright Renewed. Reprinted by permission.

Example 8-6: "Piano Sonata, Number 3, II" (mm. 1-15) by Norman Dello Joio. Copyright © 1948 by Carl Fischer, Inc.; New York. Copyright Renewed. Used by permission.

Example 8-7: THE ENGULFED CATHEDRAL, PRELUDE I, by Claude Debussy. Public domain.

Example 8-8: A THREE SCORE SET by William H. Schuman. Copyright © 1944 (Renewed) by Associated Music Publishers, Inc. (BMI) International Copyright Secured. All Rights Reserved. Reprinted by permission. (mm. 1-4.)

Example 8-9: "Ostinato" MIKROKOSMOS, Vol. IV, No. 146 by Béla Bartók. © Copyright 1945 by Hawkes & Son (London) Ltd.; Copyright Renewed. Reprinted by permission of Boosey & Hawkes, Inc.

Example 11-8a: Prelude to "The Afternoon of a Faun" (mm. 1-4, flute solo) by Claude Debussy. Public domain.

Example 11-9: VILLAGE SCENES (No. 4, Lullaby) by Béla Bartók. © Copyright 1927 by Universal Editions; Copyright Renewed. Copyright and Renewal assigned to Boosey & Hawkes, Inc., for the U.S.A. Reprinted by permission of Boosey & Hawkes, Inc.

Example 12-1: "Hindemith's Series I" from THE CRAFT OF MUSICAL COMPOSITION, BOOK I, by Paul Hindemith. Copyright © 1942 (Renewed) by Associated Music Publishers, Inc. (BMI) International Copyright Secured. All Rights Reserved. Reprinted by permission.

Example 12-2: "Hindemith's Series II" from THE CRAFT OF MUSICAL COMPOSITION, BOOK I, by Paul Hindemith. Copyright © 1942 (Renewed) by Associated Music Publishers, Inc. (BMI) International Copyright Secured. All Rights Reserved. Reprinted by permission.

Example 12-4: "Resolutions of 'tense' harmonic intervals" from MAKING MUSIC: AN INTRODUCTION TO THEORY by Alvin Etler, copyright © 1974 by Harcourt Brace & Company, reproduced by permission of the publisher.

Example 12-6: "Neotonal Models" from MAKING MUSIC: AN INTRODUCTION TO THEORY by Alvin Etler, copyright © 1974 by Harcourt Brace & Company, reproduced by permission of the publisher.

Example 12-7: "Analysis of a Neotonal Melody" from THE CRAFT OF MUSICAL COMPOSITION, BOOK I, by Paul Hindemith. Copyright © 1942 (Renewed) by Associated Music Publishers, Inc. (BMI) International Copyright Secured. All Rights Reserved. Reprinted by permission.

Example 12-8: "Hindemith, Nobilissima Visione Suite I, (Introduction or Meditation)" from *The Music of Paul Hindemith* by David Neumeyer. Copyright © 1986 by David Neumeyer. Reprinted by permission.

Example 12-9: "Meyer-Narmour Analysis of a Neotonal Melody" from MAKING MUSIC: AN INTRODUCTION TO THEORY by Alvin Etler, copyright © 1974 by Harcourt Brace & Company, reproduced by permission of the publisher.

Example 12-10: "Analysis of a Neotonal Melody" from MAKING MUSIC: AN INTRODUCTION TO THEORY by Alvin Etler, copyright © 1974 by Harcourt Brace & Company, reproduced by permission of the publisher.

Example 12-11: "Two-Voice Model" from MAKING MUSIC: AN INTRODUCTION TO THEORY by Alvin Etler, copyright © 1974 by Harcourt Brace & Company, reproduced by permission of the publisher.

Example 12-12: From *The Study of Counterpoint* by J.J. Fux, Figure 22, p. 40. Reprinted by permission of W.W. Norton & Company.

Example 12-13: "Two-Voice Model with Both Voices Decorated" from MAKING MUSIC: AN INTRODUCTION TO THEORY by Alvin Etler, copyright © 1974 by Harcourt Brace & Company, reproduced by permission of the publisher.

Example 12-17: Hindemith PIANO SONATA, NO. 2, © B. Schott's Soehne, Mainz, 1936, © renewed. All Rights Reserved. Used by permission of European American Music Distributors Corporation, sole U.S. and Canadian agent for B. Schott's Soehne, Mainz.

Example 13-1a: Hindemith A SWAN (Six Chansons), © copyright 1943 by B. Schott's Soehne, Mainz, 1936, © copyright renewed. All Rights Reserved. Used by permission of European American Music Distributors Corporation, sole U.S. and Canadian agent for B. Schott's Soehne, Mainz.

Example 13-2: MIKROKOSMOS, Vol. VI, No. 149, by Béla Bartók. © Copyright 1945 by Hawkes & Son (London) Ltd.; Copyright Renewed. Reprinted by permission of Boosey & Hawkes, Inc.

Example 13-3: "Neumeyer's Reductions of Hindemith's Interlude in G" Ex. 3.2 and 3.3, from *The Music of Paul Hindemith* by David Neumeyer. Copyright © 1986 by David Neumeyer. Reprinted by permission.

Example 17-3: LES MOUTONS DE PANURGE, The Basic Melody, by Frederic Rzewski from *The Time of Music*, 1988, by Jonathan Kramer. Copyright by Zen-On Music Co. Ltd., Tokyo.

Example 18-1: Rochberg, CARNIVAL MUSIC IV, © 1975 Theodore Presser Company. Used by permission of the publisher.

Example 18-3: "Three-Part Sinfonia No. 9 in F Minor" (mm. 15-23) by J.S. Bach. Public domain.

Example 18-4b: "Capriccio in C, Opus 76, No. 8" by Johannes Brahms. Public domain.

Index of Score Excerpts

Page numbers of complete pieces or movements are shown in bold type. Page numbers of analysis exercises and projects that refer to score excerpts are marked with an asterisk (*).

Index of Topics and Names